Strategic Marketing:
Cases, Concepts and Challenges

Strategic Marketing: Cases, Concepts and Challenges

John Atkinson and Ian Wilson

HarperCollins*Publishers*

Published in 1996 by
HarperCollins
77–85 Fulham Palace Road
Hammersmith
London W6 8JB

British Library Cataloguing in Publication Data is available upon request from the British Library

ISBN 0-00-499037-4

Typeset by Harper Phototypesetters Limited, Northampton
Printed and bound by Scotprint Ltd, Musselburgh
Cover design by The Senate

Contents

Acknowledgements

Our thanks are due to:

Prentice-Hall for reproducing 'What distinguishes the good negotiators from the crowd', *International Marketing Strategy,* Bradley 1991.

Butterworth-Heinemann for reproducing 'The eight stages of market segmentation', *Strategic Marketing Management*, Wilson, R. *et al.* 1992.

Mike Tarrier, Total Communications for reproducing a Media Schedule.

Brian Asquith of Asquith Design for information on the product design industry.

Students of both Staffordshire University Business School and Cheltenham and Gloucester College of Higher Education for working with the draft case material.

We would also like to express our thanks to Bob Grinham, John Scarman, Liz Wilson, Helen Colderick, Pauline Chidlow, Steve Worthington, Sue MacKenzie and John Williams.

Every effort has been made to contact copyright holders, but if any have been inadvertently overlooked the publishers will be pleased to make the necessary arrangements at the first opportunity.

Introduction

This case book is designed to assist both students and practitioners in their desire to understand and implement marketing strategies in the wider organisational context. Marketing strategies and programmes are explored in a variety of organisational and national environments. The case material encourages participants to find solutions in situations where the imperative of dynamic change requires a reappraisal of strategic intent.

The Style and Distinctiveness of the Case Material

Problems of case material

These cases were developed following student feedback that case material was frequently based upon secondary material provided by well-known organisations which sometimes appeared to be flat and unrealistic, however professional the content. Rather, students wanted to feel that they were *insiders,* actively involved with the constraints and opportunities of the subject organisation.

The difficulty for the case writer is that organisations are normally unwilling to allow controversial decisions and situations to be the subject of overt case material. Such corporate sensibilities are the first consideration for case writers, given the necessity of securing the information. This constraint, together with an *arms-length* approach, may result in less stimulating material. More seriously, if minimum mention of such key issues as corporate crisis and failure is *de rigueur,* cases may be perceived as public relations exercises for wider audiences. In addition, given the nature of the business cycle, the health of the subject organisation frequently deteriorates subsequent to a successful period. In such a situation, where the 1980s corporate success story is often the 1990s problem company, a credibility gap appears.

'Towards insiderisation'

What is different about these cases is that they are all based upon primary information and many are complemented by financial data (an increasing requirement of external examiners, teachers and students alike). The financial detail is frequently used to emphasise the reality of the changing environment facing the organisation; additionally, it serves to constrain students from proposing marketing strategies with minimum reference to the financial health of the business.

Many of the cases have been concealed to preserve confidentiality. This allows us to identify and discuss the more difficult issues, which would normally be understated, given the potential for embarrassment to the subject organisation. This approach allows for the development of more sensitive (but equally important) issues, such as time pressures, limited resources, lack of working capital, crises, conflict and the difficulties of personal relationships. Above all, the student can be given the taste of the live commercial situation. In this way they are encouraged to become true insiders.

The cases are linked together by the common theme of organisations that need to respond to the environmental imperatives of change (and/or crisis change). Such conditions frequently serve as the midwife to strategy development. For example, it may be the decisions taken in a crisis situation which determine the survival of an organisation. In this situation the case material can be used to encourage students to analyse how environmental change has come about and to recommend forward strategic directions, taking into account both short-term survival imperatives and longer-term objectives. The emphasis is placed on the systematic development of intended marketing strategies, given the inability of students working on cases to participate in practical decision-making over time. Emergent strategies can, however, be emphasised in the analysis stage, when participants can be encouraged to act as external commentators seeking patterns in the stream of past events.

The Scope of the Text Material

Marketing orientation is frequently claimed to be the driving force of successful organisations. The 'classic marketing companies' provide the obvious examples (these include such major multinational enterprises as Procter and Gamble, Mars, 3M and Coca-Cola). With such examples, any distinction between corporate strategy and marketing strategy may be slight. This may not be true, however, of more diversified enterprises (examples, Hanson, British American Tobacco), where the linkage, for example, between, asset management strategies and functional marketing strategies, may be obscure. Equally, successful Japanese multinational enterprises are proving difficult to classify as 'classic marketing companies' given an emphasis on enabling technologies and competencies rather than products and markets. (Indeed, Honda is frequently quoted as operating without formal marketing departments). Such considerations have stimulated our theme of *cases, concepts and challenges*. In order to create a bridge between theory and practice, the text includes three chapters on the theme of concepts and challenges.

The first chapter discusses the nature of the strategy/marketing interface and attempts to provide a framework for the exploration of marketing philosophy in the context of organisational strategies. Chapter 2 will review the conventional approach to strategic marketing planning, emphasising outputs rather than processes. Chapter 3 will then develop the theme of challenge to the conventional tools of strategic marketing still further.

The text also includes learning texts and notes on a variety of topics relating to the case material.

The Scope of the Case Material

The 17 cases include:

- National and global environments
- Small/medium sized enterprises and multinational enterprises (MNEs)
- Industrial, consumer goods and service organisations.

The individual cases are in most instances supported by questions, exercises and suggested solutions.

The Layout of the Book

Text chapters: Part I

Chapter 1: The Strategy/Marketing Interface
Chapter 2: The Strategic Marketing Planning Process
Chapter 3: Challenges: Old Dogs . . . and New Tricks?

The case material: Part II

Given the strategic focus of the material, all cases cover many aspects of marketing strategy. The specific emphasis of individual cases is indicated in the summary below.

4. **Betaware Housewares Limited:** Developing survival strategies for a medium-sized 'UK metal basher'.
5. **Banking on a Winning Strategy:** The search for competitive advantage in retail banking.
6. **Après Shower:** Developing positioning strategies for an innovative new product.
7. **British Safety Razor Case A: Strategy for Developing Economies.**
8. **British Safety Razor Case B: The Negotiation Exercise.**
   A MNE targets developing countries as part of a global expansion strategy; issues of market entry strategy and marketing ethics. The case incorporates a negotiation exercise relevant to the formation of a joint venture as Part B.
9. **The Boston Candy Co. in Peru:** A MNE seeks greater control of its distributors in South America; incorporates a negotiating exercise.
10. **Carenet:** The relevance of marketing strategy to non-profit organisations.
11. **The Mortimer Arms:** Marketing leisure services by a UK West Country hotel; stressing the importance of market segmentation, targeting and positioning (STP).
12. **G'day FNQ:** Applying the principles of 'STP' to leisure services in Far North Queensland, Australia.
13. **Carlsberg Ice Beer:** Positioning, segmentation and branding strategy for a new product.
14. **Montpellier Spa Water:** Deciding how to enter the UK mineral water market.
15. **Roses Grow On You:** Growth and positioning strategy for a smaller business.

PART I

Strategic Marketing: Concepts, Processes and Challenges

1
The Strategy/Marketing Interface

In baiting a mouse-trap with cheese, always leave room for the mouse
(Saki 1924)

The Marketing Concept

It is hard to choose two more difficult themes than marketing and strategy, given the myriad interpretations associated with each concept, as well as the growing area of common ground. Equally, it is difficult to avoid semantics, but we will endeavour to leave room for the mouse! We assume that most readers are familiar with the wide range of definitions relating to the marketing concept. In the context of the strategy/marketing interface the dual nature of the marketing concept, marketing as a management philosophy and marketing as a function, will first be revisited.

Marketing as a philosophy is often seen as the driving force for successful organisations and associated with customer focus and the pursuit of competitive advantage. Marketing as a function may refer to a set of techniques or tools, that might be employed, for example, by a marketing department. The 'marketing mix' could be referred to in this context. Philosophical and functional marketing approaches normally complement one another, presenting an integrated marketing offering. Philosophy and function may also exist independently. For example, many successful market-oriented organisations operate without formal marketing departments. Equally, the existence of a marketing department does not necessarily mean that an organisation has a market-oriented philosophy.

> Significantly, Japanese companies operate almost entirely without marketing departments or market research of the kind so prevalent in the West . . . they deliver irresistible value everywhere, attracting people with products that market research technocrats described with superficial certainty as being unsuitable and uncompetitive. (Levitt 1983)

The marketing paradox

Subsequent to the 'marketing revolution', marketing as a philosophy is increasingly being integrated into the wider domain of strategy. The vision of earlier writers, who sought to reject the narrow, specialist view of marketing, has now been widely accepted. This vision, frequently echoed today, was expressed by both academics and practitioners. For example, Hugh Davidson in 1972, a former Proctor and Gamble manager, wrote:

> There is no such thing as marketing skill by itself. For a company to be good at marketing it must be good at everything else, from R&D to manufacturing, from quality controls to financial controls.

Peter Drucker's classic definition of marketing is equally relevant:

> Marketing is so basic that it cannot be considered a separate function within the business, on a par with others such as manufacturing or personnel. Marketing requires separate work, and a distinct group of activities. But it is first, a central dimension of the entire business. **It is the whole business seen from the point of view of its final result, that is, from the customer's point of view**. [Authors' emphasis].

The integration of the marketing philosophy into the wider strategy process, in part reflects the reality that strategic decisions are relevant to the Business Unit level, where strategic marketing is focused upon product/market decisions. None of this is especially surprising as the proponents of the marketing philosophy have long believed marketing to be both the beginning (or inspiration) and the end (or implementation) of business strategy.

Marketing's identity crisis?

As the scope for the application of marketing principles widened and the interface with other management disciplines increased, the distinctiveness of the marketing concept has become blurred. Marketing as a philosophy may be suffering from the Icarus paradox, a victim of its own success. Marketing is now at the heart of strategy, but in a global and more complex world, the original certainties of the marketing concept, forged by the large consumer goods companies, are increasingly open to challenge. Some of these challenges we will review later in the text.

The success of marketing as a philosophy has prompted such cries as, 'the marketing department is dead, long live marketing'. In many ways, however, the opposite is true. Functional marketing applications are developing apace as the marketing evangelists have preached the marketing concept as a cure-all for all business and non-business environments alike. This may reflect contemporary trends, such as the triumph of the market economy, new technologies, multi-media opportunities, deregulation and the development of the service economy. In this situation marketing academics and practitioners have of necessity generated increasing sub-sets of the marketing function, such as internal marketing, relationship marketing, marketing logistics, green marketing and non-profit marketing.

The champions of the broader view of marketing (Kotler and Levy 1969; Kotler 1972) triggered attempts to redefine the original clarity of the marketing concept.

> Traditional notions of the 'product', the 'consumer' and the marketing 'toolkit' had to be redefined in non-business terms and attempts made to transfer the principles of effective marketing management . . . to the marketing of services, persons and ideas. (Brown 1995)

Bartels (1974) cited by Brown (1995) predicted that this would:

> only serve to direct attention away from important but neglected areas of marketing activity (like physical distribution), lead to an emphasis on methodology rather than issues of substance, and give rise to an increasingly esoteric and abstract marketing literature.

By contrast, contemporary challenges to marketing as a philosophy are fundamental. The starting point of customers and markets, the raison d'être of marketing, is being questioned by such writers as Prahalad and Hamel (1990), whose emphasis is on organisational collective learning and 'core competencies' rather than the resulting product and market activities. Innovation theory continues to question the fundamental tenet of the marketing concept, the focus on the existing customer base. For example, the investment in assets across an industry by a spectrum of manufacturers, channel members and customers, is a potent force for preservation of the status quo. This perhaps is the explanation why innovation normally occurs from outside an industry. The focus on customers is all very well, but the problem is which customers?

> The demands of these (large) customers can lead a firm down the garden path to spending royally on marginal improvements for older concepts, all the while ignoring newer customers in small but growing markets that support new concepts. This advice is especially valuable in view of the current doctrine to 'listen to the customer'. But which customers should firms listen to? (Utterback 1994)

Many marketing writers have themselves concluded that the marketing concept if not flawed is perhaps unsuited to a more complex world. Brown cites Piercy 1992, Thomas 1993, Gummesson 1987 and others in this context. The marketing 'toolkit', comprising such dated tools as product life-cycle and portfolio models, appears to many to be of limited relevance in the global environment of technological innovation, instant communications and strategic alliances designed to build competencies by technology capture.

These considerations and perhaps the recognition that marketing is now too important to be left to the marketing people alone, has provoked a marketing identity crisis. The advice of Davidson and Drucker and others appears to have been accepted. Marketing is no longer the only function that interfaces with the customer. This, for example, is evident in service industries.

> Had it all seemed too easy then? Management had left the delicate job of customers to a single function, which happened to be marketing. Yet, it was impossible for any one function to handle alone because, as became increasingly clear, a focus on customers is an attitude rather than a task, a state of mind as opposed to a functional responsibility. Marketing was also placed in the double bind of having to care for customers on the one hand, but also sell as much to them as possible on the other. In practice, this led to complex and divergent relationships with the other functions, as well as ambivalent goals. (Vandermerwe 1993)

Out of this identity crisis may yet emerge a revised and more relevant marketing philosophy or concept. It seems to us that the paradigm-shift in marketing thinking should be away from the dated toolkit and tendency to introspection, towards a re-emphasis on wealth creation. A new marketing philosophy would then be relevant to:

> inventing new markets, quickly entering emerging markets, and dramatically shifting patterns of customer choice in established markets . . . creating products that customers need but have not yet even imagined. (Prahalad & Hamel 1990)

The case material provides the opportunity to test some of the tools of strategic marketing in a variety of environments all of which are subject to the imperatives of crisis and change. We believe that all the cases will demonstrate that marketing is the responsibility of the whole business, rather than the responsibility of a marketing department alone.

Use of Terms

In order to explore the strategy/marketing relationship further, we will begin to use the term 'strategic marketing' in the context of the strategy/marketing philosophy interface and the term 'marketing strategy' in the context of the marketing philosophy/marketing functional interface.

The Hierarchical Nature of Strategy

The relationship of strategy and strategic marketing becomes somewhat clearer in the context of the hierarchical nature of the strategic process. Senior management, for example, may refer to strategy in relation to the whole corporation, whilst the salesperson sitting in the car prior to the sales call, may refer to strategy in relation to winning the next order. This has been variously expressed; for example:

Strategy depends upon where and when you sit (Mintzberg and Quinn 1991)

One person's strategies are another's tactics (Mintzberg citing Rumelt 1974)

A number of writers have distinguished between levels of strategy, generally identifying three or four such levels:

1. The Corporate level.
2. The Business or Strategic Business Unit level (SBU).
3. The Functional level (normally referring to the marketing, finance, operational human resource functions).
4. The Operational level.

This distinction helps to explain why business unit tactics, for example, may become strategies to the functional departments (see Table 1.2).

The differing perspectives inherent in the hierarchy of strategy model implies that there are also hierarchies of objectives, programmes and budgets, as strategy involves both formulation and implementation. In the Royal China case, for example, although the perspectives on the issue of disposing of unbalances stocks will differ (from the TTi main board perspective to that of the individual managers in the factory or concession stores), the board is dependent on these junior managers for a 'strategy of disposal'. This raises the issue of operations, or tactics-led strategy. Strategy does not necessarily have to cascade down from on high through these four identified levels. As operating managers may themselves create strategy by their actions, such 'bottom up' strategies could also be considered as a starting point in contrast to the more conventional 'top down' intended model. In this case:

What seems tactical today may prove strategic tomorrow (Mintzberg and Quinn 1991)

The 'M.O.S.T.' acronym (Mission, Objectives, Strategy and Tactics) relates to the integration of formulation and implementation. In this context it is the responsibility of senior management to establish the mission and objectives and the number of business units. Strategy and tactics are then developed for each business unit; hence the oft-quoted expression, 'mission/objectives down, strategy/tactics up'. Many variations to the M.O.S.T model have been proposed. For example, Mintzberg and Quinn (1991) have referred to 'middle-up-down management', which allows middle managers (and SBU managers), to set their own objectives within the organisational context. These ideas are illustrated in Tables 1.1, 1.2 and 1.3 below.

Table 1.1 Organisational hierarchies

- Decide the unit of strategic planning
  - Corporate level
  - Business unit level
  - Functional level
  - Individual level
- Strategy depends upon *where* you sit . . . 'one person's strategy is another's tactics'.
- And *when* you sit! 'What seemed tactical yesterday might prove strategic tomorrow.'
- Imposed, top-down; M.O.S.T. or
- Should we start with operational programmes to encourage experimentation and commitment?

Table 1.2 Strategy hierarchies

Corporate	Objectives	Strategy	Programmes	Budgets
Business Unit		Objectives	Strategy	Programmes
Functional			Objectives	Strategy
Individual				Objectives

Table 1.3 Process hierarchies

- Hierarchies of Objectives; strategies; programmes; budgets
- Rational way of presenting strategy; but, *what is the order of the hierarchy*?
  - Do objectives drive strategy or strategies drive objectives?
  - Do operational programmes drive strategy?
  - Do budgets make, express, respond to, or exist free of strategy?
  - Do decisions (capital expenditure) drive strategy?

Strategic marketing and the business unit level

Many writers (for example, Cravens 1994) believe that the essence of strategic marketing relates to decisions at the business unit level, as it is normally the principle responsibility of business unit management to decide product-market investment strategy and within that framework to develop a sustained competitive advantage. The view that strategic marketing relates mainly to the business unit level will be explored later in the text; first we will start by exploring the nature of strategy in the wider context.

The Generic Nature of Strategy

Strategy is not only a highly intangible concept, but it has strong, almost archetypal associations. One of these relates to the original meaning of the word, from the Greek *Strategos*, the art of generalship. For example, Mintzberg and Quinn (1991) quote the American Civil War Union General (later President), Ulysses S. Grant.

> Strategy is the deployment of one's resources in a manner which is most likely to defeat the enemy.

Transferring this to the organisational context

> Strategy is the means an organisation uses to achieve its objectives. (Kerin *et al.* 1990)

Implicit in these definitions is the view that strategy is an intentional process designed to achieve pre-determined objectives by the selected allocation of scarce resources (for example, allocations to functions, business units, regions, product categories or technological competencies).

The wider domain of strategy

> Most companies don't have a strategy. They just talk about it, like they do the weather. (Henderson, Boston Consulting Group, cited by Thompson 1990)

The domain of strategy is wider than an intentional process designed to allocate resources between business units and or product/market units. It is wider than the co-ordination of strategy formulation and implementation within a corporate hierarchy. The domain of strategy in the wider context relates to vision and the encouragement of strategic thinking. In this context strategic thinking is concerned with such issues as the following.

Receptivity to new ideas
Although the aim of strategy is rarely to formalise the status quo, an openness to alternative ideas (especially those presenting challenges to current practices) is difficult to achieve. This may require the fostering of an open culture or even the culture of irreverence (Kanter, 1983), rather than an emphasis upon a set of corporate values (for example, 'the IBM way').

Future orientation
A focus on the longer-term destiny of the organisation and the active consideration of alternative scenarios. This in turn requires familiarity with such issues as market/competitor orientation, the encouragement of experimentation and technological innovation,

Nurturing of core competencies
An emphasis upon the creation of linkages between corporate competencies (for example, exploiting converging technologies), upon which future successful

products and services may depend (in contrast to the conventional marketing approach which takes as the start-point existing product/market orientation).

Developing positive attitudes to unexpected events

In crisis situations, for example, organisations may rapidly 'discover' the imperative for a strategic direction. Decisions taken during a crisis period frequently have a significant impact on an organisation's strategy. Examples include, how Perrier responded to the benzene crisis, how Gillette responded to the Bic challenge and more generally how organisations respond to external innovation and global competition. Unexpected events, whether or not resulting in crises, often destroy established paradigms and become drivers of new strategic directions.

The purpose of strategy is to achieve the outcome, to defeat the enemy, to save the business or to make the right move on the global chess board. This requires an emphasis on the generation of alternatives, rather than the relative safety of analysis. The case material is designed to generate a number of alternatives and provide the opportunity for students to justify their choice of strategic direction rather than linger in the analysis stage.

Classifications of strategy

The generic nature of strategy can be further explored by considering Mintzberg's classifications of strategy as well as considering how strategy comes about.

Mintzberg (1987) highlighted five classifications of strategy which he referred to as the Five P's.

1. Strategy as Plan

The intended or deliberate strategy process emphasising a logical, structured sequence of events, designed to result in the identification of alternatives. Most business people will be familiar with this approach and may have specific experience of strategic planning. The strategy process should not be confused with the annual budget process, where the emphasis is normally upon short-term planning with minimum challenge to current assumptions.

2. Strategy as Ploy

An intended strategy can be general or specific; Strategy as Ploy relates to the latter and is often a specific programme, tactic or manoeuvre to outwit competition. Sales promotional programmes are frequently designed to 'wrong foot' competitors. For example, competitors may be denied dealer attention or supermarket shelf space. Sales promotional 'ploys' may provide further examples of Mintzberg's point that what is tactical today may prove strategic tomorrow. Consider, for example, the now classic sales promotional ploys of Miss Pear's Soap, A Tiger In Your Tank, The Homepride flour graders and Arthur, the famous white cat, the star of so many cat food commercials (and so successful that few can now recall the brand Arthur was promoting; it was subsequently re-branded Arthur!). It's a safe bet that the original sales promotional programmes were not intended to take over the complete marketing strategy (and in some cases the complete identity of the product or company). To summarise this point on a higher note than cat food, a good example from literature of strategy as ploy is Farquhar's comedy *The Beaux Stratagem*.

3. Strategy as Pattern

Strategy may also be a consistency in behaviour. It may subsequently be post-rationalised by, for example, an external observer finding a pattern in the stream of events, or as Mintzberg and Walters (1982) observed, 'a pattern in the stream of decisions'. Such an emergent strategy, for example, might be perceived by a City financial analyst and subsequently presented in financial journals as the organisation's corporate strategy. Strategy, therefore, may be emergent as well as intended. For example, the organisation may start with clear objectives or intentions, but be forced to modify intentions by the dynamic of the environment, resulting in a strategy that could be identified on a point between the two extremes of a wholly intended strategy and a wholly emergent strategy.

4. Strategy as Position

This refers to the organisation's choice of positioning (or positioning by default) in its industry environment. This normally refers to technology, capabilities, scale and markets served relative to direct competition. Strategy in this example is determined by the organisation's position relative to competition. Industry positioning in this context should be distinguished from marketing positioning, which normally refers to positioning within a market sector which has been defined by customer-oriented market segmentation. In the wider strategic context, positioning is the mediating force or match between the organisation and its wider environment.

5. Strategy as Perspective

The perspective from the internal or corporate view of the world. This may result from the sub-total of intangible shared values, attitudes and beliefs. If, for example, the corporate view or culture is regarded as the distinctive strategic asset, the organisation will be concerned to extend these values to different locations and to new employees. The organisation presumably will be equally keen to reject ideas that do not fit with corporate norms.

These alternatives should be considered in the context of the conventional emphasis on the intended, deliberate strategy as articulated by a planning process. In the real world, however, the remaining classifications of strategy may be more representative, especially so as it is the minority of organisations that have formal strategic planing processes.

How does Strategy come about?

A number of writers have provided useful summaries of strategy models (for example, Mintzberg and Walters 1982; Chaffee 1985; McDonald 1992). The summary below is adapted from and is based upon Mintzberg and Walters' continuum, distinguishing between deliberate and emergent strategies. At the one extreme of the continuum, a perfectly deliberate strategy would be characterised by articulated common management intentions and an outcome realised exactly as intended. This implies that the organisational environment is static, predictable or under the control of the organisation (or any combination of all three). At the other extreme, an emergent strategy is characterised by the absence of intentions or emerges despite any such intentions. Here the environment 'directly imposes a pattern of action on an organization' (Mintzberg and Walters 1982). Even in the absence of management decisions, observers external to an organisation may still be able to perceive a pattern in the stream of events. Working from more deliberate models towards more emergent models:

- **A planning model:** Characterised by precise intentions and supported by formal plans. Such a plan has been requested by TTi for the Royal China Group. The planning model attempts to reduce uncertainty by charting a direction, defining the organisation, focusing effort and providing consistency.
- **A visionary leadership model:** The leader's vision may not be articulated in formal plans, but it is intended. The vision, however, may prove to be untimely, wrongly conceived and too dependent upon the strategic leader. In the case of the Mortimer Arms it is doubtful if the tavern manager ever had any formal plans, rather the success of his activities related to his vision and leadership.
- **An ideological/interpretative model:** The shared attitudes and values may lead to self-fulfilling prophesies and the rejection of ideas seen to conflict with a shared view of the world. The direction remains mainly intentional. In the British Safety Razor case the shared attitudes and values of the introverted AAA Group have led them into a declining business situation as well as questionable marketing ethics.
- **A political model:** Strategies may emerge as the result of stakeholder power broking. This refers to alliances, for example, between internal (the management), external (the banks) and market (the distributors) stakeholders. The Mortimer Arms case provides an example of similar stakeholder alliances.
- **A logical incremental model:** Quinn (1980):

  Strategies . . . tend to emerge step by step from an iterative process in which the organisation probes the future, experiments and learns from a series of partial (incremental) commitments rather than through global formulations of total strategies. (Quoted in Thompson 1990).

  The incremental model also assumes that the organisation is progressing towards intended goals seeking stable equilibrium within the wider environment. The case example of Kowloon Oils and Essences is an example of a small organisation proceeding incrementally towards an international strategy.

- **A consensus model:** A consensus may emerge around environmental imperatives, not necessarily related to management intentions. In the Betaware case there is evidence that a consensus is emerging as to the difficulty of competing in the small electrical appliance market. The Royal China case, by contrast, provides an example of a marked lack of any consensus which is paralysing strategic initiatives.
- **An imposed ecological model:** Success depends upon adapting to the changing environment. Strategy is mainly a reaction to unpredictable

environmental factors. The survival of the fittest, a Darwinian view of the world. Many of the cases use the imperative of corporate crisis to highlight the adverse effects of an imposed environment.

In practice organisational strategy is likely to come about as a hybrid of the above models. Given the nature of student learning in the context of case material, we will place the emphasis on students acquiring a structured approach to strategic decision making. Our emphasis, however, will be on the importance of outputs. We will also highlight the constraints of the process and suggest modifications.

Although we will emphasise strategy as a process, it is not necessarily a top-down process. The initiative for strategic thinking may well be reversed, so that operations may drive strategy with or without strong leadership.

Strategy is not to be viewed as a point of arrival towards which organisations are constantly striving. Strategy remains a dynamic, intangible concept. Baden-Fuller

---

LEARNING NOTE on environmental influences on strategy

The usefulness of the various models may also relate to the nature of the organisational environment. Duncan (1972) has highlighted the relationship between the ways in which business decisions are made and the level of complexity and stability in an environment. He distinguishes environments that are static from those that are dynamic, and environments that are complex from those that are simple, to categorise four archetypal environments.

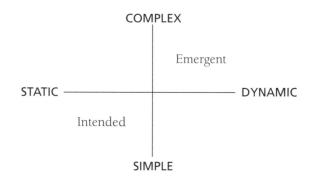

It could be argued that different strategy perspectives or models would be more or less appropriate to each of these distinctive archetypal environments. For example, the static/simple quadrant characterised by a predictable environment would be appropriate to the deliberate/ planning model, whilst the quadrant representative of complex/dynamic environmental conditions would be more appropriate to a form of emergent strategy.

and Stopford (1994) recommend that managers view their actions as steps on a 'strategic staircase' which requires the co-ordination of discrete activity phases to ensure that there is a cumulative effort to mount the whole staircase.

The dominant strategy paradigm

All of these models accept the dominant strategic paradigm, the inseparability of the organisation and the environment. Stacey (1993) summarises this as:

> the belief that organisations succeed when they operate in states of stability and harmony to adapt intentionally to their environments.

The idea that to be successful organisations need to pursue harmony and stable equilibrium with their environments underpins conventional approaches to strategy. Stress is placed upon the need to balance internal strengths and weaknesses with external opportunities and threats. The domain of strategy is believed to be limited by the concept of 'E-V-R' congruence; the overlap between the external Environment and corporate Values and Resources.

The Fruits of Disorder: Challenges to Strategy as Stable Equilibrium

The intentional pursuit of stability, balance and harmony is designed to reduce the level of surprise and increase the level of predictability. The management emphasis is one of shared visions, missions and culture; of consensus, team-building and consistency. Such uniformity and order has to be reconciled with the fruits of the rule of disorder.

> The overwhelming majority of successful innovations exploit change. (Drucker 1985)

Drucker's maxim could also be re-written to read that the majority of successful strategies create or exploit change. This implies that they should seek conditions of instability rather than conditions of stability. As Peters (1987) has commented:

> The winners of tomorrow will deal proactively with chaos, will look at the chaos per se as the source of market advantage, not as a problem to be got around. Chaos and uncertainty are market opportunities for the wise.

Some authors take the view that successful organisations are not those that attempt to adapt harmoniously to a given environment, but are those that can cope with instability and are able to harness the resulting tension as a catalyst to creating new opportunities and environments. Silicon valley, the M4 corridor and the Italian shoe industry are examples of industries creating environments, rather than adapting to existing environments.

This point is made by Stacey (1993), who believes that successful organisations are 'not simply adapting, they are creating'. He further suggests that:

> creativity is closely related to destruction, that instability is required to shatter existing paradigms so making way for the new . . . Success therefore is strongly

related to the maintenance of contradiction: developing configuration and then breaking it.

The hypothesis is that organisations may at first seek and achieve success from configurations of consistency and harmony in pursuit of the paradigm of stable equilibrium, but then face the paradox of failure when developing the configurations to excess. This implies that continuing conventional attempts to balance internal strengths and weaknesses with external opportunities and threats, may sow the seeds of disaster. The almost unparalleled success of the Model T Ford generated a corporate climate of stability and over-confidence which in turn contributed to Ford's resistance to changing market conditions and the new process innovation of all steel bodies.

Previous writers have made similar points (Miller 1990 and Pascale 1990). Miller rewrote the old adage that nothing succeeds like success by postulating that:

> Success leads to specialisation and exaggeration, to confidence and complacency, to dogma and ritual.

Rather than making the conventional either/or choices required between opposites, it is perhaps those organisations that best learn to live with and manage the tensions created by instability that succeed. Goold and Campbell (1987) have identified five such tensions:

1. Multiple perspectives v. individual responsibility
2. Planning v. entrepreneurial decision-making
3. Strong leadership v. business autonomy
4. Long-term v. short-term objectives
5. Flexible strategies v. tight controls

In the context of innovation this is expressed by Utterback (1994) as follows:

> Typically top management is pulled by two opposing, responsible forces: those that demand commitment to the old, and those that advocate for the future. Unfortunately, advocacy tends to overstate the market potential and understate their costs. Management, then, must find the right balance between support for incremental improvements and commitments to new and unproven innovations. Understanding and managing this tension perceptively may well separate the ultimate winners from the losers.

And in the context of strategy, Johnson (1989) has commented:

> If strategy is to be managed effectively, adaptively there must exist a 'constructive tension' (Kanter, 1983) between that which it is necessary to preserve and that which must be changed.

Specific examples of some of the tensions included in the case material are:

- Short-term profits v. market share growth. Case example, Carlsberg.
- Loose v. tight controls. Case example, Boston Candy.
- Decentralisation v. centralisation. Case example, Banking on a Winning Strategy.
- Individual inspiration v. team co-operation. Case example, Philips.
- Product proliferation v. product rationalisation. Case example, Betaware Housewares.

- Reduce direct product costs v. increase quality. Case example, Royal China.
- Setting up joint ventures in developing markets v. retaining export revenues. Case example, British Safety Razor.
- Premium image products v. competitive pricing. Case example, Benetton.
- Improve service delivery quality v. reduce service staff. Case example, Banking on a Winning Strategy.

A new paradigm could then be formulated which would be based upon the creative tensions engendered by instability, and the relationships between crises, destruction and creativity. The suggestion is that in these conditions inspired strategic leaps are possible in the face of the imperative to survive destructive forces.

Examples of internal and external crises

Greiner (1972) has developed a crisis-based model of organisational development. In this model strategic change is based upon five phases of growth punctuated by crises. In order to progress to each phase of growth the organisation must first resolve a crisis. He identifies five growth phases and related crises:

- Growth through creativity leading to a crisis of leadership
- Growth through direction leading to a crisis of autonomy
- Growth through delegation leading to a crisis of control
- Growth through co-ordination leading to a crisis of red tape
- Growth through collaboration leading to a possible crisis of psychological saturation

This internal view of organisational development needs to be complemented by externally-induced crises. For example, these may result from market shifts, changes in customer demand, competitive activity and innovation. As innovation frequently occurs from outside an industry this can result in crisis situations for the existing manufacturers.

One of our case examples refers to the global wet-shaving market. The 'British Safety Razor' case is based on the experiences of the major global players, who in common with most businesses can identify a succession of external crises. In the razor and blade market these have included:

- Expiration of patents on safety razors
- Monopoly of captive razor systems by competitors
- Introduction of new technology, stainless blades
- Introduction of twin systems
- Introduction of disposables

Similarly, Henry and Walker (1991) cite five historical external crises for Harley-Davidson:

- Customers switch to cars for basic transportation in the 1920's
- The Great Depression of the 1930's hits, just as the first crisis is survived
- Military orders for motorcycles nose-dive from the late 1940's

- Post-war demand sags as veterans concentrate on the basics of housing and other necessities
- The fifth crisis (possibly the most threatening) was the Japanese motorcycle invasion of the 1970's

It is at such times that strategy is 'discovered'. The decision taken at a time of crisis is frequently critical to corporate survival. Authors such as Argenti (1976) and Slatter (1984) have written comprehensively on corporate collapse and recovery. Slatter's work is especially helpful in summarising internal and external crises and the relationships between them. Slatter (1984) defines a crisis situation as 'one characterised by surprise, short decision time and a high threat to important values' and highlights 11 interrelated causal factors of corporate decline which may trigger crisis:

- Lack of financial control
- Inadequate management
- Price and product competition
- High cost structure
- Changes in market demand
- Adverse movements in commodity markets
- Lack of marketing effort
- Big projects
- Acquisitions
- Financial policy
- Overtrading

Many of these points are included in the case material and students should attempt to identify these points as part of the resource and environmental analysis.

Organisational unlearning

Slatter also anticipated many writers with his concept of 'organisational unlearning' which linked crisis to recovery. He maintained that the destructive process of disintegration and crisis could facilitate recovery providing that organisations unlearn their recipes and are open to reprogramming. This destructive/creative process prompted by crises is developed further in the Mortimer Arms, Betaware and the Royal China Group case material.

This process of organisational unlearning has been developed by Mintzberg and Quinn (1991), summarising the work of a number of authors as:

- Organisations have to unlearn what they know before they can learn new knowledge
- Organisations have to lose confidence in their old leaders before they will listen to new leaders
- Organisations have to abandon their old goals before they will adopt new goals
- Organisations have to reject their perceptual filters before they will notice events they previously overlooked
- Organisations have to see that their old methods do not work before they will invent and use new methods.

Unfortunately, crisis-ridden organisations may learn that their old methods do not work, and yet they may not learn new methods which do work. (Mintzberg and Quinn 1991)

Towards a Focus for Strategic Marketing

A number of writers have defined strategic marketing in the context of a process (Kotler, Cravens and Kerin). This process is characterised by an emphasis upon business units, on product/market decisions and on the principles of segmentation, targeting and positioning (STP). For example, Cravens (1994) defines strategic marketing as:

> the process of strategically analysing environmental, competitive and business factors affecting business units and forecasting future trends. Participating in setting objectives and formulating corporate and business unit strategy. Selecting target market strategies for the product-markets in each business unit, setting marketing objectives, and developing, implementing, and managing the marketing program positioning strategies designed to meet the needs of customers in each target market.

A critical part of the process of strategic marketing, emphasised by many authors, is the development of sustained competitive advantage. For example:

> The strategy concept can be encapsulated into two core elements: the product-market investment decision . . . (and) the development of a sustainable competitive advantage to compete in those markets. (Aaker 1984)

Cravens' definition continues the process of integrating strategic marketing into corporate strategy, whilst focusing the distinctive marketing contribution at the SBU level. The relevance of business units to the strategic marketing process is suggested by:

1. The logic of strategy integration may depend upon the need to decide specific business unit strategy (so that there is a focus and rationale for ordering activities and allocating resources)
2. The need to ensure that planning is not separated from implementation
3. Implementation is normally dependent upon product/market strategy
4. This is especially relevant when it is remembered that separate business units will most probably comprise a number of distinct Product Market Units (PMUs), each requiring a distinctive marketing mix
5. The relevance of the principles of 'STP' to the 'PMUs'

Others writers, such as Wilson *et al.* (1992), also suggest that the essence of strategic marketing includes the principles of Segmentation, Targeting and Positioning. This concept, pertinent to much of our case material, is developed further in Chapter 2. That chapter also reviews the process view of strategic marketing, complementing it with our emphasis on outputs rather than analyses.

Competitive Advantage

What business strategy is all about – what distinguishes it from all other kinds of business planning – is in a word, competitive advantage. Without competitors there would be no need for strategy, for the sole purpose of strategic planning is to enable the company to gain, as efficiently as possible, a sustainable edge over its competitors. (Ohmae 1982)

The effectiveness of any business unit's product/market strategy (aided by the application of the principles of STP) is therefore determined by the strength of the underpinning competitive advantage. According to Cravens, competitive advantage occurs when:

> an organisation's capability exceeds the strongest competitor for a buying criterion that is important to buyers. Competitive advantage is gained by finding an aspect of differentiation that targeted customers will perceive as superior value and that cannot be easily duplicated by the competition. (Cravens 1994)

Examples of competitive advantages include:

- Superior product benefits
- Superior image benefits
- Superior service benefits
- Superior relationships
- Scale advantages
- Legal advantages
- Functional marketing advantages

In the pursuit of competitive advantage, firms normally attempt to benchmark their nearest competitors with similar technology and infrastructures. This approach is dangerous in the context of dynamic change and market discontinuities, as the most threatening competition normally comes from the unexpected direction. For example, even in the low-tech/no-tech Betaware case (which covers the mundane low-priced hollowware industry), whereas incremental product development is being driven by domestic competition and the dominant retail trade, discontinuous innovation is being driven more by the Continental and Italian designers, designing for other markets.

> Ironically, following advice to be market-driven in pursuing innovation, delighting one's customers through continuous improvement of products, and seeking out lead users may be powerful concepts for success . . . but when applied to a discontinuity, they may lead a strong firm into a dangerous trap. Similarly, ideas such as lead manufacturing (with regard to product and manufacturing competencies) and mass customisation (with regard to marketing and distribution competencies) may be thought of as a way to build core competence and to be highly successful in differentiating well-known products. But these concepts may lead to a dead end when radical change is in the wind. (Utterback 1994)

Key factors for success

The allocation of scarce corporate resources to create competitive advantage, requires focusing upon those areas where differentiation can provide the most benefits. Without a structure the search for the elusive competitive advantage begins to resemble the marketing equivalent of the philosopher's stone.

Ohmae (1982), in *The Mind of the Strategist*, provides such a framework by introducing the concept of Key Factors for Success (KFSs). In any industry or market, Ohmae believes there are specific factors, which if identified, can be the keys to successful performance relative to competition. KSFs can then be employed to provide both a framework for the allocation of resources and a focus for competitive advantage. Allocating resources in a similar way to competition, Ohmae stresses, is unlikely to lead to a competitive edge. Given the dynamic nature of industries and environments, competitive advantage may be achieved more by the 'reconfiguration' of the key success factors rather than by their passive acknowledgement.

Strategic thinking, therefore, might be assisted if we could identify these key success factors. The intentional approach to marketing strategy should include, as part of the 'External Audit of the Business' (see Chapter 2), an attempt to identify these factors. Once identified the quest for competitive advantage, it is argued, becomes more relevant to market needs and better focused.

To summarise, Ohmae believes that the term 'strategy' should be reserved for:

> actions aimed directly at altering the strength of the enterprise relative to that of its competitors.

This can be achieved by identifying the KFSs and . . .

> then to inject a concentration of resources into a particular area where the company sees an opportunity to gain the most strategic advantage over its competitors.

As Ohmae points out, if resources are allocated in the same way as competition there will be no change in the relative position of the company.

The difficulty is how to identify the factors. Not only will they vary by industry, but they will also vary by the desired objective, (for example, short-term profit v. longer-term market share). Ohmae's guidance for identifying KFSs is to understand your market segmentation and understand the conditions for success or failure in your industry.

The table below illustrates possible key factors for success for four markets covered by the case material in the text:

Table 1.4 Key factors for success

The Royal China Group	SilverWorks Design	Montpellier Spa	The Mortimer Arms
Traditional Fine China	*Product Design*	*The Mineral Water Market*	*A Country Hotel, Leisure Market*
Stock levels	Design integrity	Distribution costs	Service delivery
Control of distrib.	Quality of service	Access to distribution	Staff training
Design and market segmentation	Link design and application	Branding/positioning	Location, facilities ambience
Heritage and image	Culture of creativity	Pricing	Reputation
Reliability of supply	Product field expertise	Purity	Target market
		Scale	

Strategic degrees of freedom

Assuming that such Key Factors can be identified, the next step is to determine how to concentrate competitive advantage against the identified areas.

In this context, Ohmae highlights the exploitation of 'Strategic Degrees of Freedom' as they apply to each of the identified key factors for success.

In the mineral water example above, there is limited room for exploiting degrees of freedom in pricing decisions, as the mineral water market is normally highly competitive, characterised by low margins with the majority of the retail price accounted for by trade margins. By contrast, taking the example of an insurance brokerage (where the premium rate or price has been identified as a key factor), there is normally considerable freedom to exploit the price factor. The insurance 'product' is mainly intangible, dependent upon personal skills and an empathy with specific client situations. It is difficult therefore to make direct comparisons with competitors, as each client's 'risk' is specific to that client. In this situation there is freedom to exploit the price factor, but there is also the associated risk of error. Strategic degrees of freedom, therefore, need to be qualified by a consideration of the organisation's objectives.

Of core competencies, core products and end products

The terms 'differentiation' and 'distinctive competence' are normally used to refer to discrete competencies. More recent work by Prahalad and Hamel (1990) has stressed the ability of global organisations (specifically Japanese) to develop combinations of core competencies (technical, managerial, cultural), which are more likely to lead to sustained competitive advantage, rather than the identification of unrelated competencies. This raises a challenge to the traditional product/market emphasis. Markets are, then, the results of nurtured core competencies rather than the starting point for product opportunities.

Prahalad and Hamel have provided a fresh perspective on competitive advantage. They accept that in the short-term a company's competitiveness derives from:

> the price/performance of current products . . . in the long run competitiveness derives from an ability to build, at lower cost and more speedily than competitors, the core competencies that spawn unanticipated products . . . Competencies are the glue that binds existing businesses. They are also the engine for new business development. Patterns of diversification and market entry must be guided by them, not just by the attractiveness of markets.

The analogy of the tree is evoked, with the root system as the core competence; the trunk and limbs as the core products; the smaller branches as the business units; and the leaves and fruit as the end products. This analogy suggests that marketing may be little more than a short-term function; deployed for example when there is a necessity for market communications. The challenge to the starting point of market transactions, focusing on customers and competitors, questions the whole relevance of the traditional marketing philosophy. For example, market share, focusing on the end product, is then only one indicator of success. Similarly, competitive analysis needs to look beyond existing product-market configurations;

additional measures are needed to monitor competitive core competencies and core products.

> Unlike the battle for global brand dominance, which is visible in the world's broadcast and print media and is aimed at building global share of mind, the battle to build world class competencies is invisible to people who aren't deliberately looking for it. (Prahalad and Hamel 1990)

Identifying core competencies

Prahalad and Hamel propose three tests; a core competence should:

- Provide potential access to a wide variety of markets
- Make a significant contribution to the perceived customer benefits of the end product
- Be difficult for competitors to imitate

Some of these conditions may be found in the multinational companies covered in the cases. These include Benetton, Carlsberg and Philips as well as the concealed multinationals of Boston Candy and British Safety Razor.

In the Carlsberg example (United Breweries of Denmark), the core competencies relating to this relatively low-tech industry would include:

- The global strategic alliances to secure distribution.
- The sale of technology overseas by their associated company, Danbrew Consult Ltd. This emphasises the point that more money can be made in some markets by selling brewing technology than by marketing beer. The starting point is the competence in brewing technology which is difficult to match.
- The difficulty of imitating the intangible global creative positioning for Carlsberg.

> The old arguments about technology-push and demand-pull may today have a different outcome. Certainly, the innovations produced by the subjects of Hamel and Prahalad's enquiry are not of the 'bigger fins and stripes in toothpaste' variety. (Wilson 1994)

Strategic Business Units (SBUs)

In Chapter 2 we will review the intentional planning model of strategic marketing. Given that the organisation cannot normally be 'planned' as a single entity, the planning process first requires the identification of the core planning units which form both the unit of analysis and the unit of projection. In other words, are plans to be produced by region, by market, by product group, by customer group, by function, or some other sub-grouping relevant to the organisation? For larger organisations the conventional approach is to identify strategic business units as the core planning units.

McNamee (1992) defines the strategic business unit as:

> A natural strategic grouping within a company which:

- Allocates resources
- Is a focus for strategic effort
- Provides strategically useful performance measures
- Forms the core planning unit

Increasingly, organisations set different objectives and expect different results from the component parts (or SBUs) of the organisation. Referring to Ansoff's classic matrix (Ansoff 1957), why, for example, should existing products in new markets be expected to contribute equally to overall corporate objectives? After all, this is the basic rationale for the distinctiveness of the SBU. As Abel and Hammond (1979) have commented:

> Not all units and sub-units need to grow at the same rate; not all units and sub-units need to produce the same level of profitability; not all units and sub-units must contribute equally to cash flow objectives.

How to recognise an SBU

McNamee (1992) highlights the identification process for business units. This is based upon an analysis of the existing business resulting in a 'disaggregation' of corporate activities into the company's products, markets, customers, technologies and geographical components. These constituent parts can then be clustered into unique combinations which serve as candidate SBUs. The criteria below can then be applied as a check to whether or not core planning units have:

- Common product families?
- Common technologies?
- Common end-user groups?
- Common distribution channels?
- Common geography?

Do the resulting groupings require:

- Different strategies?
- Different base technologies?
- Different competitive positions?
- Different management accounts?
  (as the management accounts should be keyed into each resulting SBU)
- Different markets/end-users?
- Different products/services?
- Different prices/cost structures?

Given the importance of the business unit in the context of strategic marketing, we have provided the opportunity for students to attempt the identification of SBUs and PMUs.

Dangers of the SBU mind-set

As we have seen earlier, Prahalad and Hamel (1990) provide a different perspective on a company's competitiveness. They distinguish between core competencies, core products and end products in a global competitive environment where competition is played out under different rules at each level (distinguishing, for example, between brand share and manufacturing share).

They believe that the SBU in this context is, 'an anachronism, an organisational dogma for a generation', which was devised 20 years ago when competition was purely domestic. They highlight the dangers of regarding organisations as portfolios of businesses, rather than portfolios of competencies. The SBU mind-set, they suggest, may lead to investment and divestment decisions which ignore competencies. Such competencies represent the collective learning of the organisation. Under a SBU structure, for example, no single unit may have the resources to invest in building the core competencies required for global leadership; and if divestment is involved:

> When it comes to core competencies, it is difficult to get off the train, walk to the next station, and then reboard. (Prahalad and Hamel 1990)

Summary

Marketing as a business philosophy is now at the heart of strategy and it is becoming increasingly difficult to recognise any boundaries. Although strategies may come about in a number of ways, we will continue to stress the intended strategy process in order to provide a disciplined framework for students. This framework will be considered in more detail in Chapter 2.

Strategic marketing has many faces, some more tangible than others. Where strategic marketing deals in known facts its contribution to the strategy process appears to be focused mainly at the business unit level, with the consequent emphasis upon supporting product/market decisions with a sustainable competitive advantage. Where strategic marketing deals with the part known and the unknown, the strategic marketing perspective is that of the change agent providing a focus for challenges to existing thinking (rather than being the means to existing ends).

Challenges to the credibility of the marketing concept itself will be further explored in Chapter 3. The marketing concept might have come of age, but a marketing identity crisis appears to have been provoked as the marketing concept is increasingly subsumed within the fields of corporate strategy, total quality and organisational dynamics. This trend becomes more evident as the marketing concept spreads to non-competitive environments. Given the relationship between creativity and crisis, which is one of the themes of this text, a new marketing concept may well emerge more suited to the contemporary environment of dynamic change and globalisation. In the meantime the credibility of the marketing concept is not helped by the rusting of some of the tools in the 'marketing toolkit'.

2

The Strategic Marketing Planning Process

Unhappy the general who comes on the field of battle with a system.
(Napoleon 1804)

Although there are a number of approaches to strategic marketing, the case material requires a disciplined approach emphasising the intended, systematic approach to developing marketing strategy. We now begin to use the term 'marketing strategy' in the context of an intentional plan.

The literature is inconclusive as to the practical benefits of the formal planning process, given the practical difficulties for researchers to isolate the specific contribution of planning. The difficulty of such research is the complex nature of the numerous interrelated factors. Nevertheless, research by prestigious academics (Ansoff et al. 1970) suggests a positive relationship between profitability and the planning process. The more general advantages of formalised strategic thinking, however, are easier to summarise. The summary below is adapted from Greenley (1989).

- Forces management to assess the appropriateness of the current strategy.
- Forces management to consider alternatives.
- Requires future orientation and the reconciliation of short-term with longer-term decisions.
- Reduces the tendency to focus energy and resources on problems.
- Provides a framework for resource allocation.
- Takes account of internal strengths and weaknesses in relation to external opportunities and threats.
- Introduces logical and systematic thinking (rather than *ad hoc* decision making).
- Provides a vehicle for communication, co-ordination and control.
- Provides an opportunity to improve morale by involving employees in the strategic process.
- Helps to reduce resistance to change by such participation.

There are many models of the formal process but most are based upon the three-phase structure articulated by Johnson and Scholes (1989).

- **Where are we now?**: The situation analysis, out of which alternatives become more obvious. In the context of marketing planning this includes an external and internal audit which will be addressed in greater depth later in this chapter.
- **Where do we want to go?**: Formulating objectives relating to the strategy hierarchy referred to earlier, resulting in a hierarchy of objectives.
- **How are we going to get there?**: Deciding the vehicle of strategy, which normally includes the product/market mix.

A fourth stage of implementation, co-ordination and control, would require detailed operational plans for each part of the marketing mix.

The three tables below illustrate the phases in the development of strategic planning, the limitations of budgeting divorced from strategy and an overview of the strategy process.

Table 2.1 Phases in the development of strategic planning

---

1. Financial planning
   – Emphasis: annual budgets
2. Forecast-based planning
   – Emphasis: longer time required for investment paybacks and commitments
3. Externally orientated planning
   – Emphasis: a process; formal situation analysis generating strategic alternatives
4. Strategic management
   – Emphasis: on nurturing strategic thinking; on results integration of hierarchies;
   – Informal; flexible procedures; open dialogues; no committees!

Source: adapted from Gluck, Kaufman and Walleck (1982)

Table 2.2 Budgeting divorced from strategy

Problems:
• Short termism
• Once a year horsetrading ritual
• Underlying assumptions remain unchallenged
• Misallocation of resources; under-investment in growth businesses whilst subsidising marginal business?
• Confusion, frustration, conflict

Table 2.3 The strategy process

• Strategy formulation:
   – Thinking
   – Creating the guidelines
   – Mission, objectives, strategies, policies
• Strategy implementation:
   – Acting
   – Programmes, budgets, procedures
   – Performance and feedback
• Strategy coordination
   – Where are we now?
   – Where do we want to go?
   – How are we to get there?

In order to anchor the strategic marketing planning process to the wider strategic planning process on the one hand and to the detailed marketing operational plans on the other, variations of the following model are examples of the externally orientated planning process refered to in Table 2.1 above. Such models serve to

Figure 2.1 A strategic marketing planning model

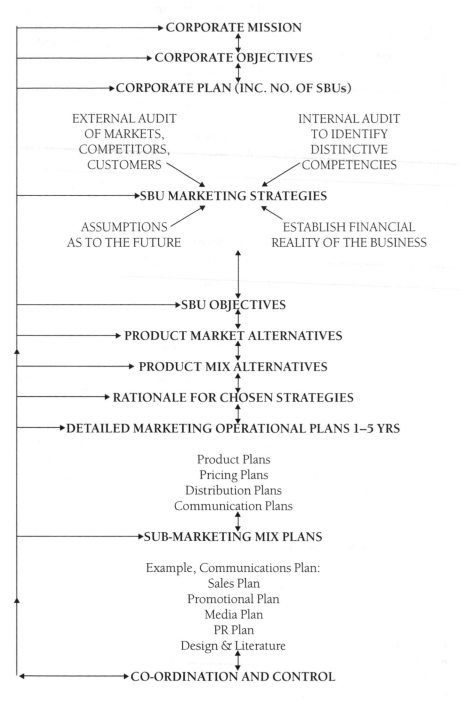

CORPORATE MISSION

CORPORATE OBJECTIVES

CORPORATE PLAN (INC. NO. OF SBUs)

EXTERNAL AUDIT
OF MARKETS,
COMPETITORS,
CUSTOMERS

INTERNAL AUDIT
TO IDENTIFY
DISTINCTIVE
COMPETENCIES

SBU MARKETING STRATEGIES

ASSUMPTIONS
AS TO THE FUTURE

ESTABLISH FINANCIAL
REALITY OF THE BUSINESS

SBU OBJECTIVES

PRODUCT MARKET ALTERNATIVES

PRODUCT MIX ALTERNATIVES

RATIONALE FOR CHOSEN STRATEGIES

DETAILED MARKETING OPERATIONAL PLANS 1–5 YRS

Product Plans
Pricing Plans
Distribution Plans
Communication Plans

SUB-MARKETING MIX PLANS

Example, Communications Plan:
Sales Plan
Promotional Plan
Media Plan
PR Plan
Design & Literature

CO-ORDINATION AND CONTROL

illustrate some of the complex inter-relationships.

Other writers have provided sequential and interactive models of the marketing planning process. McDonald (1989) explains the sequences and interactions in his book *Marketing Plans*. Such representation of the marketing planning process inevitably appears to be more linear and sequential than the reality. Models have been criticised as oversimplifications which 'make no attempt to capture the richness of unarticulated management experience' (Piercy and Giles 1989). Accordingly, the model is not intended to be a straightjacket or a form of relay race between fixed points, rather to serve as stepping stones for students wishing to explore the process without losing sight of the path. The emphasis of the process, however, should be on outcomes and actions rather than the process itself. We will return to both these points in the critique of the process at the end of the chapter. Referring to the model, we will now highlight the main constituent parts of the process.

Mission Statements: The Lost Opportunity?

Mission statements are much abused and the subject of much cynicism. Unbelievers will point to people and organisations without formal mission statements, but with obvious zeal and sense of purpose. By analogy, this is equivalent to pointing out that St. Paul had so strong a mission, he had no need of a mission statement! The starting point of the strategic marketing planning process, however, is to relate marketing strategy to the vision of the key stakeholders including the senior management. If there is no vision, platitudes will not suffice. This vision is normally referred to as the organisational mission statement and is defined by Thompson (1990) as 'the overriding *raison d'être* for the business'.

Organisational stakeholders are 'any group or individual who can affect or is affected by the achievement of an organisation's purpose' (Freeman 1984). Writers, including Greenley (1989) and Wilson *et al.* (1992), have classified stakeholders as: Internal (owners, managers, other employees); Marketplace (customers, competitors, suppliers) and External (Government, trade associations). Depending upon the extent of their power and interest these stakeholders have the opportunity to define the vision of the future.

Effective mission statements

According to Ackoff (1986) the mission statement should act as 'an invisible guiding hand' for the organisation; 'it should not be what the company needs to do to survive, but what it should do to thrive', and is more likely to be effective if the following points (loosely adapted from Ackoff) are addressed:

- Provide a framework for setting corporate objectives
- Articulate the essential purpose of the organisation
- Provide unanimity of purpose
- Provide long-range vision
- Differentiate the organisation from the competition

- Be relevant to all stakeholders
- Motivate, Excite and Inspire

Pearce and Robinson (1985) also suggest criteria. These include a statement of markets to compete in; customers to be served; core technologies; and products/services to be offered.

Compared to these criteria it is hard to disagree with Ackoff (1986), that: 'most corporate mission statements, are worthless'. Sadly we have seen the proliferation of banal, platitudinous statements, most of which inspire nobody and almost always avoid the issues of differentiation and definition of business domain. The situation we believe has not improved since Professor Ackoff's comments. Our acid tests for mission statements are:

- Whether or not it is possible to disagree!
- Whether or not the statement could equally apply to other market contenders.
- Does it inspire ?
- Does it serve as a starter for strategy development?

Even a simple sentence can be more definitive than politically-correct platitudes. For example, in the Royal China case study, the following statement from 'H.H.' and the directors would provide a clear direction, improve morale and, more importantly, exclude the consideration of alternatives.

> Our mission is to manufacture locally and market internationally the finest tableware in the world under our two historic company names. (H.H. Royal China Group)

Dangers of effective mission statements

Bearing in mind the point in the first chapter that strategy may emerge incrementally, the danger of definitive mission statements is that the mission becomes too prescriptive, actively discourages initiative or, worse, becomes the introduction to the corporate credo. Mission statements may then become inflexible monuments to corporate thinking, out of key with the wider environment. It is important therefore that the corporate mission is regularly revisited to reflect the dynamic environment. The vague, platitudinous statements, however, will require little modification, as these platitudes are not only irrelevant but timeless; for example, 'we are dedicated to customer delight!'.

Setting Objectives

The discipline of establishing an effective mission statement and clear objectives ensures that the process begins and remains strategic. Ansoff's classic definition of an objective is:

> A measure of efficiency of the resource conversion process. An objective contains three elements: the particular attribute that is chosen as a measure of efficiency, the yardstick or scale by which the attribute is measured and the goal – the particular value on the scale which the firm seeks to attain. (Ansoff 1968)

An example of the three elements might be: market share, measured in value terms, with a target ten per cent share.

When considering objectives, factors to take into account include:

- The hierarchy of objectives
- Long and shorter-term trade-offs
- Trade-offs between seemingly irreconcilable objectives
- The nature of the strategy process

The hierarchy

Organisational objectives normally need to relate to the levels of strategy identified in the first chapter (corporate, business unit and functional). In the model, marketing objectives relate in the main to the identified business units. These SBU objectives then need to be reconciled to the overall corporate objectives on the one hand and to the product/market and functional objectives on the other. Product/market objectives may include:

- New product investment v. Existing product investment.
- Entering foreign markets v. Extending local distribution.
- Rationalising distribution channels v. Market coverage.
- Increasing the product range v. Rationalising the product range.

Long and short-term trade-offs

Taking account of the fact that one person's strategies are another's tactics, integration of the hierarchy also includes a recognition of the relationships between longer-term and shorter-term objectives. There may be potential ambiguity between longer-term objectives, relating to a planning horizon of perhaps five years ahead, and the shorter-term objectives driving the activities of the operational units.

Trade-offs or resolutions of paradox may be concerned with:

- Short-term profits v. Longer-term share growth
- Cashflow v. Retention or growth of a skilled workforce
- Sales revenue growth v. Cash flow
- Qualitative (for example, company image and customer perception) v. Quantitative (number of complaints)
- Return on net assets v. Increased stock holdings

Strategy is about the future. Shorter-term operational activities should be tracking towards the longer-term strategy horizon. Where operational plans are limited to short-term horizons (one year), without reference to the longer-term strategic plan (if it exists at all), the process has ceased to be strategic. In this situation the organisation may be dominated by the *ad hoc* ritualistic horse-trading that so often comprises the annual budgetary circus. There is no intention to suggest that budgets and forecasts are unnecessary, only to ensure that short-term budget objectives are based upon and build towards the longer-term goals of the organisation. The danger of the shorter-term approach in isolation is that the process ceases to be strategic, as assumptions for the future will not have been considered, nor will existing policies and procedures have been subject to challenge and review.

Objectives and the nature of the strategy process

The setting of objectives may also relate to the nature of the strategy process discussed in the first chapter. For example:

- In the visionary, leadership model, objectives may be highly dependent upon the strategic leader.
- In the political model, objectives will depend upon the realities of power and may not be agreed until compromise/conflict has been resolved.
- In the logical incremental model, objectives may be less succinct and shorter-term, emerging as events unfold.

Analysis

Going beyond the S.W.O.T.

It can be misleading to refer to an analysis phase, as information collection and interpretation as an on-going activity, rather than a one-off discrete phase of the strategy process. This approach may also alleviate the 'paralysis by analysis' syndrome, where the strategy process is bogged down at the start point attempting to answer the basic 'where are we now?' question from both the internal and external perspectives.

The audit or analysis phase may erroneously suggest to students a passive listing of internal strengths and weaknesses and external opportunities and threats. If internal corporate competencies underpinning competitive advantage are to be understood, it is important to go beyond the 'shopping list' approach of the normal S.W.O.T.[1] and P. E.S.T.[2] student audit. Taking the example of the internal resource audit, the analysis should include such considerations as:

- The effectiveness and efficiency of resource deployment (doing the right things rather than doing things right). Effectiveness relates to considerations such as the deployment of people, capital and marketing resources, whilst efficiency measures the productivity of these deployments in such terms as yields, utilisation and profitability.
- The priorities of the business in relation to the deployment of scarce resources.
- The balance of resources. An imbalance in the resource base might be identified if the board, for example, are all accountants or the salesforce skill base is confined to 'order-taking'.
- Changes in resources over time, as revealed by balance sheets and evidenced by acquisitions and disposals.
- Linkages between resources which can be explored by value-chain analysis.

[1] Strengths, weaknesses, opportunities and threats.
[2] Political, economic, social and technological environmental analysis.

- Reviewing the criteria for measuring success/failure, so that conclusions can be reached as to past performance.
- Comparisons to competitor resource deployment.

In similar vein the external analysis is sometimes confined to the macro environment given the logic and security of a P.E.S.T. analysis rather than the difficulties of summarising key information relating to customer behaviour, market structure and competitive intent. Given the importance of market segmentation to the analysis phase and the importance of targeting and positioning to product/market choices, the concept of 'STP' is covered under a separate heading. As the marketing literature is replete with advice for structuring the marketing audit, we will suggest two checklists, for the external and internal marketing audits (although we acknowledge that the marketing audit is part of the wider business audit discussed above).

Table 2.4 Analysing the SBU

- *External*
    - Environment, industry opinion leaders, key factors for success
    - Market, competitors, end-users
- *Internal*
    - Resource analysis; change, balance, effectiveness, efficiency
    - Linkages between resources
    - Resource priorities v. competitive priorities
    - Financial reality; stakeholder reality
- Avoid simple lists of strengths and weaknesses and 'paralysis by analysis'
- Make assumptions about the future

Figure 2.2

Example of an external marketing audit
Identify the opportunites and threats as a result of analysing:
- The market industry environment
- The key factors for success
- Market size/trends
- Market life cycle
- Market segmentation
  Is the segmentation mode correct/ relevant?
- Identify major competitors
- Summarise their market targeting/positioning
- Identify the channels of distribution
- Identify the key customer groupings
- Identify the key end-users groupings
- Specific analysis of direct competition
  (competitors in the same market sector)

Example of an internal marketing audit
Identify the Strategic Business Units (SBU's)
- Are they similar/different to those suggested in the case?
- Identify the major product market units (PMU's) within each SBU

- Identify strengths and weaknesses as a result of internal analysis:
  a) Segmental analysis:
     Summarise sales by SBU
                       by product group
                       by product
                       by outlet type/distribution channel
                       by customer
     As above by net profit or profit contribution
  b) Review the current marketing mix for the identified SBU's/PMU's (individual product groups), making comparisons to major competition where applicable:

     Branding/corporate identity strategy
     Width of range
     Depth of range
     Quality/price positioning
     Customer philosophy
     New products programme
     Positioning v. competition
     Pricing strategy
     Distribution strategy
     Communications strategy
        - selling
        - promotional activity
        - PR/exhibitions
        - advertising
  c) Review organisation, planning and financial data

     - Marketing organisation
       - integrated marketing areas/efforts?
       - integrated with other functional areas?
       - new product development organisation
     - Marketing planning and control
       - how frequently is objective information collected?
       - how strategic is the marketing planning process?
       - how formalised is the marketing planning process?
     - The financial base of the business
       - balance sheet
       - profit and loss statement
     - Summarise current marketing strategy

Market Segmentation, Targeting and Positioning (STP)

Many distinguished writers, including Kotler (1988) and Wilson *et al.* (1992), believe that STP is the essence of strategic marketing. Given that markets may be viewed as the sum of aggregate customer demand, it is more often than not sensible to question whether or not this demand is of a homogeneous nature. If it is not, distinct sub-sets of customer demand may be recognised within the market. The process of breaking markets down into distinct sub-sets or sectors is the process of market segmentation. This approach is well established. Over 20 years ago Levitt was urging marketing practitioners to:

> Stop thinking of . . . customers as part of some massively homogeneous market . . . start thinking of them as numerous small islands of distinctiveness, each of which requires its own unique strategies in product policy, in promotional strategy, in pricing, in distribution methods, and in direct selling techniques. (Levitt 1974)

The starting point for segmentation should be customer demand rather than manufacturers' modes of supplying that demand. This ensures that segmentation is based upon the ways in which the different customer groups perceive the products or services in the market place. The danger of defining market sectors from the internal view of the organisation should be avoided. Charles Revson, the founder of Revlon Inc., is reputed to have recognised this difference with his reference to selling hope (in bottles), rather than products.

Market segmentation therefore recognises the diversity of demand in the market place. It recognises that the needs and wants of customers or consumers are unlikely to be identical. This leads to the opportunity for marketing-oriented organisations to target distinct marketing mixes at distinct market sectors.

To summarise therefore, market segmentation is:

1. Sub-dividing markets into distinct sub-sets of customer demand or market sectors

Figure 2.3 The eight stages of the segmentation, targeting and positioning process

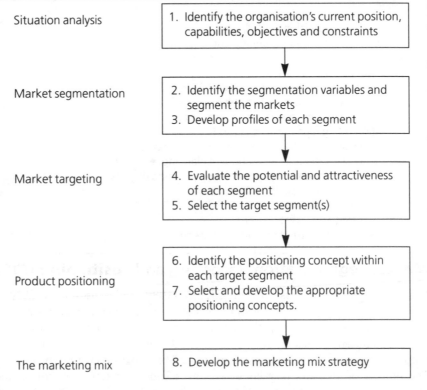

Situation analysis	1. Identify the organisation's current position, capabilities, objectives and constraints
Market segmentation	2. Identify the segmentation variables and segment the markets 3. Develop profiles of each segment
Market targeting	4. Evaluate the potential and attractiveness of each segment 5. Select the target segment(s)
Product positioning	6. Identify the positioning concept within each target segment 7. Select and develop the appropriate positioning concepts.
The marketing mix	8. Develop the marketing mix strategy

2. Where any market sector can be viewed as a distinct target market
3. Against which an organisation can deploy a distinct marketing mix to achieve competitive advantage

Wilson *et al.* (1992) have identified eight stages in the process. These are set out in Figure 2.3 (page 32).

The process of 'STP' is predicated upon a sound in-depth knowledge of customer perceptions. As this is often a daunting task, scepticism is common and may be voiced, for example, as: 'Why should we segment our market in a situation where our products have broad-based appeal; we would only be turning away good business and what is the sense in that?' Although this is true in some market situations (for example, those markets at the development stage of the market life-cycle), competitive advantage is unlikely to be achieved by such a broad-based appeal.

Counter segmentation, the dangers of introspection

- Customisation may sound great on the lips of the consumer worshippers, and the advertising industry, anxious to have a distinct profile of the target group, but satisfying customers at a loss is hardly a challenge. Profits are normally enhanced by standard products and service mixes. (Witness the trends towards global brands exploiting global market segments; for example, Seiko, Hertz, Haagen Dazs, Coca-Cola.) Normally, there should be a convincing argument for incurring the additional expenses of specific marketing mixes targeted at specific sectors. The resolution to this paradox is an opportunity for innovation. All too often marketing people can incur such additional expenses by the proliferation of additional lines, flavours and sizes which may flow from a desire to exclude competition rather than from market segmentation. There is a danger of marketing people becoming obsessed with the techniques of segmentation, rather than concentrating on the overall market trends and competitive activities. Segmentation should be taken with a few grains of salt with the emphasis, as many writers have suggested, on segments being Measurable, Accessible and Substantive.
- The environment is increasingly unpredictable, especially so in the dynamic/unstable conditions characterised by new-technology-based industries. This somewhat stable environmental marketing concept could be less than helpful in these circumstances. What may be more important, for example, might be the convergence of separate market sectors or the convergence of separate markets. Whereas, in established markets, a competitive innovator may achieve success by identifying a viable fast-growing market niche, another may originate from outside the market (perhaps because the innovator is not part of the dominant paradigm of the industry). The techniques of market segmentation are by definition introspective to the market under consideration. This problem is compounded by poor or misleading market definitions. Again quoting Levitt (1983):

> Two vectors shape the world, technology and globalisation. The first helps determine human preferences; the second, economic realities. Regardless of how much preferences evolve and diverge, they also gradually converge and form markets where economies of scale lead to reduction of costs and prices.

● The difficulty or impossibility of attempting segmentation in practice. This problem relates to the difficulties in choosing a mode(s) of segmentation. The danger is selecting an unsuitable mode upon which to base the subsequent targeting, positioning and development of a marketing mix. Peters (1987), in *Thriving on Chaos*, sets out the case for 'niche or be niched' and encourages this as an approach to market creation rather than market sharing. Market sharing focuses on establishing a position in existing markets, whilst market creation is the entrepreneurial activity of new ideas, new technology, new standards and new industry infrastructure. Peters' analogy is that market creation is about creating a bigger pie, or better still baking a new pie, rather than taking a bigger slice of the existing pie. To put this advice into practice, the strategic focus should be more on what markets might become, rather than on becoming obsessed with current market structures.

The paradox is that a concept close to the essence of strategic marketing could in some circumstances act as a restraint to strategic thinking.

Table 2.5 Summary of market segmentation, benefits and pitfalls

Benefits	Pitfalls
Staying close to the customer	Applying segmentation to emerging/technology-based markets
Knowledge of customer behaviour	
Focus for competitive advantage	Segmentation in manufacturer's/provider's terms
Specific marketing mix	
Opportunities become apparent	Fragmentation
Identification of positioning v. direct competitors	Lost in the techniques
	Markets incorrectly defined
Specific targeting for marketing communications	Poor information base
	Marketing introspection

Unfortunately, there is no one 'right way' to segment a market (whereas there probably are a number of very wrong ways). Another common problem is attempting to reconcile the different marketing strategies that might emerge if different, but equally viable, modes of market segmentation were employed. This point is illustrated in the insurance brokerage example in the section on 'Targeting' opposite.

As well as there being no one right mode, it is unusual to segment on the basis of a solus mode of segmentation. More often solutions can be found by combining modes. For example, a combination of geographic and demographic segmentation modes would result in geo-demographic market segmentation. Examples of combined modes of segmentation are found in the commentaries following both the Mortimer Arms (demographic, geographic and lifestyle segmentation) and the Royal China Group (lifestyle/demographic segmentation) case studies.

Getting the information: Identifying the mode of segmentation

A comprehensive review of modes of market segmentation is beyond the bounds of this practical case book and we are assuming a knowledge of the basic approach. For further study there are a number of excellent texts on the subject. Amongst these are Wilson, Gilligan and Pearson (1992) *Strategic Marketing Management*, Chapter 8; Lancaster and Massingham (1993) *Essentials of Marketing*, Chapter 7; and Walters (1988) *Strategic Retailing Management*, pp. 10–37.

The starting point for segmenting markets is an understanding of customer behaviour. The organisation needs to determine the ways in which their customers think, verbalise and react to their products or services. Generally, such information relates to the *Five W's of customer analysis*: who, where, what, when, why, and usually involves a significant amount of primary, mainly qualitative data. For example:

- Who they are: *Demographic* (age, sex, class, family life cycle)
- Where they are: *Geographic*
- What benefits they seek: ⎫
- How often they use/buy: ⎬ *Behaviourist*
- How loyal are they: ⎭
- Their attitudes, values, interests and lifestyles: *Psychographic*

Targeting

Targeting addresses the question: in which market segment or segments does the organisation wish to compete? Subsequent to the targeting decision, the organisation would then develop a specific product or service concept to aid the development of a specific marketing mix for a specific target segment(s).

In order to demonstrate the relevance of this approach to smaller businesses (given that such techniques are often thought to be more useful to larger organisations), set out in the table below is a 'targeting matrix', which is based upon a commercial insurance brokerage. This theme is further explored in the context of the Mortimer Arms, one of the cases included in the text.

The brokerage has been 'disaggregated' into its component parts, which are its clients and its services. The vertical axis on the product/market matrix below

Table 2.6 Targeting matrix for a commercial insurance brokerage: assuming two related but different modes of market segmentation

A. Client size by premium income Products/Services	Over £20k	£5–20k	Below £5k
Capital rewards	√		
Corporate pensions	√	√	√
Legal liability	√		
Car fleet insurance	√		
Stock damage	√	√	√
Non-payment risk	√		
Fixed assets	√	√	
Employee liability	√		

B. Client by industry type Products/Services	Industrial	Commerce	Service
Capital rewards		√	
Corporate pensions	√	√	√
Legal liability		√	
Car fleet insurance		√	
Stock damage	√	√	
Non-payment risk		√	
Fixed assets	√		
Employee liability	√	√	

tabulates the insurance brokerage's major product/service groups, whilst the horizontal axis tabulates the identified market segments in terms of client premium revenues. In order to illustrate the possible effects on marketing strategy of two different segmentation modes, the second part of the table changes the horizontal axis from client size to client industry type.

The process of targeting enables the brokerage to target specific market sectors; this in turn allows a specific marketing mix to be assembled, taking into account the distinctive needs of the targeted sectors. In so doing the brokerage will be deciding to 'position' themselves within the sector relative to the direct competition.

This example demonstrates that the mode of segmentation chosen will influence the decision as to the final marketing mix. The mix, however, becomes more or less specific depending upon how the market has been segmented.

Positioning

In the example above, the resulting marketing mix(es) will depend upon how the brokerage positions its products and services within the target market sector. The important point about positioning is to remember that it is the organisation's position as perceived by the customer, rather than its own internal perception. Indeed, the starting point is to determine customers' current perceptions and compare them with the organisational perception. The difference, or gap, between the two indicates the success or otherwise of the intended positioning. Customers' perceptions of competing firms in the same market segment may then be illustrated by means of perceptual maps. These for simplicity normally take the two key dimensions of customer choice (established by customer research), and plot the resulting competitive positioning, market clusters and gaps. Continuing the example of the brokerage, if we use two of the key factors for success mentioned in the first chapter (service and the level of premiums), the resulting perceptual map might appear similar to Figure 2.4 (next page).

The case material offers a number of opportunities for students to develop positioning strategies. The Royal China and Mortimer Arms cases are especially helpful in this context.

The term 'concept' is sometimes substituted for positioning. This substitution makes clearer the dependence of the marketing mix on the guiding product or

Figure 2.4 Car fleet insurance for commercial clients

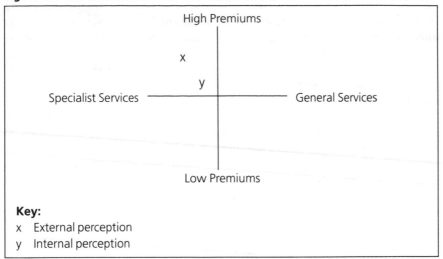

High Premiums

x

y

Specialist Services ———————————— General Services

Low Premiums

Key:
x   External perception
y   Internal perception

service concept. Cravens defines positioning strategy as:

> the marketing program a firm uses to position itself against its key competitors in meeting the needs and wants of the market target . . . The positioning strategy **provides the unifying concept** for deciding the role and strategy of each component of the mix (my emphasis). (Cravens 1994)

An organisation's target market positioning as perceived by the customer is normally most visible in the form of marketing communications. Positioning may also be defined in this context:

> the process of designing an image and value so that customers within the target segment understand what the company or brand stands for in relation to its competitors. (Wilson *et al.* 1992)

Positioning decisions are concerned with not only deciding where to compete within the segment, but also on what basis to compete and with whom to compete. Most writers acknowledge the following bases for positioning decisions. Positioning by:

- Attribute, or product/service benefit (fluoride toothpaste or 'chunky' dog food).
- Price/quality (Kwik Save and Sainsbury in retailing).
- Use/application (Microsoft Windows and laptop PCs in PC technology).
- The end-user, or lifestyle positioning (fragrance and cosmetics in fashion businesses).
- Association with a distinctive product class (top-loading washing machines or digital watches).
- Competitor, choosing to position against a specific competitor and deciding whether to challenge or to follow.

Alternatives

Analysis in isolation rarely results in strategic marketing initiatives. Although analysis is normally the starting point, it is important not to become lost in the detail (and possibly the wrong detail), and lose sight of the necessity for analysis to result in action. The bridge between analysis and action is the essence of the strategy process as it is at this stage that assumptions about the future are made and alternatives considered.

An objective analysis should lead directly to both the ability to make logical assumptions about the future and the generation of alternatives. For example, if market trend data has been reviewed over the last five years and the environment scanned for change, assumptions as to future trends have a sound base on which to project. It is at this point, however, that many people experience the most difficulty. Leaving the relative security of analysis may be difficult, but strategic thinking has little relevance to the past.

> The evidence is overwhelming that a great many students try to seek refuge in analysis and come to their examination desks hoping that inspiration will suddenly flow . . . There is an apt Chinese proverb which says, ' He who deliberates fully before taking a step will spend his entire life on one leg'. The question of taking decisions is a conceptual leap for many students. They need help. In the absence of full information, they have to make assumptions, use their judgement and be prepared to back it up on paper. (Chartered Institute of Marketing, Tutorial Text)

The danger of over-emphasising analyses can be reduced if the purpose of the strategy process is kept in mind. A counter emphasis on outcomes, such as the generation of alternatives, is more likely to keep the process strategic (especially in dynamic environments).

> . . . the outcome of planning need not be a plan. Rather than trying to produce a watertight document covering the next ten years, planning as an exercise should concentrate on identifying and evaluating alternative courses of action for the business, so that more opportunities are created. Planning therefore increases awareness. (Thompson 1990)

A useful starting point for the consideration of alternatives is the 'no change scenario' which in effect is the first alternative. 'Business as usual' is not the same as a 'do nothing' (almost impossible) scenario. The forward projection of business as usual normally demonstrates very clearly the need for strategic change. This approach could be usefully applied to most of the case material as it also identifies the 'planning gap', the difference between future revenue and profit expectations and the reality of the no-change projection. The strategic marketing process must demonstrate how this gap will be closed.

Deciding between alternatives: Ten points to consider

1. Is the chosen strategy compatible with the organisations or business units' mission, objectives and wider purpose?
2. Is the strategic alternative compatible with the corporate or business unit

strategic direction? For example, an expansionist strategy would be inappropriate for a business unit which was intended for 'managed decline'. Marketing strategies therefore need to be supportive of the wider corporate/unit strategies and reflect the underpinning core competencies, so that the internal capabilities of the organisation are balanced with the external opportunities and threats. Compatibility with internal strengths and weaknesses may include such considerations as the fit with the existing corporate culture and synergy with the existing business portfolio.

3. Is the strategy compatible with the financial resources of the business or business unit? What are the financial implications of each alternative? In reality this requires financial projections for each identified alternative (profit and loss statements, balance sheets, cash flow statements and capital requirements). Are these financial implications acceptable? Are the underlying assumptions behind the figures relatively safe? What is the up-side/down-side potential?

4. Is the strategy compatible with important non-financial criteria or considerations, such as the need to hold on to the goodwill of important stakeholder groups (for example, key customers)?

5. Is the timing feasible? For example, will it take years rather than months to develop new products for new markets. Like military strategy, timing is often the crucial decisive factor. Have short and longer-term criteria been considered? From a strategic perspective the focus is normally on the longer term. In crises situations, however, this may not be possible as pricing and rationalisation decisions (dictated by cash flow imperatives) may adversely impact on a longer-term perspective.

6. Is the strategy flexible enough to be able to adjust to the unexpected? (For example, a market in flux or a competitive challenge.)

7. Does the strategy build on the competitive advantages identified in the analysis phase; are these advantages easy/difficult for competitors to copy?

8. Does the strategy synergise with other business units? For example, can advantage be taken of shared resources? Marketing examples might include common channels of distribution, common sales administration, common product development programmes and common branding/identity?

9. Which strategy is most easily understandable by all levels in the business/business unit? Can the chosen strategy be communicated with minimum confusion?

10. Will the chosen strategy give a clear direction? Will it act as a unifying or dividing force?

Detailed Marketing Plans: The Concept of the Sub-Marketing Mix

The concept of the hierarchical nature of strategy was introduced in Chapter 1. There is also an identified hierarchy of marketing operational plans. These may be viewed as:

● The overall rationale or plan for the business unit's marketing strategy, setting out the number of products/services and markets contested.

- The individual product or market plans setting out the required marketing mixes.
- The detailed sub-marketing mix plans for each of the identified products/markets.

Detailed action plans (and budgets) are generated by exploding the identified strategic marketing direction into detailed marketing operational plans. The following figures illustrate the sub-marketing plans normally required (see Figures 2.5, 2.6, 2.7). They also take the example of the sales plan and show how this is related to the marketing communications mix.

This process may be time-consuming where large numbers of products/markets are involved, all of which may require specific mixes and detailed financial projections. Hopefully the process ensures that:

- Individual product/service marketing mixes are integrated
- Shorter-term objectives (budgets) relate to longer-term objectives
- Co-ordination and control is a reality
- Individual product strategy is integrated to the overall strategic marketing intent

Figure 2.5 Planning marketing operations – specific examples

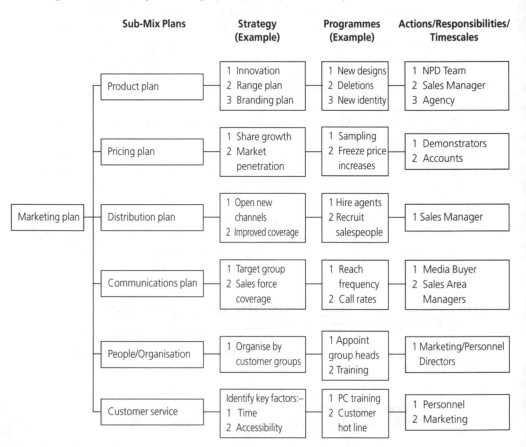

Figure 2.6 The concept of the sub-marketing mix

Example: The Marketing Communications Mix

The Marketing Plan → Marketing Communications Plan →

Advertising Plan
– Theme
– Scheme

Public Relations Plan

Selling & Sales Management Plan

Exhibition Plan

Sales Promotional Plan

Design Plan:
– Corporate related
– Product related
– Environment related
– Literature related

Figure 2.7 The concept of the sub-marketing mix

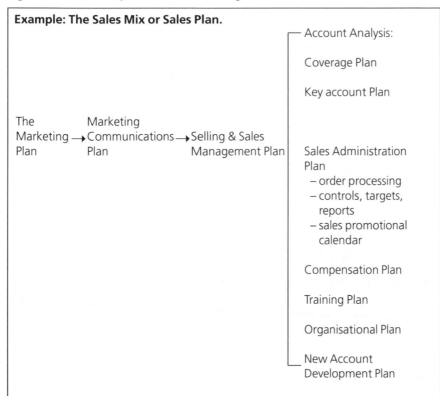

Example: The Sales Mix or Sales Plan.

The Marketing Plan → Marketing Communications Plan → Selling & Sales Management Plan

Account Analysis:

Coverage Plan

Key account Plan

Sales Administration Plan
– order processing
– controls, targets, reports
– sales promotional calendar

Compensation Plan

Training Plan

Organisational Plan

New Account Development Plan

Given the amount of work involved there is the danger (as we saw with the marketing audit) of becoming lost in the detail or, worse, repeating the process if the alternatives need to be reappraised. Once again the process is ceasing to be strategic if the imperative of establishing budgets and control systems is the driving force.

The formal planning approach to strategic marketing needs therefore to be complemented with a more flexible approach. We conclude this chapter with a plea for a modified approach similar to the strategic management phase illustrated in Table 2.1 (page 24).

Flexibility: Avoiding the 'SPOTS' by Emphasising Flexibility and Creativity

Why should the process be sequential?

Piercy and Giles (1989) reminded many practitioners of the 'SPOTS' syndrome (Strategic Plan On The Shelf). There are many managers who would empathise with the feeling that strategic planning does not appear to relate to the realities of the current business. It is seen more as an additional burden and interference to running the business. Piercy and Giles suggest that in order to encourage commitment and incremental discovery, a process of tactics-driven strategies might be more useful.

> Given the reality of how managers actually do their jobs, we suggest that there are advantages in starting with the detail of implementation and tactics to gain commitment and involvement, and work back from this to the development of strategic directions.

This requires the inversion of the classic sequential model so that:

> planners move backwards and forwards in the planning system, to test the implications of each new analysis or piece of information on analyses already completed, and to consider their importance for what has yet to be done. (Piercy and Giles 1989)

Flexibility and creativity

We have attempted to stress that strategic marketing implies a challenge and a review of established practices. The problem with a too disciplined approach to marketing strategy is that:

> Indeed the very fact of having a strategy, and especially making it explicit (as the conventional literature implores managers to do), creates resistance to strategic change! (Mintzberg and Quinn 1991)

The formalised approach to strategy needs to include the flexibility to cope with the unexpected. A balance has to be found between the needs for centralised control and decentralised experimentation. Innovation and creativity requires the support systems of compatible corporate cultures. Keeping strategic thinking alive is the acid test of the strategic approach to marketing. All too often such thinking is construed as a threat and is too easily snuffed out in the morass and rigour of the strategic marketing planning model. Military analogies are replete with the importance of flexibility and timing. This comment on the von Schlieffen plan makes the point on a wider scale:

The plan of campaign was as rigid and complete as the blueprint for a battleship. Heeding Clausewitz's warning that military plans which leave no room for the unexpected can lead to disaster, the Germans with infinite care had attempted to provide for every contingency . . . Against that elusive, that mocking and perilous quantity, the unexpected, every precaution had been taken except one . . . flexibility. (Tuchman 1962)

The need for inspiration in the strategic process is also emphasised by Goddard.

The kernel of a strategic plan is the rule that it breaks, the orthodoxy that firm is choosing to challenge . . . This has to be a jump of the imagination. A plan that doesn't make such a jump is a fraud. In other words a strategy cannot be fully rationalised. It has to be an act of faith. (Goddard (1985) cited by Baker 1991)

Summary

This chapter has presented the conventional sequential model of strategic marketing planning. We have placed the emphasis of the intentional planning process on outcomes, such as the generation of alternatives and the fostering of strategic thinking. In this context we have stressed the need for flexibility and experimentation in order to rise above the excessive pursuit of analysis and detailed planning. We have reviewed the principles of segmentation, targeting and positioning, which are at the heart of the strategic marketing process. It has been stressed that despite the evident logic, the sequential process should be used more as a guide rope, rather than as a straightjacket, given the problems of relating the process to the reality of organisational dynamics. As Piercy and Giles have remarked:

It is a perfectly valid model for presenting the results of planning to top management, but it does not adequately or validly represent the human and organisational realities that we and others have experienced in the practice of planning. (Piercy and Giles 1989)

Figure 2.8 Concluding practical advice

Proceed cautiously	Making it work and avoiding the SPOTS!
• Be informal and encourage open discussion • Be flexible with regular scheduled reviews • Base decisions and resource commitments on the outcomes; no decisions = SPOTS • Stress outcomes, rather than the process • Avoid uniform procedures and massive paperwork • Avoid formal presentation and numerous participants • Avoid the substitution of a five-year budget for a five-year strategic plan	• The outcome of planning need not be a plan! • Rather than a watertight document ... stress the importance of identifying alternatives • Nurture flexibility, creativity and insight • Informality • Allow people to experiment and make mistakes; strategy by learning • Cultivate strategic awareness

Although strategic marketing planning may do little to reduce the level of uncertainty, if a less rigid approach is adopted, what we can hope for is a commitment to strategic awareness from market-oriented managers which should result in alternative visions of the future and the active encouragement of experimentation on the path towards that goal. Without this emphasis attempts to introduce strategic marketing initiatives may be diminished and discredited; for as Mintzberg has remarked,

> ....strategies are to organisations what blinders are to horses: they keep them going in a straight line, but impede the use of peripheral vision.

> ....strategies (and the strategic management process) can be vital to organizations, both by their presence and by their absence. (Mintzberg 1987)

3
Challenges:
Old Dogs . . . and New Tricks?

Later sections in this chapter challenge both the novelty and the appropriateness for marketing strategy of such concepts as internal marketing and relationship marketing. We first consider a situation where marketers have apparently ceded domination over an original and core proposition of the marketing philosophy.

Marketing is full of paradigms and paradoxes. We live, for example, in an age of both globalisation and fragmentation of markets and media. This chapter contrasts some of the much vaunted, but outdated, tools of strategic marketing with the application of marketing to ever increasing circles. It is not surprising that the former opens marketers to criticism of their practice of strategy while the latter raises challenges to the scope of such strategy.

Old Dogs . . .

Feeling boxed in?

> No planning system guarantees the development of successful strategies. Nor does any technique. (The Boston Consulting Group, Annual Perspective 1981)

Perhaps in view of this opening quotation, we need not be too concerned at the apparent failure of many strategic planning models to penetrate the real world. Research conducted for the Chartered Institute of Marketing in 1983, for example, revealed that under ten per cent of respondents used the 'Boston box' regularly.

And yet, models such as the product lifecycle and the Boston matrix, typically occupy large chunks of textbooks on marketing and corporate strategy, and indeed often infiltrate textbooks on finance and manufacturing as well. One partial explanation of this strange phenomenon is that while such models have failed to achieve breadth of penetration, in the commercial world they have achieved depth of penetration in some sectors, particularly in large businesses where the hand of consultants is often to be seen at work. Another partial explanation appears to lie in the apparent simplicity of their construction and prescriptions. Unfortunately, while the reduction of the complexities of the market place to a four quadrant matrix has a tantalising appeal, it is also bound to be a gross, and possibly dangerous, over-simplicity. As Pearson (1994) says in respect of one of the most well-known models, 'Fortunately, many managers were too shrewd, or optimistic, to follow through the Boston prescription. They used the Boston model very widely, but apparently did not take its prescriptions too seriously if they did not accord with what they were going to do anyway!'

The most popular portfolio planning matrix is that known as the Boston Matrix, BCG Matrix or Boston box. Its popularity – despite the recognition of its inadequacies, nearly 15 years ago, by its inventors – probably rests in its positioning as simple, first to market and the one with the catchiest names. Like most products it has been modified over the years and one of its most recognisable manifestations is shown below (Figure 3.1). It is typically used by marketers as a means of classifying products according to their cash generation or consumption characteristics.

Figure 3.1 The Boston Matrix

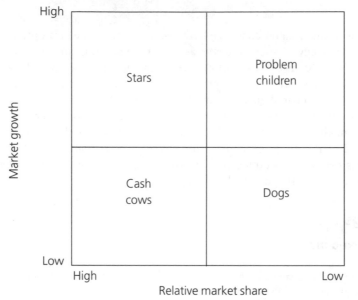

The crux of the Boston Matrix is the logic that as costs fall with experience, the highest market share should lead to highest profits. Experience gains should be even greater in a faster growing market. But the empirical basis of the model were commodity products which are characterised by a lack of differentiation and a general price level. A further problem, recognised by Boston, was that the cost-reducing effects of experience were only significant where market growth rates exceeded ten per cent. The prescriptions of the matrix were therefore not generally applicable – indeed they were inappropriate for the situations faced by most firms. They could lead, for example, to an unjustified preoccupation with market share or to a premature decision to withdraw from low-growth, low-share markets. Perhaps even worse, they could lead to the milking of cash cows to fund new brands and products when much of the evidence of the last few years points to the high failure rates of new products and the profitable longevity of established brands if treated to a continual diet of product quality improvement, manufacturing and promotional investment.

Are there then any useful lessons to be gained from the Boston Matrix? Yes, but perhaps little beyond reminding us of some fairly obvious lessons. First, as with the product life cycle, there is the lesson that, unless managed, products will migrate on their own from one state to another, but not necessarily into the desired state. Second, as with the product life cycle, it behoves a firm to have a balanced portfolio so that some products are generating cash to allow the funding of new products and the transition of others to a more successful state. Third, for some firms, there is the notion that it may well be worthwhile sacrificing short-term profits to build longer-term market leadership. Fourth, it forces firms to analyse products and markets and therefore is likely to produce a more logical allocation of resources across the available options. As with other models, the aforementioned logicality assumes that definitions of products, business units and markets are themselves made logically. Of course, as with other models, this and the information necessary to operationalise the model, are frequently the most problematic issues.

Often, then, the model is used not as a tool for diagnosis, and not as a tool of strategic choice, but as an aid to presentation of choices already made. As an aid to strategy, subsequent developments of portfolio matrices promised more in that they incorporated more variables then merely market share and market growth rate. Typically they measure market/industry attractiveness against competitive position/business strength. Examples, which are described extensively elsewhere, include those of General Electric, Shell (Directional Policy Matrix), Abell and Hammond (investment opportunity) and Arthur D. Little (strategic condition).

However, most of these are best used for making resource allocation and strategic objective decisions *amongst* SBUs, rather than *within* SBUs. For this latter purpose marketers can obtain more mileage from developing their own criteria for evaluating which product-markets or segments to compete in. The list below suggests some typical segment selection criteria, which can then be weighted in terms of relative importance to the firm. (Similar specific criteria can be developed to aid product introduction or deletion decisions.)

1. Size and growth rate of segment
2. Prevailing price and profitability levels
3. Durability and stability of demand
4. Strength of existing competition
5. Ease of entry for potential new competitors
6. Ease with which customers can be identified and uniquely targeted
7. Cost of customisation (i.e. additional fixed and variable manufacturing and marketing mix costs needed to adapt to needs of new segment)
8. Degree of interdependence with other segments (for example, a replacement parts manufacturer may find it necessary to enter the original equipment segment of the market in order to stimulate the demand for spares)
9. Degree of marketing control achievable
10. Level of risk
11. Degree of consistency with overall SBU marketing objectives, policies and positioning.

A firm in the position of Après Shower, for example, might be wondering whether to enter a new market segment. As well as analysing the above factors it would also need to consider the new mix of product and offer attributes preferred by the segment and its strength – relative to competition – in providing these attributes (and where it lacked the desired attributes, its ability to develop them or to change customer perceptions as to its possession of them, or to alter the importance the customers attached to the missing attributes).

Real direction?

Developed by Igor Ansoff (1968), and hence more commonly described as Ansoff's matrix, the growth vector matrix is useful in helping to develop both marketing objectives and marketing strategy. It is a reminder that marketing objectives have to be specified in terms of product and market sales volumes, value (and share) as well as timescales. It also provides a framework for generating alternative strategies by suggesting alternative growth directions. Ansoff's original matrix is shown below.

Figure 3.2 Ansoff's matrix

Products Markets	Present	New
Present	Market penetration	Product development
New	Market development	Diversification

As with all models, it is deceptively simple. In particular there are difficulties of logic as well as definition.

Typically, students will take 'new products' to mean new product classes. In this way an example of 'new products to present' markets (product development) might be provided by fountain-pen manufacturer, Parker, entering the ball point market, or by Gillette entering the disposable razor market. In fact the above example is extracted from O'Shaughnessy (1988) where he also refers to a radio manufacturer moving into tape recorders or Elizabeth Arden moving into age-combating products as (concentric) diversification.

The different categorisation presumably reflects that in the former examples, product class remains the same (while product form differs) while in the latter case, the product class also changes. However, the change in technology from manufac-turing a radio to manufacturing a tape recorder may be small (would it worry Sony?) while a plastic disposable razor is a different technology from an anodised aluminium one. Not only is it a different technology it is a different market. The only similarity between buyers of plastic disposables or buyers of the 'best a man can get' is that they are male. Surely, then, this is an example of market development (i.e. new segments) which requires a new marketing mix including a new product variant. But if it is a new market and a new product it must be a case of diversification after all!

As with many tools in marketing, definitional variations can make the most apparently simple concepts seem much more problematic when subjected to close scrutiny. The main point Ansoff was making was that the greater the move away from existing markets and products, the riskier is the strategy. He made the point in particular in relation to diversification which usually would necessitate new skills, techniques and facilities and therefore 'almost invariably leads to physical and organisational changes in the structure of the business which represent a distinct break with past business experience'.

It is clear, therefore, that diversification is a decision which has to be made by corporate level strategic decision makers. It is beyond the options available to a marketing strategist operating at the SBU level.

From the point of view of SBU marketing strategy, the growth vector becomes of more practical use if it is removed from the confines of a matrix and is elaborated. Interestingly, when he first used the concept, Ansoff did not put it in matrix form. Also, interestingly, Ansoff subsequently added an additional dimension to the matrix to allow for present and new geographical markets.

The opportunities for growth via product development represent a continuum as follows:

1. Range updating , i.e. new versions of the existing brand brought about by (hopefully) improvements in terms of quality, style, features or image (perceived, but only cosmetic change) which result in replacement product items.
2. Range extension, i.e. additional versions of existing brands brought about by new sizes, flavours, colours or packages which result in extra product items.
3. Segment factoring whereby new brands aimed at existing customers are introduced in order to restrict or preclude competitor entrants, thus producing additional product items. The new brands will cannibalise existing brands to some extent. To the extent that they don't, it could be argued that they are reaching new market segments. It all depends on how segments are defined!
4. New (to the firm) product ranges. These could come in terms of new product forms (e.g. a convertible version of a saloon car, which constitutes much more of a change than new versions of existing ranges) or new product classes (e.g. a saloon car manufacturer introducing a range of high-performance motor bikes).
5. New to the world products. By definition, such products create new markets (in the product sense) but could be sold to customers of existing products. The Sony Walkman is a well-worn example.

The opportunity for growth via market development but using present products is relatively limited since entering new markets or new market segments will usually call for some product adaptation if not range updates, extensions or new ranges. For example, geographical expansion usually requires new and different product standards to be met. However it may be possible to broaden a product's appeal thus making it attractive in larger segments. A product could be made available through additional marketing channels and reach a different customer in that way.

Alternatively the product could be repositioned so as to appeal to a wider age range, for example, or to heavier users, or to users on different occasions. A jogging shoe could be re-positioned as a more general purpose leisure shoe. A breakfast cereal could also be promoted as a bed-time snack – although this last example could also be a form of market penetration (i.e. increasing the frequency of usage by present customers). As usual, it all depends on which variables are chosen as the basis for segmenting the market.

Paradoxically, a strategy of growth through market penetration permits a wider range of sub-options. Thus higher sales in the present market using present products could be achieved by:

1. Increasing frequency of usage (as noted above) of existing customers.
2. Increasing amount purchased on each purchase occasion.
3. Converting non-users (within the same segment) to users.
4. Converting lapsed users to users.
5. Attracting product users away from competitors to your brand.
6. Reducing defection to the competition.

It should be noted that strategies 1 to 6 are brand strategies which result in smaller shares for competitors. However, they may have the side effect of increasing sales of the product class in total. If there is a deliberate intention to stimulate demand for the whole product class this should really be considered to be a strategy of market expansion rather than market penetration.

Relating Ansoff's matrix to the concept of positioning strategy, we can make the following observations:

1. Market penetration is really confirming the current strategy. It seeks to grow by functional marketing strategies, i.e. doing more of the same or doing it better.
2. Market development essentially requires a change in positioning or additional positionings. However, where market development takes the form of geographical expansion – although a major strategic decision – some marketing theorists would take the view that global marketing means addressing the same segment, which just happens to cross national boundaries.
3. N.P.D., depending on what degree of newness is meant implies either strengthening the current positioning, re-positioning or creating new positionings.
4. Diversification is most likely to involve additional positionings and in the case of conglomerate diversification and some types of concentric diversification will probably involve new SBUs.

Oh! Mr Porter . . . What shall we do?

Porter's generic strategies model (1985) has probably had more impact on the teaching of marketing strategy (and has certainly influenced more business people) than any other model in the last 15 years. Yet, even when not misused (as it usually is), it is a blunt tool with the potential to mislead and side-track marketers. Following a brief exposition of the model we will consider just a few of the reasons why this is so.

Porter's most recent version of his model is shown in Figure 3.3 on the next page.

Figure 3.3 Porter's generic strategies model

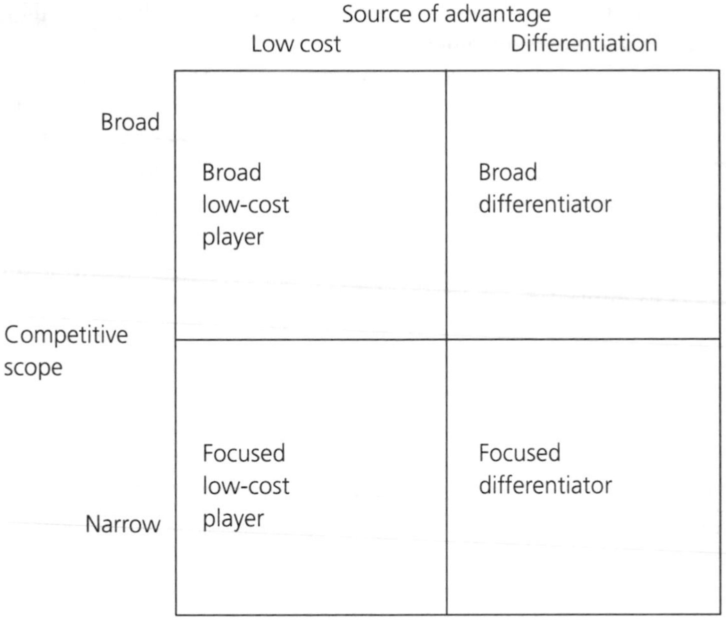

Source of advantage

	Low cost	Differentiation
Broad	Broad low-cost player	Broad differentiator
Narrow	Focused low-cost player	Focused differentiator

Competitive scope

His premise is that, to achieve above average performance in the long run in an industry depends (save in a few exceptional situations) on the selection and rigorous prosecution of one of the strategies. Although Porter himself does not elaborate on the reasons for this, it can be deduced from his work that the different 'generic' strategies each require a different mix of skills, resources and organisational structures, and that any compromise will necessarily lead to organisational inefficiencies. According to Porter, cost leadership (broad cost) can only be achieved by *one* firm. To do so it must pursue all sources of cost advantage but it must also be able to command average prices by achieving proximity (parity). Parity can be considered as a minimum level or combination of benefits equally desired by buyers across the market place.

Differentiation (broad differentiation) strategy requires a firm to be unique along some dimension(s) widely valued by buyers throughout the industry. Provided the price premium earned by this differentiation exceeds the cost of providing it, then the firm will earn above average profit. In focus strategies, firms target a particular segment within the overall market and tailor their offering to it, so as to meet its needs better than firms with broad focus. Within this narrow target firms must still choose to compete as low-cost producers or differentiators in order to earn above average profits.

What, then, of the criticisms in the context of marketing strategy?

First, although developed in the context of competitive advantage, Porter's model is not really a (wholly) marketing model. Cost leadership is not a marketing strategy. It is simply a way of explaining how margins can be bigger if costs are the lowest and prices are average. Exactly what advantage does cost leadership offer the customer? None, unless it is translated into lower prices – and then, of course, it becomes differentiation. On top of this academic point there is also the practical question of why would anyone buy the 'standard' product when there are differentiators around offering added customer value?

Second, it is not clear at what level the model applies. Does it apply to firms, business units or single product groups? Porter's main example of a cost-leader is Ivory Soap. But Ivory Soap is one of many soap brands marketed by Procter & Gamble. Many of these other brands will be differentiated in alternative ways to appeal to multiple segments. Does this not make Proctor and Gamble a differentiator? Would this result in organisational inefficiency or would it depend on the way the brands' manufacturing and marketing organisations were structured? Most of Porter's examples are conveniently based on individual products or on single product firms or business units.

Third, referring again to the example of Ivory Soap as a cost-leader, Ivory Soap is a long-established leading brand. Being a brand, which clearly has different product features, packaging and pricing from other brands, it must be differentiated from other soaps? Further, why can't other products be both differentiated and cost-leaders? Indeed, technological innovation or quality leadership might be the bases of differentiation which lead to market share leadership and economies of experience which in turn lead to the firm becoming the cost-leader!

Fourth, what is the difference between differentiation and focus? Again, by definition, a differentiator appeals to a group of customers who are prepared to pay for an offering tailored to their needs, i.e. a market segment. Perhaps the logic of Porter is that focus implies a niche (a very small segment or a sub-sector of a segment) whereas his differentiator harbours the hope that his offering will become the largest segment or even the industry standard?

Faulkner and Bowman (1992) take the view, along with others (particularly devotees of the presumed Japanese approach to customer benefit features plus high quality plus low cost) that organisations can, and should, aim for both low cost and differentiation. 'The prime issue is not which strategy to adopt, but how most effectively to operationalise the only sustainable strategy, low-cost differentiation, which enables the firm to compete through higher perceived use value, and also on price, if the circumstances demand it.'

Pearson (1994) comes to a different, but equally critical conclusion. He suggests that Porter's model fails to indicate how differentiation can be achieved and for this, 'we have to look for more orthodox marketing methods, of which Porter himself appears to be virginally innocent'.

Who needs strategy anyway?

Richard Schonberger (1987), the world-renowned authority on manufacturing, has subtitled his 'World Class Manufacturing' text *The Lessons of Simplicity Applied*. Schonberger writes, 'The text books talk about finding your competitive niche or area of "distinctive competency". Perhaps your company is the cost-leader in the industry. Then, the book will say, you should expect your quality to be somewhat lower, your response time a bit slower, and your flexibility less. If you get the product out of the door faster than everybody else, then your quality is unlikely to be as good and your costs are higher, so charge more. Now we know that all that is balderdash. The best manufacturers of the world are likely to be good in *all* those areas.'

Schonberger thus doubts the value of strategic planning at all. He argues that with today's technology, it is no longer appropriate to agonise over which particular set of advantages to focus on in order to provide a clear (unique) market positioning. A firm can effectively fulfil a wide variety of segmental needs, and in some cases, individual customers' needs.

. . . New Tricks

The marketing of quality and the quality of marketing

One of the striking features of management education, development and strategy of recent years has been the increasing emphasis on the quality issue. Of particular interest to us at this juncture, is the convergence of interpretations of what marketing is and what quality is. This convergence has largely resulted from the way in which views on quality have changed and expanded.

Initially, quality was a term primarily applied to the manufacture of a product. It focused on techniques aimed at reducing the number of faults occurring in such products. Since then, its scope has broadened considerably and its philosophy has also changed. In the 1980s it would not be an unfair generalisation to say that quality gained pre-eminence as a basis of competitive advantage and many well-known organisations invested heavily in training aimed at raising quality levels. It also became clear that cost and quality did not have to be traded off against one another. New thinking, spread by Japanese organisations, suggested that better quality was a principal route to lower costs, proving that you could have your cake *and* eat it. Further it became possible to talk – in some situations – of achieving not just better quality, but even zero defects.

However, it also became clear that what mattered most was the customer's perception of quality, whether it be the quality of the product, the quality of customer service or the quality of the relationship between supplier and customer. Thus the 'quality industry' now defines quality as 'meeting customer needs'. The philosophies of marketing and TQM, then, are currently very close. (Marketers see this both as a vindication of their ideas but also as a threat to their ownership of them.) There are some differences. Marketing orientation requires focusing on company capabilities and competitors as well as customers, for instance. However, TQM does seem to have 'scored over' marketing in respect of the implementation of customer orientation amongst all members of the organisation. While marketers have frequently talked about the need for internal marketing and for recognition of the role of part-time marketers, the marketers of TQM have developed frameworks for the quest for quality at an operational level.

Quality Circles, for example, involving direct customer contact by production staff have instilled the need to be responsible for customer satisfaction and the means by which to achieve it. As Strauss (1994) says of marketers, 'There is a lack of understanding that Total Quality Management is a scheme that adopts the conceptual core of marketing, further develops it, and thus rivals marketing as an autonomous discipline'. The challenge facing marketers is to decide whether to respond to the challenge posed by the quality industry.

Internal marketing – strategy imperative or pilfered politicking?

Increasing attention today is being paid to the problem of making marketing strategy happen. Thus one of the criteria which should be used in helping to select from amongst alternative marketing strategies is the implementability of those strategies, i.e. their acceptability both in the market place and also to those employees who are charged with operationalising the strategy. In addition to this, it has been suggested that an internal marketing programme be developed as well as the external programme, which specifically addresses constraints and barriers within the organisation and that this is an integral part of the total marketing planning process. Christopher, Payne and Ballantyne (1991) define internal marketing as 'any form of marketing within an organisation which focuses attention on the internal activities that need to be changed in order that marketing plans may be implemented'. The implication is that marketing management must learn not only how to understand and persuade customers but also colleagues.

One way of thinking about this is to use the analogy of the organisational salesperson. He or she will probably have a mental model of the sales process they typically follow and of the structure of the customer's buying process. They may well also have a model of the persuasion process and, in particular, a set of relationship strategies for dealing with specific individuals.

Table 3.1 The strategy sales process model

---

1. Set objectives
   - what is our timescale for selling the strategy?
   - have we planned phased stages?
   - do we have fall-back strategies if our full preferred strategy proves unacceptable?
2. Sell benefits
   - more profitable and secure organisation?
   - reshaped job roles?
3. Overcome objections, e.g.
   - ignorance of the need for change
   - inertia
   - resistance to marketing
   - lack of faith in strategy
   - loss of status or power
   - resistance to commitment to plans
4. Close
   - use of pressure?
   - obtaining support of a 'sponsor'?
   - modify the strategy?
   - offer an inducement?

The models shown below are incomplete and hybrid. Their purpose is to show a few examples of how a Sales Process model could be applied to an Internal Marketing Plan (see Figure 3.1).

Piercy (1992) has suggested that the internal plan can also be seen in terms of the '4 P's' in the same way that the external plan might be elaborated. As an example, the Product would be the new strategy itself. The Price might manifest itself in various guises and would probably constitute a major objection. For some members of the organisation the new strategy may mean loss of control, reduced resource allocations and lower status. For others it may mean additional work. For everyone it will be the psychological cost of change and the opportunity cost of the alternative strategies which have been forgone. Communications (Promotion) targets may require classification in terms of decision-making role (see below), job function, job level, opinion leadership, power and influence (see later) and even individual employees' attitudes and values. Communications media might include meetings, seminars, training programmes, social occasions and appropriate use of the grapevine. A key medium will be the Marketing Plan document itself. Careful thought needs to be given to the size, structure, content, language and dissemination of the plan. Clearly, as far as this last issue is concerned, the right balance between the need to know and the need to safeguard confidentiality must be achieved. In terms of Place, Piercy suggests that 'the real distribution channel is human resource management, and in the lining up of recruitment, training, evaluation and reward systems behind marketing strategies, so that the culture of the company becomes the real distribution channel for internal marketing strategies'.

As noted earlier, one way of defining communication targets is to draw an analogy with the concept of a buying centre or decision-making unit (DMU) within a customer organisation.

- Users – those who will have to carry out the strategy, e.g. brand/product managers, sales persons, manufacturing and logistics managers, advertising agencies
- Influencers – those, who by dint of power, will have a strong say in the acceptance of the strategy
- Deciders – those who either recommend or take the actual decision, e.g. Marketing Director, Managing Director
- Approvers – those whose formal authorisation, to sanction funds, etc., is needed, e.g. Finance Director
- Gatekeepers – those who may be able to spread (grapevine) or inhibit the flow of information and rumour

Marketers need to understand the composition of these groups at different stages in the strategy-selling process. They need to recognise that employees have a perspective and pre-disposition which results from their job function in the organisation and from their background. Marketers also need to recognise that, as human beings, employees have individual personalities and styles of behaviour. Third, they need to recognise their different power sources.

Power has been defined by French and Raven (1959) as 'influence potential' and as having seven possible sources. The internal marketer needs to be able to recognise his own sources of power and the power bases of individuals he needs to influence. The seven types are:

- Expert power resulting from perceived useful expertise
- Information power resulting from access to perceived useful information
- Referent power resulting from perceived attractiveness of interaction
- Legitimate power resulting from position in the organisation
- Reward power resulting from ability to provide benefits or solve problems
- Connection power resulting from perceived association with influential bodies
- Coercive power resulting from perceived ability to invoke sanctions

Having identified targets, their roles, their power, their values and their likely attitude (and the strength of it) towards the proposed strategy an appropriate relationship and influence strategy needs to be designed. For example, powerful players thought to be in favour of the strategy might be used as sponsors - to advocate the strategy in high places. They could perhaps be used to help neutralise or sideline powerful opponents. When trying to persuade neutral or unsympathetic targets, marketers must be careful to use an appropriate negotiation strategy.

Many of the above processes are, of course, undertaken intuitively by marketing and other functional managers in an organisation. The notion of an internal marketing plan simply provides a more structured, actionable, predictive and controllable framework to the task of selling and implementing marketing strategy within the organisation.

However, the question has to be raised as to whether the broader view of internal marketing, as expressed by Fifield and Gilligan (1995) for example, is really overextending the skills and jurisdiction of marketers. They write that it is 'concerned with creating the sort of culture and climate within an organisation in which there is a far clearer understanding amongst all staff of the objectives, the key values and the sorts of implementation issues that need to be addressed'.

Clearly the notion of one functional area treating others as internal customers has many attractions. But should not the prime responsibility for organisational cultural development lie with general management and human resource specialists?

The start of a new relationship or the return of an old friend?

It is perhaps strange that the notion of relationship marketing has only in recent years come to the fore, particularly in marketing academia. Strange, because decades ago Drucker defined the purpose of a business as being 'to create and keep a customer', i.e. to establish and maintain a relationship. Maybe the answer to this conundrum lies in the possibility that relationship marketing is yet another buzz phrase for something that is both fairly obvious in principle and moreover has been in common practice in some organisations for a long time. There is also, however, the possibility that what has been a long established and simplistic notion has been refined in the light of new perspectives and in the recognition of the gap between the theory and the reality.

One of the notions behind relationship marketing is that firms should pay more attention to keeping existing customers in the longer term rather than focus too much effort on creating new customers or winning customers from competitors.

As Worthington (1994) says, 'Customer retention is the key element in a relationship marketing strategy, as loyal customers are both the most profitable customers and the most effective form of advertising'. Retention costs are typically a fraction of customer conversion or creation costs. Conversely most customers are lost through neglect and bad service. Thus the second key concept behind relationship marketing is that of commitment to customer service. The people and processes involved in activities which impinge on customer service must provide a quality of service which is in line with (some would say, exceeds) customer needs and expectations. A third element is the emphasis on 'opening relationships' rather than 'closing sales', i.e. building long-term relationships with specific customers instead of seeing business as a series of one-off transactions. A fourth element, high customer contact, is perhaps a natural progression from the preceding points.

For someone who learned their marketing in a well-managed industrial marketing firm, none of the above would create a great stir. In many markets for industrial goods, business generally has been based on trust and on service developed over many years of co-operative relationships. Stimulated by the need to co-operate over technical and service issues (and more latterly also by the needs of Just-in-Time operations) complex networks of contacts between supplier and buyer employees have developed.

Huge investments in time and other resources are needed to build such relationships, and because of this they are not easily rent asunder by offerings of lower prices from competitors. Indeed, there is much evidence to suggest that relationships between, for example, technical staff from a supplier firm and a buyer firm may be closer and better than those between different departmental functions within the same firm – to the extent that such employees strive to maintain harmony with 'colleagues' from another firm at the expense of conflict within their own firm.

The importance of relationships has also typically been recognised by small firms and by service firms, whereas (generalising again) consumer goods firms have often failed to recognise either the importance of relationships within the marketing channel or with individual consumers. Thus relations with the trade have often been adverserial (this is also frequently true of industrial marketers) while at the same time, many firms have also lost their consumer franchise. Loyalty has shifted from manufacturer brands to retailers who now feel that they 'own' the customers. Some consumer goods firms have tried to come to grips with this situation by seeking more co-operative and stable trade relationships but also by trying to build relationships with individual consumers, other than through media advertising. Such attempts have generally been restricted hitherto to direct mailings and to loyalty cards aimed at communicating product or special offer information. However, as more information is collected about individual consumers, the opportunities for developing a continuous, long-term and selling relationship will develop. Service organisations like the banks and motoring organisations are already well down this route, aided by rapid advances in information technology power and reductions in its costs.

The heightened awareness of the value of quality of customer service leading to increased long-term customer satisfaction and retention is therefore at the heart of the concept of relationship marketing. The attention paid, particularly in high profile service industries, to the training of people and the development of processes to bring desired quality improvements into effect, has added to the awareness.

Christopher, Payne and Ballantyne (1994) propose further that relationship marketing should be interpreted more widely than pertaining to buyer-supplier relationships. Rather like the several markets or audiences which may be the target of public relations activity, they suggest that relationship marketing should also include supplier markets, employee and recruitment markets, influencer markets (e.g. financial markets, government), referral markets (e.g. financial agents) and internal markets. In this last context, relationship marketing and internal marketing become virtually synonymous.

An even broader view of relationship marketing is taken by Gummesson (1994) who sees it as 'a new paradigm and the beginning of a new marketing theory'. He claims that 'relationship marketing is marketing seen as relationships, networks and interaction'. He goes on to define some 30 types of relationships incorporating relationships with customers, suppliers, the law, ecology and many others including internal customers and collaborating companies.

The 'new paradigm' inevitably strikes at the concept of the marketing mix since mixing four or seven ingredients to stimulate the appropriate customer response seemed unrealistic in the context of the complex negotiations, joint new product developments and long-term contracts which often characterise many businesses, particularly those in industrial marketing. Some further challenges to the mix follow.

The myth of the marketing mix?

While to the general public the most visible face of marketing is advertising, the most visible aspect of marketing to the student is the marketing mix itself, most universally expressed in McCarthy's Four P's mnemonic. And yet this article of faith has been subject to increasing doubts. There are several reasons.

One criticism grew with the growth of interest in services marketing. The crucial roles played by the *People* who provide the service, the way the service *Process* is managed and the *Physical* evidence surrounding its performance were not adequately reflected in the Four P's and led to the growth of these extra three P's. Kotler has proposed six P's (and also four C's). Others have suggested 15 and even 28 P's.

A second criticism was that the four P's seemed not to allow for the crucial importance of customer service and long-term co-operative relationships and that it emphasised promotion and place which could be almost irrelevant in some situations.

Another criticism reflected the reality that in many (most?) organisations, not all the P's were under the control of marketing. Price, for example, often remains the prerogative of the chief executive.

A more philosophical criticism is that pre-occupation with the P's might lead to focusing on the 'trappings' of marketing rather than the 'substance'. Thus the presence of a promotional campaign might hide the lack of genuine marketing orientation or the existence of a clear marketing strategy. In short they emphasise the company and not the customer.

Wilson (1994) has suggested that the P's (plus the vital element of customer service) should be considered not as the 'marketing mix' but as the 'positioning mix' because of their key role in helping the customer to correctly position the company and its offerings.

For the time being the notion of the P's serves as a useful checklist for thinking about the implementation of marketing strategy. However students and practitioners should not feel constrained by it and the search for more appropriate paradigms should continue.

PART II
Case Studies

4

Betaware Housewares Limited[1]

Background

Betaware Housewares Limited (BHL) was established in 1991 by a Dutch whole-saling group, following the sequential purchases of three separate production and distribution companies in the West Midlands, specialising in hollowware and small electrical appliances (SEAs).

The acquisitions involved were:

- **Betaware Housewares, Hall Green, Birmingham; a manufacturer of aluminium hollowware**

The factory at Hall Green was, by 1993, producing aluminium hollowware to a net sales value (after trade discounts) of some £5.7m. The resulting products comprised lower-priced saucepans, kettles, percolators and tea sets. The kettles and percolators are subsequently transferred to the Willenhall factory for wiring and electrical assembly/testing. This aluminium hollowware is sold as 'own label' products to such major retail chains as Argos, F. W. Woolworth, Tesco and Asda. The own-label strategy, combined with competitive pricing, are the principle key factors for success in a business which started as a 'tinkering' operation, with a corporate culture of 'never being knowingly undersold'. This requires a low-cost manufacturing base allied to a responsive key account selling operation.

- **UniPress, Stainless Steel Consumer Hollowware, Earlsdon, Coventry**

Associated with the UniPress acquisition was the well-established 'Avon' branding which had been used extensively in establishing export markets in Scandinavia. The Avon branding was applied to stainless steel kettles and percolators. The stain-less steel percolators had been discontinued shortly after acquisition in 1991, following an agreement with the Swedish distributor to manufacture under licence. Today the royalties accrue to the holding company. Nevertheless, the UniPress acquisition did introduce an exporting culture into the business as well as the right to use the 'Avon' brand name.

By 1993 the value of the Coventry factory's output of stainless steel saucepans and kettles was equivalent to some £2.5m, at net sales value (NSV). The kettle bodies are also transferred to Willenhall for electrical assembly. The Betaware brand name has now been extended to the majority of Coventry produced

[1] Market data and product information has been modified so that this case should be used for teaching purposes only and not for factual information.

products. To date, only limited distribution has been achieved with stainless steel saucepans in the major UK retailing chains. This limited distribution is also based upon an own-label strategy.

- **Electrical Assemblers Ltd, an electrical appliance assembler, sourcing materials and assembling for other manufacturers and retailers, based in Willenhall, North West Birmingham**

This electrical appliance assembly unit distributes its products under Betaware or own-label branding. The electrical division sources the 'bodies' of the stainless steel and aluminium kettles from the Coventry and Hall Green factories; the majority, however, are still of polypropylene (PP) specification. Given the difficulty of being perceived as a one-product 'kettle company', the range of small electrical appliances has been expanded recently to include the factoring of heated trays, toasters, microwave ovens, coffee-makers and electric irons. Factoring refers to finished products bought in for resale from other manufacturers and re-branded Betaware. Willenhall production in 1993 (including product transferred from the other group factories) was valued at some £6.5m (NSV).

All these acquisitions subsequently traded as Betaware Housewares Limited from January 1992.

Performance After Consolidation as BHL

The following financial tables (Tables 4.1–4.6) refer to:

1. Balance Sheet as at 31 December 1993
2. Profit and Loss Statements for the years 1992 and 1993
3. Key ratio analysis
4. Sales and Margin Analysis by Product Category 1993
5. Sales and Margin Analysis by Commercial Unit 1993
6. Sales by factory unit 1993

The new organisation faces a number of problems. These are summarised as financial, organisational and marketing issues.

Financial issues

There is immediate cause for concern for the Dutch holding company financing the enterprise.

- BHL is essentially a kettle and cookware company, with high direct costs (for example, materials are 58 per cent of net sales).
- An expansion in sales revenues 1992/93, but a decline of almost £500,000 in operating profits resulting in a situation close to break-even.
- A decline in gross margins from 33 per cent to 29 per cent influenced by increasing quantities of factored products (offered to accounts to balance the product range) and rises in raw material costs.

Table 4.1 BHL balance sheet

Balance Sheet	£000's
	At Dec 93
Assets	
Current Assets	
Cash	80
Debtors and Prepayments	1,788
Raw materials	1,034
WIP	403
Finished goods	1,554
Total Current Assets	4,859
Fixed Assets	
Factory/Plant Assets	1,780
Lease	56
Total Net Fixed Assets	1,836
Total Assets	6,695
Liabilities and Owners Equity	
Current Liabilities	
Trade Creditors	1,699
Bank overdraft	650
Due to holding Co.	750
Accrued Expenses	267
Other Current Liab.	209
Total Current Liab.	3,575
Long Term Liabilities	
Instalment Debt Payable	590
Other L-T Liabilities	238
Total L-T Liabilities	828
Total Liabilities	4,403
Owners Equity	
Brought Forward	409
Retained Earnings	29
Share capital	1
Holding Co.	1,853
Total Owners Equity	2,292
Total Liabil. and Equity	6,695

Table 4.2 BHL profit and loss statement

Income Statement £000's	BHL Ltd		Prepared: Jan. 1994	
	Dec. 1992	per cent	Dec. 1993	per cent
Gross Sales	12,025		14,176	
Net Sales	11,238	100	13,540	100
Direct Materials	5,995	53	7,913	58
Direct Labour	1,577	14	1,674	12
Cost of Sales	7,572	67	9,587	71
Gross Profit	3,666	33	3,953	29
Overheads (Operations)				
Electrical	267	2	325	2
Cookware	289	3	545	4
Procurement	104	1	139	1
Quality	69	1	80	1
Depreciation	203	2	257	2
Overheads (Marketing)				
Sales admin.	50	0	59	0
Distribution	344	3	452	3
Selling	603	5	606	4
Service	50	0	72	1
Product development	150	1	159	1
Ad. and promotion	145	1	254	2
Depreciation	121	1	130	1
General management	221	2	267	2
Other overhead	221	2	267	2
Rent/Rates/professional	135	1	145	1
Total Operating Expenses	2,972	26	3,757	28
Net Operating Income	694	6	196	1
Interest Expense	83	1	152	1
Net Income before Tax	611	5	44	0
Tax	202	2	15	0
Net Income	409	4	29	0

Table 4.3 Key ratio analysis

Key Ratio Analysis 1993	
Profit B.I.T./Net assets	1.4
Net Income/Sales	0.3
Gross Profit/Sales	29.2
Operating Exp./Sales	27.7
Sales/Net Assets	4.3
Sales/Fixed Assets	7.4
Sales/Stocks	4.5
C. Assets/C. Liab.	1.4
Acid Test	0.5

Table 4.4 Product category analysis

Actuals 1993 Contribution By product group	£000's Alu. C'ware	S/steel C'ware	Percs	Kettles	Other Elect.	Teaware	Factored Electrical	Total
Sales Revenue	2,998	1,260	1,196	4,587	754	859	1,886	13,540
Revenue %	22	9	9	34	6	6	14	100
Gross Margin	1,131	491	215	1,514	181	137	283	3,953
GM %	38	39	18	33	24	16	15	29
Allocated O/H's								
Cookware	201	85	80	121	0	58	0	545
Electrical	0	0	59	228	37	0	0	325
Prod. Develop.	50	21	0	76	12	0	0	159
Total Allocated	251	106	140	425	50	58	0	1,029
Net Margin	880	386	75	1,089	131	80	283	2,924
Net Margin %	29	31	6	24	17	9	15	22
Non-Allocated O/H's in prop. to sales	600	246	246	928	164	164	382	2,728
Contribution	280	140	–170	161	–33	–84	–99	196
Contribution %	9	11	–14	4	–4	–10	–5	1

Table 4.5 Commercial unit analysis

£000's Business Unit Analysis, 1993	Key Accounts	Field Sales	Export	Total
Gross Revenue	6,120	5,349	2,707	14,176
Net Revenue	5,733	4,900	2,707	13,540
Discount %	−6	−8	0	−4
Gross Margin	1,682	1,665	606	3,953
GM %	29	34	22	29
Total Allocated	1,622	1,418	717	3,757
%	28	29	27	28
Contribution	60	247	−111	196
Cont. %	1	5	−4	1

Table 4.6 Factory analysis

Net Sales By Manufacturing Centre, 1993	Factored Elect.	H'Green (Alu)	Coventry (SS)	W'Hall (SEA)	Total
Totals £000's	1,886	5,700	2,503	6,537	16,626
Alu. Cook	0	2,998	0	0	
Alu. Kettles	0	647	0	647	
Percs.	0	1,196	0	1,196	
Teaware	0	859	0	0	
SS. Cook	0	0	1,260	0	
SS. Kettles	0	0	1,243	1,243	
SEA's	1,886	0	0	754	
Other Kettles	0	0	0	2,697	
Reconcile Factory Transfers					3,086
Net Sales					13,540

- The balance sheet shows that assets are being financed by trade creditors, bank overdrafts and the holding company.
- A continuing liquidity crisis with a quick ratio of only 0.5.
- Significant working capital requirements and a sales to stocks turn of 4.5 which decreased to 3.9 when the factored products are excluded.
- Unprofitable product groups and distribution channels on a fully absorbed basis (after the full allocation of corporate overheads).
- Inadequate leadership and central control functions; importantly the absence of a Chief Executive and the clear allocation of responsibilities.

- Large amounts of information appertaining to separate parts of the business which have not been analysed, co-ordinated or summarised.

Organisational issues

In addition to three different production cultures, there are three different commercial cultures, given that the selling operations are now organised in three units:

- The key account team
- The field sales force
- The export sales division

As well as this matrix of three production units and three commercial units, the business has at the centre in Willenhall a Financial Controller and a Marketing Manager. Executives from the holding company oversee the business by *ad hoc* visits from Groningen or long sessions on the phone involving the financial controller. Other management functions are as follows:

- Production and quality assurance are based in the separate factories, with the exception that Hall Green is now responsible for Coventry's production.
- The new product development function (an individual) had been acquired as part of the Coventry acquisition and is still based in Coventry.
- An export operation has also been acquired with UniPress. This too is still based in Coventry.
- The management team in Willenhall therefore includes a Financial Controller, a Marketing Manager and a Key Account Manager.
- The Financial Controller is seen as MD Designate, whilst the Marketing and Key Account Managers are regarded as equals.
- The national field sales force reports to the mainly office-bound, Willenhall-based Marketing Manager.

These organisational constraints resulting from a rapid acquisition policy have implications for marketing strategy.

Marketing issues

These are contained in the marketing audit for both cookware and SEAs summarised below.

The marketing audit

Cookware summary

The cookware market
By 1993 the cookware market had grown to some 14 million units representing some £114m in the latest period (see Table 4.7). This relatively high level of real growth is surprising in such a well-established market.

Table 4.7 UK cookware market segments

	1993 Volume	1993 Value	1994 (Estimated) Value
Alum. non stick	50%	46%	40%
Alum. uncoated	8%	1%	1%
Glass	12%	9%	6%
Stainless steel	11%	15%	20%
Enamelled steel non stick	10%	14%	20%
Enamelled steel	5%	7%	5%
Cast iron non stick	1.5%	3%	5%
Cast iron	1.5%	4%	3%
TOTAL	14m units	£114m	

Market trends include:

- The dominant aluminium non-stick market sector, in common with the generic aluminium saucepan is in decline; but nevertheless is still estimated to account for 40 per cent of the market value in 1994.
- A contributing factor to the decline of the aluminium sector is concern as to the aluminium oxide effect; this concern is further compounded by the trend towards healthier eating and the possibility of Europe-wide legislation.
- Within the large aluminium sector, design and aesthetics have now become major trade and consumer concerns; simple polished aluminium hollowware is declining faster than the sector average, whereas anodised/strong primary coloured hollowware is increasing in unit terms. By contrast the first generation basic designs are declining in line with the overall market sector.
- There is evidence that product design is beginning to have a major impact on this household market. Increasingly, continental designs are being introduced, highlighting continental style, shapes and decorations; this is particularly true of the stainless steel and enamel steel sectors.
- Accordingly, unit growth is projected in the stainless and enamelled steel sectors, where products are becoming vehicles for continental designs. This in turn is adding value to products and increasing the average price of these product categories.
- The historical pattern of strong retailers dealing with a large number of fragmented 'me too' manufacturers is slowly breaking down with the emergence of stronger, design-based, mainly foreign, manufacturers.
- Although there is evidence of increasing consumer sophistication, and increasing frequency of purchase, almost 60 per cent of the market volume is still accounted for by aluminium products.

Betaware positioning and market share

The following positioning map (see Figure 4.1) illustrates the polarisation of the market between the added value brands, Swan and Tower, and the own-label sector. The two major dimensions of customer choice used for the axes of the positioning map are Price and Added Value/Aesthetics.

Figure 4.1 Cookware positioning map

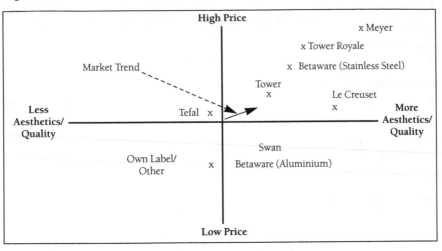

Relevant decisions for BHL are:

- Have they segmented the market correctly?
- Which resulting sectors best allow BHL to develop a distinct competitive advantage?
- Which sectors are they best equipped to contest?
- How should they communicate their offering?

BHL's total cookware volume in 1993 approximately equates to an overall unit market of 4.5 per cent (or 6 per cent of the aluminium sector). This compares with Swan 17 per cent, Tower 17 per cent and Tefal 19 per cent.

Market related
- Betaware is losing share in a growing market.
- Their hollowware products are mainly confined to aluminium, the stainless steel opportunity is not seriously addressed; there are as yet no facilities to manufacture enamel on steel products.

Product related
- The bulk of Betaware products are aluminium-based and down-market.
- The Hall Green factory is unsuited to the manufacture of up-market products with high added value design elements.
- Cookware generates the highest margins in the company, together with 214 per cent of BHL profit contribution.

Branding related
- Branding is focused on the Betaware identity or a retailer's own label. There is evidence that this strategy is only viable for the lower-priced market sectors.
- The Betaware branding is practically unknown, given the dominance of the own-label business.

Competition related

● Betaware increasingly adopts a 'me too' position in the face of competition, either branded or own-label, in the lower-priced cookware market sector.

Price related

● A heritage of competitive pricing and being 'never knowingly undersold'.

Distribution related

● Significant opportunities in cookware outside of the aluminium sector being relayed back by the salesforce.

Customer related

● Generally satisfied key account/regional account buyers. (Refer to limited trade research summary following.)

Summary of trade research

Based upon feedback from 20 national and regional accounts who have experience of dealing with BHL mainly (in relation to hollowware).

● Betaware is perceived as lower priced, own label merchandise.
● Key account service is generally of a high standard.
● Packaging is perceived as down-market.
● Product quality is perceived as average.
● Design is perceived to be weak relative to competition.

The marketing audit

SEA summary

The SEA market

In 1993 the total market for small electrical appliances (SEA) was some £245m at manufacturers' selling prices (MSP). Of this, kettles accounted for 29 per cent; food processors for 13 per cent; and toasters for 12 per cent.

   BHL summarised the current trends in the SEA market as below:

● Increasing consumer sophistication.
● Increasing concern with safety.
● Increasing demand for convenience (for example, cordless products; and the ongoing question as to when, if ever, will the UK ever join the rest of the world and sell SEAs with plugs!).
● Increasing demands for colour co-ordination for matching products.
● Increasing polarisation of the SEA market between the 'Quality' brands and the 'Economy' brands; perceived danger of being 'stuck in the middle'.
● Trend towards higher prices for the added value products.
● Increasing concentration of trade buying points.

BHL's Small Electrical Appliances

If factored products are excluded, some 86 per cent of BHL's total SEA sales and some 89 per cent of SEA gross margin in 1993 was generated by the kettles product group. The importance of kettles to the total BHL business was

Table 4.8 Electric kettles, market volume

1985	2.7m units
1989	4.1m units
1992	4.3m units
1993	4.5m units

Table 4.9 Trend by sector of electric kettles (per cent of volume)

Variant	1990	1993	Trend (Estimate)
Traditional auto.	28	25	Falling
Jug auto. inc. WG	32	30	Static
Jug auto. exc. WG	20	15	Declining
Cordless	10	25	Growing
Other	10	5	Declining

Table 4.10 The electric kettle competitive situation (per cent unit share by market sector, 1993)

Sector/ Brand	Traditional	Jug inc. WG	Jug exc. WG	Cordless
Russell Hobbs	28	18	14	–
Swan	24	19	24	–
Tefal	–	–	–	28
Philips	–	–	–	25
Haden	12	16	15	30
BHL	10	1	3	7

emphasised in Table 4.4 on page 65 which shows that the product group generated 34 per cent and 33 per cent respectively of total sales and gross margins (39 per cent and 41 per cent excluding factored products).

The market for electric kettles

Trend data for the kettle market sector is set out below:

Market related

- The market for electric kettles is growing at 5 per cent in volume terms, mainly as a result of cordless developments.
- The traditional automatic kettle sector is forecast to decline from a 25 per cent volume share.
- The automatic jug kettle sector is forecast to hold a 45 per cent volume share.
- Cordless kettles are estimated to grow from a current 25 per cent volume share.

Product related

- BHL is positioned in the declining standard jug kettle sub-sector.

- BHL has yet to establish its Avon branded cordless product to take advantage of market growth.
- BHL is marketing some 124 kettle variants despite a low share/distribution profile.

Competition related
- In the traditional automatic kettle sub-sector, Betaware is losing share to Swan, Russell-Hobbs and Haden. If Betaware is to sustain a viable business, should it defend its 10 per cent share of this market sector?

Table 4.11 Distribution, the competitive situation

Brand	Shop or Volume weighted Distribution	Sterling or Value weighted Distribution
Russell-Hobbs	57	93
Swan	55	92
Betaware	15	40*
(mainly own label)		
Avon cordless	6	17

* Betaware because of its focus on major key accounts, can be found in only 15 per cent of all stores, but these 15 per cent account for 40 per cent of the value of all sales of electric kettles.

Table 4.12 BHL, kettle volumes and margins 1993

Product type	Net sales	% of sales	Gross margin (%)
Alu. kettles	647	14	39
P. prop. kettles	320	7	34
S. S. kettles	1,243	27	33
P. P. jug	1,136	25	31
Cordless	1,170	26	36
S. S. jug	71	1	22
Totals	4,587	100	33

Table 4.13 BHL retail kettle pricing (£s)

Brand	Traditional	Jug inc. WG	Jug exc. WG	Cordless
Russell Hobbs	22.2	20.8	20.4	–
Swan	18.4	18.0	16.5	–
Morphy Richards	19.3	–	–	–
Avon	17.7	–	18.7	19.5
Haden	14.7	16.7	16.2	20.2
Betaware	14.1	15.4	12.7	–
Philips	–	–	–	24.5
Other	15.0	18.2	15.2	23.4
Average	18.1	18.7	17.3	23.7

- Betaware's minimal share of the added value automatic jug kettle sub sector is being rapidly eroded by Swan.

Distribution related
- Betaware's sterling-weighted distribution is half that of its major competitors, Swan and Russell-Hobbs.

Price related
- Betaware is occupying the lowest price point in the kettle market and is therefore vulnerable to a lower-cost competitor. Currently Haden is edging close to the Betaware price point on standard traditional automatic kettles.
- Betaware's positioning is confined to the lower-priced own-label sector.

The commercial business units

The business incorporates three commercial units with differing perspectives on the business. These are:

- Key accounts
- The field sales force
- Export

Refer to the Table 4.5 for the relative profitability of these commercial units (after allocation of overheads).

Key accounts
This unit generated 42 per cent of BHL's 1993 net revenues and 31 per cent of total BHL profit contribution. It is essentially a trade marketing operation concentrating on a limited number of major high street chain stores including Boots, F.W. Woolworth, Tesco, Asda and Argos. These five accounts currently generate some 87 per cent of the key account revenue. Products supplied by BHL are normally branded with the store own-label so that minimal BHL brand equity is built up for the company.

The Key Account manager is exposed to constant pressure to match competitive price bids when the annual contracts are reviewed. Unfortunately for BHL, these high street chain stores experience minimum disruption in changing suppliers, as competitive manufacturers seeking to generate volume for their factories will readily meet the required customer specifications.

The key success factors for this type of business can be summarised as:

- Staying close to buyers
- Empathy with buyers
- Flexibility of design and specification
- Reliability of supply
- Accepting lead times of at least 12 months for new introductions
- Willingness to co-operate with promotional activity (which may mean paying for it!)
- Attempting to build in product and service quality, so that price is not the only criteria of selection

Field accounts

The field sales force of six sales people is concentrated on the major cities of the Midlands and the South East. Supervision and sales coverage plans are the responsibility of the marketing manager. Unfortunately, he has little time to travel with his sales team, given the day to day demands of the business. Field accounts generated 126 per cent of total BHL profit contribution in 1993.

The field sales force services all regional accounts as well as the mail order and premium business. Some six sales people are employed who know the industry well, having also worked for competitors. They believe there is potential for cookware if a full product range could be assembled. They are less optimistic about appliances, given the strength of their competitors.

The export business

Facts on the export business are difficult to establish as the Export Manager is a difficult person to pin down, given both his travel schedule and his policy, whether by default or intent, of maintaining a minimal number of records.

Exports, however, accounted for 20 per cent of BHL's revenue, but only 15 per cent of total company gross margin. Some 77 per cent of the export revenue was accounted for by three product categories. These refer to aluminium percolators (now branded Avon) 39 per cent, Stainless Steel kettles 23 per cent, and Teaware 15 per cent.

Some 60 per cent of the export revenue was accounted for by two markets, Sweden and Saudi Arabia. Both these markets were characterised by a number of different entry modes. The product emphasis appears to be placed on the low profit lines, resulting in significant losses for the export unit.

The new product development function

The new product development function is co-ordinated by one individual in Coventry. Given the nature of the new organisation, there is little focus in the current new product development programme. It would appear that:

- There are few written briefs, inclusive of cost guidelines or milestones for new product programmes.
- There is little or no co-ordination, other than informal meetings arranged between the marketing manager, the key account manager and the new products manager.
- In the past, in response to pressure from the sales force, products have been launched without launch stock or with BEAB approval (for electrical products).
- Currently there are some 54 projects, none of which are prioritised on an 'ABC' basis.
- Focus is on separate products or product groups, rather than any integrating factors such as a common design theme for a range of kitchen appliances, or a common shape theme for a range of saucepans. Particular success has been achieved with the cordless jug kettle, where a major market trend was identified.
- The new product area also assists in identifying and policing the specifications for factored products.

- The salesforce has identified potential for a new range of toasters. The current range of factored toaster products are regarded as old-fashioned and non-competitive. The salesforce regard a modern toaster as an essential product to enhance the credibility of their SEA product range.

Note on toasters

Currently, Betaware branded toasters are factored via Hong Kong. These are conventional two and four slice toasters, generating sales revenues of £450,000 and gross margins of 20 per cent.

The Willenhall factory manager believes that such conventional toasters should be assembled in-house in order to foster assembly skills. Such skills would be invaluable if the Dutch holding company succeeds in its negotiations with a German manufacturer to assemble a second generation product. The product features the sales force have requested include a 'Cool-wall', variable width flexibility and both two and four slice variants.

If a licensing agreement can be reached with a European manufacturer, the sales force estimate that sales revenues could be increased by £2m, generating 40 per cent gross margins. In the short term, however, the second generation products could be factored in order to test the market prior to establishing assembly facilities.

Summary S.W.O.T analysis

Strengths
- Key account distribution
- Relatively low cost, flexible aluminium cookware factory
- A small dedicated retail sales force
- Trade recognition of the Betaware name as a low cost, reliable product
- An efficient small appliance assembly line
- Stainless steel quality products
- The Avon name, although trade awareness is rapidly declining

Weaknesses
- Dominance of a limited number of major customers and suppliers
- Only two major product categories – cookware and kettles
- High variable costs
- Low margins on percolators and teaware
- A complex culture based on three factories and three enterprise units
- A confused branding strategy with little use being made of the Avon name whilst the Betaware branding is stretched to encompass low-priced branded products and relatively high-priced stainless steel products
- Significant gaps in the cookware range
- The need to run fast to remain competitive in kettles, given the dominance of major competition
- The absence of a managing director and corporate mission to co-ordinate and focus efforts
- The uncertainty as to the future of the business resulting in short-term thinking
- No clear strategy in relation to factoring

For example, factoring objectives might include:

- A method of testing new products prior to manufacturing commitment
- Balancing the product range
- Acting as 'order-starters' for more profitable products
- Spreading the costs of the sales force
- Satisfying major customers
- Supporting a key product line

Threats

- Further cost increases (especially with imported materials)
- De-listings by major accounts
- Continuing innovation in the small appliance market raising the threshold entry costs in terms of capital investment and support
- Evidence that Haden (the major competitor in the Betaware price segment) provides superior quality at a similar price point to Betaware
- Trends in new designs and the inability to adapt to such trends within the time-frame of the fashion cycle
- Problems with the core business relating to the aluminium oxide scare and EEC legislation
- The continuing lack of focus of the business, with 'everybody doing everything and no one doing anything' syndrome

Opportunities

- The cookware market is a good match for BHL's internal resources
- The opportunity to build on the value for money reputation of the Betaware branding
- The opportunity to develop a more up-market range of well designed products to exploit the full potential of the stainless steel facilities
- The specific opportunity to develop the enamel on steel cookware category
- The opportunity for a dual branding strategy allied to the two separate market 'positionings' of value for money and design/added value
- The opportunity to develop clear pricing guidelines relating to the above two opportunities
- Specific opportunities for the small appliance area relating to:
  a) Cordless kettles
  b) Sustaining the traditional strength in traditional kettles
  c) Manufacturing state-of-the-art toasters under licence from a European manufacturer

Your Tasks

1. Complete the Marketing Audit by summarising:
   - The key success factors for both cookware and SEAs
   - Possible modes of market segmentation
   - The existing marketing mix for both Cookware and SEAs
   - The core competencies of the business
   - The financial imperatives.

2. Identify a number of alternative marketing strategies taking full account of the financial realities of the business.
3. Summarise the likely implications of each identified alternative for the business.
4. Rationalise your choice of strategic direction and recommend the marketing mixes/programmes required for implementation.
5. What marketing research activities would you recommend that BHL undertake in order to plug the gaps in their information base? Ensure that your proposals are realistic by recognising the resource limitations and by prioritising your proposals giving a clear rationale for your priorities.
6. Submit proposals to restructure the organisation taking into account:
   - The distribution channels
   - The key marketing functions
   - The discrete markets
   - The imperative to encourage new product development.
7. Recommend a revised product range strategy for both Cookware and SEAs taking into account:
   - The current confusion as to branding
   - Product positioning and pricing within market sectors
   - The number of product variants
   - The nature of competitive activity.
8. Develop specific new product development briefs for:
   - A premium range of Avon branded stainless steel saucepans
   - An economy range of Betaware branded toasters
   - Your briefs should include a profile of end-users, distribution channels, pricing guidelines, design specifications and identification of key competitors.

BHL, summary of strategic alternatives

Students should recognise that BHL is in a crisis situation which requires the application of classic turnaround strategy. There is little point suggesting that the business should be sold-off without considering the implications. Apart from the fact that a sale will take many months or years to arrange, selling at the net asset value, after consideration of the equity of the holding company (in effect a long-term loan), is not especially attractive. The sale value might be increased, however, if there is a definitive strategic plan indicating positive earnings over time.

Organisations like BHL in turnaround situations require both:

- A shorter term survival plan with the objective of strengthening the balance sheet and ...
- A longer term development plan highlighting future earnings potential.

The problem is to implement the survival plan before it is too late and to implement it without closing off the development opportunities; for example, reducing the workforce without losing skills which require long lead times to replace.

The urgent need is to develop a viable strategy which concentrates upon both the company's need for survival and the future potential of the business. In the

BHL situation none of this will be achieved unless the leadership vacuum is addressed. As with other organisations in this situation the priority is to appoint a 'turnaround manager'.

The short-term survival plan

The case material helps students recognise the interdependence between financial and marketing decisions in this crucial short-term phase. If the company is to survive, action must be taken rapidly. Any breaching of overdraft limits and/or the inability of the holding company to continue to finance the business, might at any time lead to liquidation. Students should concentrate upon the financial imperatives suggesting initiatives to strengthen the balance sheet and profit and loss projections. These might include:

● What assets can be removed from the balance sheet
● How working capital can be reduced and the velocity of the working capital cycle increased to turn over stocks faster
● How overdrafts can be reduced
● How cash can be increased
● How the profit and loss statement can be improved.

Students should be sure to set themselves clear financial targets for the survival stage. Most of this depends upon marketing decisions. For example, students need to consider the specific areas where immediate action can be taken as regards:

● Product range rationalisation
● Price increases
● Discount reductions
● Stock disposals
● Faster trade payments
● Distribution channel priorities
● Direct and indirect cost reductions
● Immediate sales increases
● Manpower reductions

The disposal of assets might include the sale of part of the business in order to focus upon the remainder. This would recognise the duality of the business as essentially a cookware and small appliance assembling business.

The longer-term development plan

Although marketing strategy has to be firmly based upon the financial realities of the business, it is strategy which enables the creation of a new financial reality. In deciding the forward direction students should determine:

● What are the key success factors for both cookware and SEAs?
● How might these two markets be best segmented?
● What are the core competencies of the business?

- What products and services result from focusing upon these core competencies?

Two possible development alternatives

1. The disposal of the small appliance business and the retention of the cookware business

This alternative might involve moving the cookware facilities to one site and concentrating on two distinct pricing segments under two different brand names.

- Betaware for low cost products, building on the key account strength
- Avon for the development of added value cookware and specifically to exploit the stainless steel facility

Possible expansion plans are included in alternative 2, below.

2. Retention of both business and expansion based upon clear priorities

An expansion strategy recognising that there is considerable distribution synergy between the existing products and that better management together with a consistent marketing strategy could regenerate the business.

Implementation guidelines

- Continued rigorous pruning of the following factored products:
  - Microwave ovens
  - Coffee makers
  - Irons
- Expansion strategy as a result of a clear focus on the following priorities:
  1. Aluminium cookware
  2. Stainless steel cookware
  3. Enamelled steel cookware
  4. Kettles and jugs
  5. Toasters
- New products such as enamelled steel cookware and state-of-the-art toasters to be introduced on a factored basis prior to full manufacture
- Loss-making products such as teaware to be phased out by price increases
- Percolators to be rationalised and two new variants developed
- The Avon brand name developed to exploit the stainless steel and enamelled steel opportunity; the Avon name to be applied to second generation toasters and other up-market products
- The Betaware branding to be confined to lower price position products; all products over a pre-determined price point to be marketed under the Avon branding
- The current kettle range to be rationalised and the 'two brand philosophy' applied on the same basis as cookware
- The cordless opportunity under the Avon branding to be pursued by considering additional items such as electric irons
- A new traditional kettle shape to be marketed under the Avon branding as well as a new shape designed for the Betaware branded traditional kettle

- Conventional toasters will continue to be branded Betaware, whilst new state-of-the-art toasters will be developed under the Avon branding
- Selective price increases to improve margins; minimum margin guidelines to be established for each product group
- Distribution to be expanded from key accounts to field accounts using the current salesforce

Organisational recommendations

Restructure to five operational directors in one geographical location comprising:

- Managing Director, with a financial and sales and marketing background
- Financial Director, also responsible for IT and business planning
- Operations Director, responsible for all manufacturing sites and purchasing
- Marketing Director, responsible for export, key accounts, field sales force, warehousing and distribution, product service and sales administration as well as marketing strategy, marketing planning and control, product rationalisation, pricing, new product development

Summary

- A rationalisation, new product, new distribution plan, requiring major cultural change.
- Hold the Betaware key account business whilst developing a differentiated Avon branded product range.
- Establish a 'two bite' market sector strategy, high price/low price.
- State-of-the-art technology and design for Avon; value for money for Betaware.
- Establish clear price guidelines for each brand franchise.
- Re-launch products to reflect these franchises.

5

Banking on a
Winning Strategy

Bob Grindley surveyed the piles of paper on his lounge floor, and wondered if it were possible to make any kind of sense of them. One pile was labelled 'Top Guns' and was a collection of quotations by senior banking and building society executives relating to the key issues and possible directions facing the financial services industry. The second pile was a summary of a consumer survey undertaken by Digital Equipment Company (DEC), a leading computer technology supplier to the financial services industry. Their 1992 survey was based on 1,000 interviews of bank account holders and included comparisons with a similar survey conducted in 1989. This pile was labelled DEC. The third pile was really no more than a series of aide-memoires relating to issues within the branch which Bob was addressing on an on-going basis. He had labelled this pile of notes 'Branch Agenda'.

Bob had been manager of a city centre branch of one of the banking majors for some six years. During that time there had been some dramatic developments within the industry and many of the environmental changes had impacted rapidly on Bob's own job, markedly affecting both the nature of his responsibilities and the manner in which he was required to execute them. Bob mentally and randomly recapped on some of the main environmental changes affecting retail banking services.

1. A long-term increase in the demand for financial services owing to growth in personal income and wealth, and to the spread of the 'banking habit'. Over 90 per cent of UK adults now had a bank or building society account.
2. Despite, or perhaps because of the above, a movement from a 'sellers" to a 'buyers" market. Consumers had become more demanding in terms of the quality and scope of service and general relationship with their local bank.
3. The deregulation of the financial services market which has allowed building societies to compete freely in segments that had traditionally been the preserve of the high street banks, e.g. current accounts, pensions and investment advice.

Deregulation, marketing channels and the main players

The structure of the financial services industry was fundamentally altered by the Financial Services Act (FSA) of 1986. This opened the way for the concept of so-called 'polarisation' which required retailers to opt for either 'tied' or 'independent' status. Independents act as agents of their customers and are free to recommend products provided by any life assurance company. Tied retailers represent a single 'manufacturer' and so can only advise on their products. The principal objective of this clarification was to protect consumers against dubious and incompetent selling practices. It also led to a realignment amongst the main players in the 'bancassurance' industry.

1. The major High Street banks and building societies, with the exception of the Bradford & Bingley, have opted for tied status, although the NatWest did not choose this route until 1993.

The tied retailers can be further segmented into those which act for a traditional life assurance company and those which have now acquired their own insurer. Examples of the former relationship include Nationwide-Guardian and Royal Exchange (GRE), Alliance and Leicester – Scottish Amicable, Leeds – Norwich Union, Cheltenham and Gloucester (C&G) – Legal and General, and Halifax-Standard Life. In 1994 Halifax moved into the second group which also includes Lloyds, Midlands, Barclays, TSB, and more recently NatWest and Abbey National (which effectively turned itself from a building society to a bank in 1989). There are some other notable variants to the above model of the main High Street retailers. One example is Direct Line Insurance, owned by the Royal Bank of Scotland (RBS), which concentrates on motor insurance sold by telephone but is also moving into additional personal insurance products. A second example is Marks and Spencer which has its own personal loan, personal equity plan (PEP), unit trust and credit card products.

2. Other banks and building societies including independent advice arms of some of the majors, which sell from any or a range of insurers. Bradford and Bingley fall into this category.
3. Insurance brokers which may offer either household, motor, life insurance, pensions or some or all of these financial products. In general terms, those brokers for whom life insurance was only a small part of their business opted for tied status while those which concentrate on life business are registered as independent advisers (IFA).
4. Insurance companies which market direct to consumers. Allied Dunbar, Equitable Life and Teachers Assurance, for example, employ large field sales forces while others like Sun Alliance use only direct response advertising.

In terms of the extent of achievement of the original objectives of the FSA, there remains some doubt. The trend from independent to tied advice might suggest a reduction in consumer protection and choice. On the other hand, research suggests that consumers are reluctant to indulge in complex search behaviour by comparing different products, particularly when they themselves have not perceived the need for the product or when the product is linked to some other purchase which may be more important to them, e.g. life cover linked to a mortgage. The number and size of fines imposed by the Life Assurance and Unit Trust Regulatory Organisation (Lautro) for misconduct also suggests that there is a long way to go before the quality of advice given by financial advisers/salespeople is at a satisfactory level. On the other hand, the industry is now taking such matters most seriously as a result of the fines and publicity. Norwich Union, for example, sacked hundreds of salespeople in 1994 and recalled further hundreds for more extensive product and ethical sales training.

The main changes in the financial institutions themselves have taken place against the above background, and Bob summarised them as follows:

1. Greater attention paid to attracting young first-time investors and, at the same time, encouraging customers to switch from competitors, owing to saturation in bank account market penetration.
2. Growth in interest in marketing as a means of responding to the more competitive climate. Bank marketing had been characterised by a senior Barclays manager as consisting of:
   a) identifying the most profitable markets
   b) assessing present and future customer needs
   c) setting business development goals and making plans to achieve them
   d) promoting the various products/services to achieve plans.
3. Cost-cutting exercises as illustrated by recent figures from the Big Four. Barclays carried out 110 branch closures and 5,000 staff cuts in 1990 (with a further 10,000 cuts planned during 1991–5). Midland closed 130 branches in 1991/2 and cut 4,100 staff, NatWest closed 117 branches and cut 6,400 jobs in the same period. Lloyds cut 7,000 jobs in 1991. (By contrast Abbey National actually increased staff numbers by almost 7,000 between 1987 and 1990.)
4. Attempts to repair their tarnished image which was brought to the attention of the nation during 1991–2 as a result of the publicity given to the banks' apparently ruthless and seemingly short-sighted treatment of small businesses. This image had been paralleled in the private retail sector where banks have been accused of (a) charging excessive interest rates on credit cards, (b) consistently making mistakes in their favour when calculating interest charges on overdrafts, (c) charging customers to advise them that they have overdrafts, (d) misleading their customers into believing it took four days rather than three to clear a cheque (thereby boosting profits from increased loan capability), (e) closing accounts (and branches) with the least profit potential, and (f) failing to offer customers their best interest rates on deposits without being prompted. Finally, (g) both banks and building societies have been accused of failing to advise customers that their money could be earning much more by transfer into more recent investments. Most banks now had codes of conduct which explained the principles on which business was undertaken.
5. The ever-increasing investment in information technology making radical improvements possible in terms of (a) reduced operating costs, (b) greater variety in service delivery, (c) enhanced ability to monitor customer accounts and 'cross sell' additional products, and (d) more efficient targeting of product to potential new customers.
6. A general trend away from the traditional core activity of administering a process towards becoming financial services retailers. Banks and their branches have metamorphosed from production units to shops. Associated with this trend has been a proliferation in the 'product range' offered by most players.

With these perspectives fresh in his mind, Bob turned to the Top Guns pile and began reading.

National Westminster

In all of our businesses, our aim is to provide a better service to our customers. We believe this to be essential to enhance the investment of our shareholders. In giving service, the quality of what we provide stands and falls on the motivation, talents and dedication of all our colleagues.

Lord Alexander of Weedon, Chairman 1992

It will steadily become important not only just having a large share of customers, but a large amount of information about them and then using the new technology and distribution channels to maximise sales based on these assets. This trend is already reflected in NatWest establishing centres of excellence, i.e. share shops, corporate business centres, credit cards and personal loans.

Stewart Legg, Director of Group Strategy

NatWest's Actionline and Primeline services indicate how little dependence there need to be on traditional branches when the power of the telephone, plastic cards and the ATM networks are fully harnessed.

The trigger to reaching our customers will be the smart card. The successful users of technology will be those who can see beyond automating existing procedures, and being able to exploit it to achieve greater results. As customer information improves as a result of new interactive databases we will be better able to deliver valued advice to customers rather than piles of junk mail.

Phil Wise, Chief Executive of Group Services

Over the past two years NatWest has been undertaking a wide-ranging exercise to develop our long-term strategy. We recognise that we must choose our future markets carefully, focusing our resources in markets where we would have a large and profitable presence. At the heart of our vision was the recognition that success in our current and future activities must reflect the fact that the customer is king.

Therefore at NatWest, we agreed that we would earn the respect of our customers through offering and delivering outstanding service, efficiently and at an acceptable price.

Derek Wanless, Group Chief Executive

Trustee Savings Bank

Our strategy is to focus on our prime business of banking and insurance services for the personal customers. Backed by excellent service, value for money products and advanced technology, bank assurance is the key to building long-term relationships with customers.

Sir Nicholas Goodison, 12 January 1994

Differentiation will continue to lead the market strategy of banks, but it cannot be centred on products. Factors such as the availability of telephone banking, access to sophisticated ATMs and contact with helpful, knowledgeable staff will be more important to the buying decision if all products are about the same and price differentials are minimal.

Future service must deliver real financial and convenience benefits. Relationship development will be the new focus. New and better ATMs will mean more frequent contact between customer and bank. Technology and expert systems will help in this. The financial retailers of the future will be guides, trusted financial friends, helping their customers through the maze of different options available and helping them make the right choice.

Peter Ellwood, Group Chief Executive

Barclays Bank

We are committed to:

- customer focus
- quality of service
- quality staff
- focused network
- social responsibility
- integrity

Andrew Buxton, Chairman

Barclays must differentiate through quality.

Alistair Robinson, Vice-Chairman and Chief Executive

Addressing our customer base, we asked what are their needs? Are we meeting their requirements? How can we quantify our performance? Embedding quality throughout our work and management processes requires real commitment and takes years.

The catalyst for change has been the humble telephone. Telephone banking is set to usher in a new era of opportunities and expansion, extending personal sector facilities beyond the branch into customers' homes and offices.

Alex Joblonowski, Managing Director of Barclays Global Services

Abbey National

We have long recognised the value of information technology as a means of providing both a higher level of customer service and more accurate and effective management information. The bank continued to invest in our branch network, modernising, refurbishing or resiting 118 branches in 1993.

Abbey National has the freedom to compete as a bank, while retaining the values of a building society; prudent, caring and trustworthy. Unlike traditional banks, we have been fortunate in that we do not need to break away from an uncaring and impersonal image.

The bank of the future will rely heavily on markets that it knows well and that have served it reliably, while diversifying cautiously into allied areas. Future branch networks will be leaner, more streamlined.

Recent market research suggests that customer visits to branches are already falling and will continue to do so. Therefore the banks and building societies will need to seek new ways of meeting the convenience need, perhaps through non-branch channels of distribution that are more segmented and targeted than at present.

- ATMs
- Direct mail
- Telephone banking
- Office and home banking through PCs
- Home visits by mortgage advisers

Interior design is also an important aspect. More selling space, service-orientated staff and friendlier atmosphere, reinforced by new technology-based distribution channels.

In the competitive world of financial services, providing the customer with a better service is the most important goal. In theory we all put the customer first, but putting the principle into practice is the way forward. We need to evaluate continuously and proactively the needs of our customers.

Peter Birch, Chief Executive

Midland Bank

As centralisation has increased, bankers have become more remote from their customers and laid the foundations for the proliferation of complaints currently being levelled at them. At Midland we are implementing a strategy which is designed to restore the best features of traditional banking to our business. The core strategy is to restore branch and area managers to a position at the heart of the community.

Midland has renewed its commitment to improving our service quality. For example, rationalisation of our product range is now well underway and our effort to improve communications with customers through the use of straightforward language has already been recognised by the Plain English Society.

The high street will remain the most competitive of marketplaces, and we aim not just to survive in this environment, but to gain a greater share. We have taken the first bold steps, against the prevailing trend, taking the bank back to our customers and I am confident that the rewards will be substantial.

Brian Pearce, Chief Executive

Customers felt that they only ever heard from a bank when they had done something wrong and their manager sent them an official letter. Changes needed to be made to alter the perceived parent–child relationship to an adult–adult relationship. By basing this relationship on mutual trust the banks would begin to deliver the service that customers required.

Kevin Newman, Chief Executive First Direct

Lloyds Bank

We believe that tomorrow's most successful bank will be built on focus, not diversity. Lloyds' policy is to concentrate its resources on those businesses in which we have the experience and ability to excel and to avoid those markets where realistically we cannot be among the leaders. The more we focus on a few major markets the more likely we are to find ways of providing better value for our customers. Our aim is to differentiate ourselves by better products, by being innovative, and above all by a higher standard of service.

Sir Brian Pitman 1990, Chief Executive

The customer has to be the first priority. The concepts of customer service and customer relationships have both come under strain during the recession.

This means organising the Bank around the customer. Lloyds is currently re-engineering its processes to improve its service to its customers. Management will have to ask themselves whether or not they are offering the best service and, if not, they must begin to do so. Progressively Lloyds has moved its non-retailing businesses out of the branches, leaving them to concentrate on retailing activities. We are retailers now. This shift towards centralisation of non-essential procedural services, such as loans, direct debits, releases more staff to act as front line contact staff.

Colin Fisher, General Manager UK Retail Banking

Girobank

The whole bank needs to be customer driven, not just those areas with direct relationships with external customers. So with little sustainable competitive advantage to be gained solely at the product level, the service with which we deliver the product moves up the customer's agenda.

Traditional competitive product attributes such as price, interest rate or speed of credit are easily and quickly copied by competitors, so they only offer short-term marketing advantages. However, if service is perceived as excellent it can offer a much greater competitive marketing edge, largely because positive service differentiation means having to improve all the 'people' aspects of the business – training, education, motivation and attitude – and not just those aspects where staff have a direct interface with the customer.

Girobank's marketing positioning as a telephone bank can be traced back to its start in 1968 when it created Telecare. By 1986 its dedicated branded customer telephone enquiry service handled more than 100,000 calls a week. A key area for improvement for the Telecare system was in the training, equipment, staffing and the availability of the working environment. The remarkable effect of quality can be seen by Telecare's changing performance. By 1988 the service was failing to meet customer service standards, so a fundamental review was carried out.

Training for the 500 or so full and part-time staff was improved dramatically and they now have an in-depth knowledge of bank products and procedures which enables them to offer a better telephone service to customers. This decision to focus on quality has been wholly justified – Girobank is the first financial institution to achieve the BS5750 registration.

To Girobank's senior management team the question now is not whether other banks and financial institutions will follow it down the quality road, but when and how fast. As with telephone and mail banking, quality of service is likely to be the only sure way of retaining the increasingly sophisticated financial consumer.

Gordon Henderson, Head of Corporate Quality

The DEC Survey

Why customers choose their bank

Customers were asked why they had selected the bank where they held what they considered to be their main account. The single most common answer by far, with a score almost double that of the next most popular, was because of the location. It was less of an issue for the under 35s (36 per cent), and overwhelmingly the most important for post office account holders (57 per cent) and socio-economic group 'C2' (49 per cent). The only category where anything other was most important was the 'AB' account holders who rated personal recommendation equally with location (30 per cent).

Personal recommendation was the second most important reason overall here, though there were differences between groups. Women rated this more highly than men (26 per cent vs 18 per cent), under 35s more highly than ever

(28 per cent vs 20 per cent) and bank account users compared with building society account users (24 per cent vs 16 per cent).

Special offers, favourable interest rates and lower bank charges were the third most popular reason with, not surprisingly given the bank's marketing activities, the biggest percentage of customers mentioning this in the under 35s (13 per cent versus 10 per cent overall).

Figure 5.1 Reasons for choosing a bank

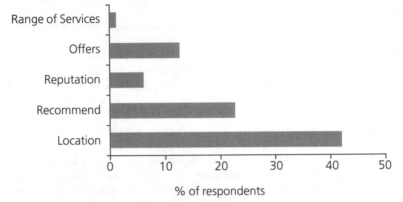

% of respondents

Customers changing their accounts

During the last three years the number of respondents who claim to have changed their main bank in the last two years has declined significantly. The figure has almost halved, from 13 per cent to 6.8 per cent. This may be a reflection of increased satisfaction with bank services or simply a reflection of the uncertainty brought about by the recession. Given the importance of location in people's choice of bank the reduced rate of house moves and job moves seen in the past few years are potentially the main reason for the fall. Equally the figure for three years ago may have been unusually high because of the then recent impact of the Financial Services Act and the promotional activities of the different financial institutions.

Customers and bank charges

Customers were asked about their attitude to bank charges. The question asked was – 'Which of the following ways of charging for bank services would you prefer?'

The responses point strongly to the conclusions that customers prefer a charging system that treats them as an individual (45 per cent wanted charges agreed for their accounts), and that customers wanted their charges to be predictable. Adding together those asking for specifically agreed charges, a flat fee, the charges absorbed in lower rates and those asking for 'no charges' gives a figure of 87.1 per cent of customers favouring a charging method that would give them a predictable charge.

The percentage of customers expecting 'no charges' appears low (only 8.2 per cent) but in the questionnaire this was not a prompted option. Evidently significant numbers still felt strongly enough to press their point on charges, indicating the bank still have to educate the public that service has to be paid for. Nevertheless, the survey does lay one of the popular misconceptions of how customers view their bank charges; they are prepared to pay charges but they want to know how much their banking will cost.

The branch and counter services

Consumers were asked how often they visited their bank branch to use the counter services. The pattern of branch visiting has not changed much since 1989 although the percentage of customers visiting their branch weekly or more often has fallen from 50 per cent to 46 per cent while those claiming to never visit has risen from 2 per cent to over 4 per cent. This compares well with research carried out by the Britannia Building Society in 1991 which had a figure of 50 per cent for branch weekly visits. Their figure of 15 per cent for weekly building society visits is, however, low compared with 40 per cent for those who are using their building society account as their main account. Under 35s are most likely to visit their branch at least weekly. Given these figures it is not surprising that customers felt strongly about branch location as reason for choosing or changing their bank.

Figure 5.2 Branch visits for counter services

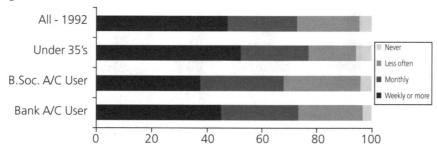

Since many banks are seeking to identify more ways of avoiding the need for customers to visit their bank branch (home banking, ATMs, direct banking, etc.) customers were asked how important it was to be able to visit their bank branch.

Figure 5.3 The importance of being able to visit the branch

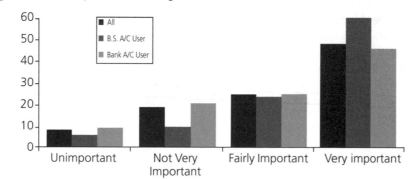

Taking those stating 'not very important' or 'unimportant' together this would indicate a potential of some 29 per cent of the banked population as potential users of non-branch based services networks. This figure was highest for 'C1' account holders with 33 per cent in these categories. The male/female split here was marked. A total of 35 per cent of men fall into the non-branch target while only 23 per cent of women do. In spite of this significant opportunity for non-branch services, 70 per cent of the sample felt it important or very important to be able to visit their branch, with a higher figure, over 80 per cent, feeling this amongst building society account users.

The question asking customers about their pattern of branch use produced few surprises. The frequency with which customers get cash is, as expected, higher than any other service. Of interest though is the relatively high frequency of making deposits, and the strong peak of 'monthly' for getting a statement and for paying bills. Paying bills is still not associated with branch visiting for nearly half the customers and financial advice scores 'never' with three quarters.

Figure 5.4 Frequency of using counter services

How do customers want to be served?

Customers were asked about how they would prefer to receive various services, at the counter in their branch, through machines, over the phone or by post.

Given the popularity of ATMs it is surprising how high 'personal service' (almost 50 per cent) reaches for even cash withdrawal. This tallies with the 1989 survey that indicated that almost 40 per cent of all account holders either did not have a cash card or had one but never used it. There is obviously still an education job to be done here.

Of equal interest on the ATM front are the low figures for deposit, transfer and bill payment which indicate an even bigger education problem if the use of self-service is to be increased in these areas.

Post is the only non-personal medium to outscore personal service in any sector, being the most popular approach to requesting a statement and collecting a cheque book.

Figure 5.5 How customers want to be served

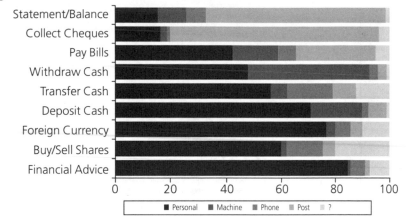

Customer satisfaction

Given the importance of being able to visit their branch how do customers feel about the way their banks perform? Asked how satisfied they were with diffferent aspects of the bank branch, customers recorded very high levels of satisfaction reaching an average of 7.8 on a scale of 2 to 10.

Figure 5.6 Satisfaction with branches

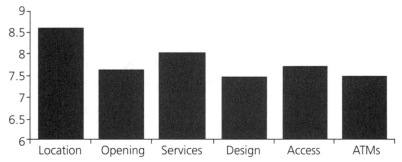

Location is, as has been seen earlier in this summary, important, and customers seem well satisfied with this aspect of their bank. They are also satisfied with the services available and with the accessibility of branches. Below average levels of satisfaction were achieved in opening hours, branch layout and in the availability of self-service machines.

When customers were asked to rate the importance of certain factors and their satisfaction with their branches for the same factors, again high levels of satisfaction with performance were shown, although in the main, levels of satisfaction were lower than the importance attached to the factor.

Interestingly the factor with the highest importance also scored the highest satisfaction – friendly staff. In this area the need for specialised staff scored a higher importance and a lower satisfaction and staff who know the customer was also in the same direction.

Figure 5.7 Satisfaction vs importance

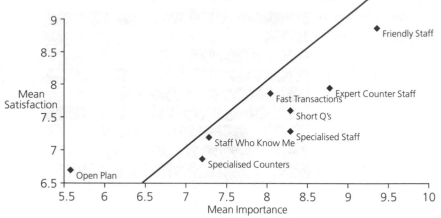

The provision of open plan branches was felt to be the least important of the items mentioned.

Source of services

When it comes to choosing the source of financial services, customers have very fixed views. Arguably there is little difference between a personal loan and a mortgage but customers very clearly prefer a building society for the mortgage and a bank for the loan. Independent advisors score highly for pension and investment advice and for insurance. The bank has become the most preferred channel for buying and selling shares – a demonstration of how a relatively new area has quickly been occupied by them. When asked about their preferred source for financial services, customers demonstrate the strong branding already achieved by the different sources of these services and at the same time show the scale of the marketing problem that faces new entrants into specific fields.

Figure 5.8 Customer's preferred source of services

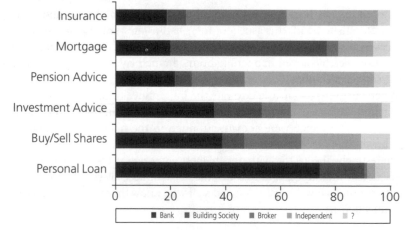

Changes?

Finally customers were asked what they would change about their branches.

A very high proportion of customers said they would change nothing (36 per cent) or were completely satisfied with their branch (11 per cent), so perhaps the greatest message to the banks and building societies is to leave well alone!

The most highly rated improvements suggested related to increasing the accessibility of bank branches. The 20 per cent figure includes requests for longer opening, Saturday opening, more branches and better parking.

Almost as highly rated (19 per cent) were the service related proposals with more tills, shorter queues, more personal service, better layout and quicker service all contributing to suggestions in this area.

Suggestions related to charges and interest rates accounted for 9 per cent.

Branch Agenda

At the top of Bob's own agenda were two items which were inextricably linked. The first was the changing nature of Bob's own job and his attempts to clarify in his own mind his key roles. The traditional notion of the Bank Manager as pillar of society, autocratic manager of a tightly-run bureaucratic ship and possessing the power to confer or deny loans, had all but disappeared. There was increasingly a new breed of manager whose job in some senses was now de-skilled, but was certainly different in many aspects. The Bank Manager was still expected to fulfil a societal role, but one based largely on the need to build the right image for the bank within the general local community and on the need to build specific relationships with key personal and corporate clients. The de-skilling of the job was largely related to the fact that decisions regarding loans, once the preserve of the bank manager, were now made by computer models. Not only did this reduce the need for the traditional manager's years of experience but it also removed much of his authority, grounded in both expert and position power. On top of this, the elements of personal discretion were removed from the process. Bob felt it was ironical that in the drive to build relationships with valuable customers, one of the manager's key tools had been thrown away. A formula response provided by a computer model could wipe out hours or even years of relationship nurturing.

Bob recognised that the role of the modern Bank Manager was increasingly that of a team motivator and it was this task which was exercising his mind in relation to a problem brought about by all the banks' recent rush to proliferate their product ranges. In particular, there was considerable pressure on the bank to boost its sales of life assurance products, supplied by its own insurance company subsidiary. The problem for Bob lay in the relationship between traditional (deposit taking) bank staff, the life product specialists and the customer. Specifically, how to effectively motivate the former two and how not to alienate the latter. Taking the customer issue first, Bob was well aware of the scope for upsetting relationships, via aggressive selling, which could manifest itself in several ways. For example, the searching of customer accounts and transactions for opportunities to cross-sell could become a nuisance if overdone. Telephoning 'valued' customers at home was a practice being employed by some managers which, he knew from friends, was annoying and was often deemed to be 'the sort of thing I would not expect a bank to do'. Even the use of branch-based computer sales quotation/presentation systems was unpopular with some customers who felt that a pressuring logic was being applied to them. (Sales staff themselves were divided in their response to the screen system. Some felt that it made their sales presentations more logical and foolproof for the customers. Others felt that it restrained their own 'style' too much and preferred not to use them. In recognition of these clear preferences Bob had allowed bank staff freedom to make their own decisions as to whether or not to use the screen system.)

The staff motivation issue was bound up with the organisational structure within the bank. It was appreciated that life insurance sales, being an investment product, were regulated by FSA standards. Not only this, but their complexity also suggested that specialists were needed to effectively advise on – and sell – such products. Consequently each branch had a small team of financial advisers who concentrated their activities on the sale of life and non-life products. They were regarded as having sales and product expertise and were rewarded by a combination of salary plus incentives. The incentives included attractive commission rates based on the value of policies sold. Although the financial advisers were free to generate their own leads through 'cold' telephone canvassing, it was accepted that the vast majority of business should result from 'warm' leads supplied by deposit-taking counter staff. Perhaps not surprisingly there was an element of conflict between deposit-takers and financial advisers and this was clearly inhibiting the provision of leads. The initial source of conflict appeared to be a culture clash. The financial advisers were relatively new, and they were seen as the 'fast track' employees within the branch. In contrast, the deposit-takers represented the remnants of the traditional banking era. Most of them had joined from school and had entered what they thought would be a career in administration. Recent years had, however, seen widespread change so that the emphasis was now on seizing the initiative in actively selling products and services to customers. Bob smiled as he remembered a well-known axiom in modern sales training, 'Telling is not selling'. The pun was a nice one. 'Telling has become selling', he thought, would be more appropriate for today's banks.

Despite a high level of investment in staff training, many still found it difficult to adapt to the new sales-and-customer-oriented culture. On top of this, they were not rewarded for their sales efforts. They neither received commission on the leads they were expected to pass on to financial advisers nor on their own sales of unregulated products. The original culture clash had thus been exacerbated by a differential remuneration system. There was no apparently easy solution for Bob since, although he was in overall managerial control at the bank, the financial advisers reported to the Financial Service Manager and the deposit-takers (selling non-regulated products and services) reported to the Business Development Manager.

The division between financial advisers and deposit-takers was reflected in the zoning policy incorporated in the re-design of branches which had been updated. Thus the financial advisers were located in individually screened areas at the rear of the branch, whereas the simpler transactions such as account openings and credit card applications were handled by deposit-takers moving into a specially designated open-plan area. The principal objectives of the re-design had been to provide a more welcoming atmosphere in terms of mix of open planning and privacy, removal of 'bandit' screens, and branch decor in order to complement other customer care improvements and to encourage an increase in traffic. The open-plan and zoning concept also reflected the desire to implement the transition of a bank branch from back-room processing department to a money shop.

There was no doubt in Bob's mind that this new role of financial retail outlet was making better use of the Bank's comprehensive branch network. Part of this had been made possible by the introduction of new technology which had made processing quotations more cost effective, improved customer service and allowed more active exploitation of sales opportunities. However, the new technology had also been partly responsible for the development of alternative service delivery channels which would reduce the need for customers to visit branches.

Bob felt he was going round in circles.

Questions for Discussion

1. Berry (1990) proposed 'Ten Commandments of Services Marketing'. These have been summarised by Baker (1993) as:
   (i) Focus on quality.
   (ii) Turn marketing into a line function.
   (iii) Market to existing customers, i.e. build on existing relationships.
   (iv) Market for employees, i.e. recruit the right people, 'the employees *are* the service'.
   (v) Market to employees, i.e. internal marketing.
   (vi) Manage the evidence, i.e. present the tangibles in the most effective way.
   (vii) Tangibilise the service.
   (viii) Manage the details – it is these that provide the differentiation.
   (ix) Improve the service architecture – i.e. the systems concerned with the creation and delivery of the service.
   (x) Brand the company.

   What is the evidence that banks are progressing along each of these dimensions of marketing orientation?

2. To what extent will the strategic 'themes' outlined by senior executives allow each bank to carve out a clear and unique positioning?
3. Is there a clear hierarchical thread between the strategic 'themes' referred to in 2 above and the competitive situation at individual branch level?
4. To what extent is the changing role of the bank branch manager making him/her into a marketing manager?
5. How should the banks respond to the apparent contradiction between the continuing priority given by customers to convenient branch locations and the growth in telebanking?

6. How reconcilable is the intention to make banks more proactive in selling whilst preserving the obligation to provide high-quality customer service and sound financial advice?
7. How should the bank re-organise at branch level in order to minimise internal conflict?
8. What can Bob do to minimise the above conflict before any reorganisation?
9. What is the role for internal marketing in shifting a bank branch from a 'production' unit to a customer-oriented financial shop?
10. What are the key issues for each element in the services marketing mix? How much can each be used as a competitive weapon?
11. To what extent should/could bank branches adapt their positioning strategy to match the needs of their local target markets?

6

Après Shower

The Easidry Body Dryer is an innovative new bathroom accessory product which was designed by Mike Godwin in 1991. The dryer unit is designed to fit in most bathing areas and shower cubicles and uses a system of warm air jets to effortlessly, quickly and hygienically dry the whole body. It is the only air dryer in the world which is patented as a total body dryer.

Après Shower Ltd was established in 1991 by Mike Godwin to manufacture and market the dryer. Although Mike was a successful entrepreneur, being a fully qualified electrical engineer and having established one of the region's most successful electrical contracting businesses, he had no previous experience of marketing products on a national scale. After some early success, Mike made limited headway and turned to his friend Kevin Pritchard, an honours graduate with over 12 years' experience in blue chip companies, specialising in the sales and marketing of new products, and business development. Impressed by the concept, in April 1993 Kevin established Après Shower Distributors UK Ltd (ASD) to market, sell and distribute the product.

Mike Godwin acts as Technical Director to ASD. His responsibilities include quality standards, new product development and, when requested by purchasers, product installation. The only other member of staff is Judith Russell, Business Manager. Judith was appointed to co-ordinate sales and marketing efforts, to develop new distribution channels, to attend exhibitions, to provide demonstrations to larger potential purchasers and to deal with office administration, invoicing and customer inquiries.

Easidry took two years to develop and was particularly designed for use within a shower cubicle, although it can be installed over a bath or on any wall. The dryer consists of an electric motor which blows jets of warm air over the body. The electric motor is encased in a tough plastic 'pod' which is installed just above the height of the shower cubicle away from the flow of water. The air, at a constant temperature of 70 degrees Fahrenheit, which cannot burn the skin, passes through a hollow 'leg', which runs vertically down the wall, and out through jets at an angle of 30 degrees downwards. The unique design of this leg ensures that the air is distributed evenly along the length of the body so ensuring even drying. An air-pressure switch was designed, opening up the product to the disabled market. This is a touch pad switch that can be located anywhere within the shower cubical, even on the floor where it can be operated with the toes.

The dryer is highly efficient at drying the body. It dries every part of the body, even the feet, leaving the body touch dry rather than towel dry. The dryer works most efficiently within a shower cubicle, where the smaller volume of warm air is recycled. The dryer is economical to use as it only costs around 3p for an average drying period. This cost compares very well with the laundry costs of towels and delivers the added benefit of warming the whole room.

The dryer works well in conjunction with specially designed shower chairs which are already in existence for those people who cannot stand in the shower. The dryer is particularly useful for people with skin complaints as it removes the need for harsh rubbing with towels, and for arthritis sufferers who cannot get into a bath but would still benefit from heat treatments.

The unique design of the 'leg' which ensures the constant air flows has been fully patented in the UK. Easidry is manufactured to BS3456 and BS800 quality standards.

ASD give a 12-month parts and labour guarantee with each Easidry. They also offer an optional maintenance contract for one or three years at a cost of £30 and £70 respectively. In fact the product is virtually fault free, and, if any problems do occur they tend to be caused by incorrect installation by the electrician or DIY installer. In the cases where ASD have been called out to a faulty dryer they simply install a new dryer free of charge as this apparently seems more cost-effective than repairing and ASD are working hard to build a quality reputation. ASD will also sell spare legs to customers if the original is broken, perhaps in collision with wheelchairs. However the legs are made of sturdy plastic and breakages are very rare.

Although ASD do promote and sell directly to end-users from their head office, they do not have the resources to set up and run a national salesforce. Therefore, rather than use a franchise system or the services of wholesalers, they have established a network of 'distributors'/ retailers. ASD currently has eight distributors countrywide. Although ASD refers to these outlets as distributors, they are technically non-exclusive retail sales outlets which sell the dryers directly to end-users and are not allowed to sell the dryer on to sub-distributors or other retail outlets.

The main business of the retailers is usually the sale of disabled equipment such as wheelchairs and specialised baths and showers. ASD is considering developing additional retail channels possibly through bathroom and home improvement centres.

ASD require most retailers to hold some stock. The discounts offered, the provision of a demonstration model and the support offered by ASD depends on what potential sales levels and promotion the distributor can offer ASD in return.

Existing end-user price is £275+VAT, plus £8 carriage, plus installation, if required, at £65. Distributors receive a discount related to the level of service and promotion they offer plus the volume of sales they achieve.

ASD employ a range of promotional techniques and media. Most media advertising is primarily aimed at eliciting a direct response, but some is also geared to increasing general awareness. An example of a recent advertisement plus the media schedule are shown below in Figure 6.1 and Table 6.1.

Kevin and Judith attend a number of exhibitions when the display is usually positioned in a level access shower cubicle to accommodate wheelchairs.

Figure 6.1

DO YOU HAVE DIFFICULTY DRYING YOURSELF?

Whether you find it hard to use conventional towels effectively because of reduced mobility or because of sensitive skin, Easidry can help you. Its gentle air jets dry the whole body effortlessly, quickly and hygienically. And this pleasurable experience is remarkably affordable – the average drying time will cost around 3p, which compares favourably with the cost of laundering towels. For a free, no obligation demonstration or further information, contact us today.

E·A·S·I·D·R·Y

Après Shower Distributors UK Limited, Unit 1 Woodhill Street, Bury, Lancashire BL8 1AT. Tel: 0161-761 3131

Table 6.1 Après shower media schedule 1994/1995

	Cost per Insert	Jan	Feb	Mar	Apr	May	Jun	July	Aug	Sept	Oct	Nov	Dec	Total
National														
1. Radio Times														
Quarter Page Central Region	800	✓	✓	✓	✓						✓	✓		4,800
Quarter Page Granada Region	560	✓	✓	✓	✓						✓	✓		3,360
Limited Mobility														
1. Multiple Sclerosis News	273				✓				✓				✓	819
2. The Messenger	679		✓											679
3. The Disability Guide	135	✓	✓	✓										405
4. Disability Now	243		✓	✓		✓								486
5. The Leonard Cheshire Wk	150						✓							150
6. The Purchasers Review	500				✓									500
7. The British Wheelchair Sports Foundation	300							✓						300
8. Arthritis News	205			✓			✓			✓			✓	820
Total		1,495	2,417	1,943	2,133		355	300	273	205	1,360	1,360	478	12,319

Mailshots are used periodically to reach a variety of targets including follow-up to exhibition enquiries. The mailshot package includes a brochure plus an appropriate letter depending on who is being targeted.

A PR agency has been appointed and Easidry has been featured in the new product sections of a variety of journals aimed at the physically challenged and also at builders and architects. Where possible, press releases have also featured case histories.

Reviewing the current situation and the progress made so far, Keith and Mike felt that they were at something of a crossroads. Limited resources meant that some critical decisions had to be taken. There was clearly much work to be done to develop the disabled market further.

Mike also recalled that the dryer had initially been conceived as a luxury product. There were, probably, other ways in which the overall market could be segmented. How many of these ways were there? Which might represent the largest potential demand? Which would be the easiest or least expensive to develop? Would it be possible to develop more than one segment? If so, how would the marketing positioning mix have to be adapted? Even if the current strategy was maintained, to what extent should any of the present approaches to the marketing mix be altered?

Further stimulus to the debate was provided when a student acquaintance of Judith's offered to carry out some preliminary market research. Pauline Chidlow began assembling information. A review of the environment concentrated mainly on factors which might affect the disability segment. A telephone survey of a sample of past customers was used to find out more about their status and behaviour. A single group discussion among some of Pauline's friends was used to generate ideas for further research directions.

Environmental review

1. Greater freedom for Occupational Therapists to select from a wider range of providers of technical aids.
2. Increasing variety of channels for technical aids – specialist shops, dedicated mail order catalogues, kitchen and bathroom showrooms, builders' merchants, DIY and homecare outlets amongst others.
3. Increasing number of organisations which will display and distribute free of charge information about technical aids, e.g. Disabled Living Centres.
4. On average, three homes modified each week by each Social Services Department to meet the needs of the physically challenged.
5. Estimated current 10 per cent per annum growth rate in shower installations into the homes of the physically challenged.
6. Over 12 million people in the UK aged over 60.
7. Estimated 6 per cent per annum growth rate in total UK shower installation. UK home penetration currently 50 per cent compared with 90 per cent in USA.
8. UK bathroom sector fastest growing segment of the home improvement market, fuelled by introduction of luxury into the washing/bathing routine, e.g. basic showers being upgraded to power showers, baths to incorporate jacuzzis.
9. Continued growth in the leisure industry including hotel breaks, health farms and sports and fitness centres.

10. According to the 1989 OPCS Survey of Disability there are 6.2 million adults in Great Britain with a disability above the threshold level. Of these, 5.8 million live in private residences and seven out of ten use some form of disability related equipment.
11. The 1994 Community Care Act will result in declining hospital beds and increased numbers of patients receiving care in their own homes.
12. Predictions in 1989 by Hay Management Consultants suggest numbers in the over-75 age group will be a quarter higher by the year 2000.
13. Breakdown of the nuclear family implies more independent living.
14. Rising expectations regarding standard of living and maintenance of that standard into old age.
15. Only 31 per cent of persons with disabilities under pensionable age are in paid employment.
16. 75 per cent of people with disabilities rely on State Benefits as their main source of income.
17. Increasing numbers of elderly people are benefiting from incomes from private pension schemes.
18. On average, for those aged over 75, the cost of the Health Service is six times higher, and the cost of Social Services 26 times higher.

Customer survey

1. 80 per cent of ASD sales currently made to the private sector.
2. Most purchases are made by women.
3. Over half of private purchases are made by those aged over 60.
4. 66 per cent of private purchasers consider themselves to have some sort of disability or physical limitation.
5. Just over half of purchasers are registered as disabled.
6. 40 per cent of purchasers learned about Easidry from an advert and 12.5 per cent through an exhibition.
7. Reasons for purchase included mobility problems, privacy, freedom, assistance to the carer, and complete dryness aiding dressing.
8. 20 per cent of private purchasers had had consultations with an occupational therapist and most of these had received some form of grant to help pay for the dryer.

Questions for Discussion

1. What sort of Mission Statement should ASD have?
2. What should ASD's priority objectives be – short-term profitability or long-term growth? If growth, should this be achieved by growing the market, by market development, by product development or by diversification?
3. Should ASD plan to stay independent or should it seek a partner of one form or another?
4. Do you see ASD's business as being in a niche market or in the early stages of a mass market?
5. How would you segment ASD's markets and how would you prioritise the resulting segments? Why?

6. Would you recommend a concentrated, undifferentiated or differentiated segment strategy? If the last, how would you modify the marketing mix for each segment?

7. How many different marketing channel strategies are potentially available to ASD? What criteria would you use to help choose between them?

8. What forms could ASD's medium- and longer-term organisational development take?

9. How significant a factor is price in each of the market segments you have identified and how would you plan the development of price in each segment over the life cycle?

10. What do you see as the main barrier to growth and the main threats to ASD's future?

11. What is the appropriate marketing communications mix for ASD? How should this develop by segment over time?

12. What objectives would you set for each element within the marketing communications mix and how can these elements be synergistically integrated?

13. How should ASD determine its communications budget?

14. What do you think of ASD's advertising in terms of advertising proposition, creative concept and media schedule?

15. How can ASD effectively motivate its distributors?

7

British Safety Razor A[1]

'THE NAME ON THE WORLD'S FINEST SHAVE'[2]

Entering Developing Markets

The British Safety Razor Company (BSR) had been operating overseas since the early 1930s. The company had survived the successive competitive challenges of:

- Stainless double-edged blades
- Captive systems
- Disposable razors
- Twin-bladed systems

These phases of innovation resulted in BSR focusing upon its product/market strengths, which were double-edged blades in the developing markets, and disposable razors and systems in more developed markets. As a result of this strategy the company's products had become international brand names. Accordingly, British Safety Razor's global business was organised into five distinct operating divisions. These were:

- The European Group based in Richmond, Surrey, UK
- The North American Group based in Charlotte, North Carolina
- The Central and South American Group based in Caracas, Venezuela
- The South East Asia Group based in Sydney, Australia
- The Africa, Arabia and Asia Group (AAA), based in London

British Safety Razor operated a decentralised international business, based upon distinct regional groupings which shadowed the world's major trading blocks. These regional groupings were supported by local manufacturing units in the principal markets of each region. The company prided itself on its international culture which was reflected in the wide mix of international personnel. For example, the General Manager of the rapidly growing South East Asian business was Dutch, whilst his country managers (for his five major markets) were two Chinese, one Malaysian, a Swede and an Australian.

---

[1] British Safety Razor is based upon a number of companies in the industry. Accordingly, as people, places and products are fictional, information should be used only for teaching purposes. Equally, the reference to Egypt in no way implies any relationship to any person or Egyptian organisation.
[2] With apologies to a well-known company!

The AAA Group's Operations

The exception to this pattern was the City of London based AAA group, which was still exporting UK manufactured blades to the open markets of the Middle East. The group had built up a complex network of linkages with international traders based in major centres such as London, Vienna and Berlin. These traders 're-exported' products to the developing economies, and given the shortage of hard currency might accept less usual forms of payment. This meant that AAA had frequent and complex dealings with all types of intermediaries, including export brokers, agents, merchants and representatives of national governments. It was felt by the rest of the company that if British colonial attitudes still existed they were alive and well and living in EC1, as many AAA markets were those parts of the map that were once coloured red.

The major markets included in the AAA Regional Group included:

Iran	Russia	Algeria
Pakistan	Ukraine	Morocco
India	Poland	Kenya
Egypt	South Africa	Iraq
Nigeria	Turkey	Yemen

LEARNING NOTE . . . 'Opening and Closing'

Closed markets for exports refer to those markets where it is difficult or impossible to import given one or a combination of the following factors:

- Import bans
- High duties/tariffs
- Administrative barriers
- Lack of hard currency
- Political instability
- Unacceptable risk of non-payment

From the standpoint of the national government such measures are important contributors to nurturing developing local industries. Markets may 'reopen' to imports if these factors are reversed.

British Safety Razor had rightly placed its priority on building its business in higher GDP markets with open and stable economies. The result was that AAA had become something of a corporate backwater and was increasingly operating independently of the parent organisation given a lower level of corporate interest in the majority of its markets. AAA provided only general reports and overviews of its operations to the Richmond office (which was also the location of corporate headquarters).

It was well known, however, that the AAA Group were experiencing increasing difficulty in achieving their sales and profit targets. This reflected the small number of really 'open' export markets that were available across this vast region of developing countries. In the past the four key AAA Regional Managers had played a balancing act between markets 'closing' and those of equal value 'opening'. Given the decreasing oil revenues in a number of major AAA markets, an imbalance in favour of markets closing had now raised serious doubts as to the viability of this traditional exporting business.

Increasing Corporate Interest in AAA Group Activities

BSR were becoming convinced that whereas, in the past it had been possible to allow the geographical divisions considerable scope in their approaches to blade marketing, the rapid development of global customer segments dictated a reappraisal of this decentralised approach. In view of both the declining revenue situation and the increasing corporate interest in having a long-term presence in AAA's major markets, it was only a matter of time before the company began to seriously reconsider its strategy.

The company now wished to duplicate their successful global formula of strategic alliances in major markets (to secure local manufacturing and distribution), in these more neglected AAA markets. The time was now right, they felt, to build upon the awareness and distribution of the traditional 'Double A' branded double-edged blades, in order to provide a launch platform for second generation global products (such as disposables). Equally, they recognised the urgency to pre-empt competitive attempts to establish local infrastructures in markets of burgeoning customer demand.

When the company began to request substantive details of the AAA business, the AAA managers maintained that in many cases they had no knowledge as to end-users as their dealings were often confined to brokers and merchants who operated as principals. Frequently they spoke of the separation of responsibilities referring to the importation and logistics by international merchants on the one hand and the distribution activities of their own agents or distributors on the other. Indeed the language of market reports was beginning to sound archaic and appeared to relate more to a bygone age than a contemporary multinational organisation. For example, unfamiliar justifications were found in the sales variance reports for specific markets. These included such statements as:

- 'The Company Manager was forced to leave the country as his visa was withdrawn at short notice.'
- 'The agent has disappeared . . . believed to have stolen part of the consignment stock.'
- 'The local distributor refuses to meet the agreed sales coverage targets . . . preferring to stock-pile in a hyper-inflationary economy.'
- 'The civil war has closed the ports, so deliveries are now pending a land convoy.'
- 'Given that we are to be paid in agricultural commodities we have yet to find a trustworthy commodity broker before we can credit ourselves with the sales values.'

The situation was put into focus at one meeting in October 1994 when the AAA Group General Manager was asked to explain the high sales levels relating to the low population economies of the Ivory Coast, Libya and Kuwait. The Richmond staff personnel had worked out that if the shipment figures were to be believed, the quantity of blades going into these markets would result in the average male shaving 20 times, 35 times and 79 times per day respectively. Whilst maintaining that export management companies or brokers acted as principals, the manager acknowledged the significance that these countries were geographically close to the major markets of Nigeria, Egypt and Iran/Pakistan/ India respectively.

For the first time the status of low-priced double-edge blades as entrepôt items was acknowledged at a senior level in the company. British Safety Razor's products, the AAA management explained, had taken on a role similar to cigarettes immediately after World War 2 in Europe. This was especially true of those countries with unstable currencies. The company began to realise the implications of losing control of their products and a consensus was emerging to minimise the activities of AAA's independent intermediaries. If the current situation was allowed to continue, the headquarters staff argued, both the company's reputation and its longer-term plans for penetration of these burgeoning markets would suffer considerable damage. This developing consensus, however, was pre-empted by the crisis in Egypt in December 1994.

The crisis breaks

That December, BSR were shocked to discover that their appointed distributor in Egypt and two of his staff had been arrested and charged with being actively involved in illegal importation and distribution. They were further advised that the distributor would maintain that he had the full support of BSR who were the chief culprits. The moral reputation of the company, carefully built up over the years, was now in peril.

Egypt was in effect a closed market for lower-priced foreign-manufactured blades (high tariffs and duties), given the desire of the national government to encourage local industry. British Safety Razor's products were, however, to be found increasingly in the major cities and throughout the Delta area. The AAA group employed an official distributor and fully supported his selling efforts. They maintained that all charges on imported blades were paid in full and despite maintaining that this was the London broker's responsibility, they provided invoices to support their statements. None of this, however, explained how market prices were so competitive.

Given both the risk of the current situation worsening and the need to safeguard the commercial potential of these AAA markets, the company moved fast and focused its attention (and its internal audit personnel) on the AAA group. It became apparent that official imports to Egypt accounted for less than 10 per cent of blade volumes. The remainder was 'smuggled' by third parties. The Board then insisted on a comprehensive review of all agreements with third parties and a greater emphasis on building a stronger local manufacturing base, with the objective of encouraging a revised consensus to operating in developing economies. Corporate thinking increasingly reflected the view that not only must AAA rejoin the corporate structure and culture, but new aggressive competition in these markets must be countered from within before they became better established in some of the most populous nations in the world. Above all, any suggestion that company personnel might be involved in questionable activities would not be tolerated.

Towards a new strategic direction

The AAA group did not rely solely on indirect or direct export to generate business. Within the group, three 'mini-plants' had been successfully established in three separate markets where majority foreign equity participation was allowed.

In addition, pilot joint-venture schemes had been established in an additional three countries. All of the joint-venture attempts had, however, run into difficulties, given conflict with local partners or political instability. By the end of 1994 none of these ventures were still trading.

The company set as its objective the phasing out of the over-reliance on the export business in favour of local manufacturing in key markets which would involve the group managing a wider portfolio of market entry modes. The question of distribution would be addressed as a separate but sequential issue. The company recognised that this involved a major escalation in commitment and investment in these developing and sometimes unstable markets. This escalation of commitment both in terms of manufacturing and distribution is illustrated in table form below.

LEARNING NOTE on international operational modes

The ladder of escalation

Manufacturing ladder
- Export broker
- Direct export
- Licensing
- Contract manufacture
- Joint ventures
- Subsidiary company
- Manufacturing alliances

Distribution ladder
- Visiting salesperson
- Commission agent
- Stocking agent
- Distributor
- Distributor/Sales co. mix
- Own selling company
- Distribution alliances

This conventional approach of incremental progression (increasing commitment and control) towards a combination of entry modes/distribution arrangements has been implemented by many international organisations. The global market imperative now presents a challenge to this approach, given the emphasis on rapid launches to global customers, rather than a market-by-market incremental approach, which appears to have characterised the BSR international strategy.

Cultural change

The company also recognised that they were embarking on a programme of major cultural change for the AAA Group which might take from five to ten years to complete. This would require new leadership and a careful blend of existing and new managers (recruited from the company's other geographic operations, such as South East Asia, which was leading the company's push towards operating inside developing markets).

The current culture of the AAA Group as articulated by the newly appointed South African Director of AAA (now referred to as The Overseas Investment Group or OIG) is contrasted below (Table 7.1) with the 5/10 year cultural objectives.

Table 7.1

AAA now	OIG will be
British	Mix of nationalities
Colonial attitudes	Global attitudes and mindset
Export orientation	Emphasis on local manufacture
Power with distributors	Power with local company
Short-term oriented	Long-term commitment
Narrow product focus	Market full range
Ad hoc	Strategic
Balancing any no. of open/closed markets	Clear country priorities
Based in City of London	Based in major markets
Institutionalised secrecy	Open door culture
Formal/non-professional	Informal/professional
Independent	Part of British Safety Razor
Loose controls	Adhere to corporate ethics

The agreed outline strategy

The revised OIG strategic plan targeted the following major markets for local manufacture and direct distribution:

Africa
Nigeria, Egypt and Morocco; the current manufacturing unit in Durban, South Africa was to be upgraded and expanded given the ending of sanctions.

Asia
Russia, India, Pakistan and Iran.

Middle East
Retain current direct export modes but attempt to convert from third party distributors to selling companies in three markets.

The preferred routes set out in the strategic plan were:

1. Local equity participation based upon the technology developed for the blade mini-plants in South East Asia (and successfully piloted by AAA in South Africa and Kenya). It was anticipated that equity participation with a local partner would be limited by the national government to a minority share, as blades were regarded as non-essential technology. Each candidate country was likely to vary with regard to its regulatory climate, so it would be necessary to negotiate from a strong position which would require the transfer of branding and technology.

2. In the event of unacceptable low minority shares (less than 25 per cent), the company would then attempt to establish a contract manufacturer allied to an existing or new distributor.

3. In the event of failure with option 2 above, develop a licensing fall-back proposal to be triggered in specific circumstances.

4. To carefully investigate the tariff and duty structure of target markets in order to check the possibility of establishing wholly-owned manufacturing companies in circumstances where import restrictions were high on finished goods, but low on components and machinery.

5. To expand and modernise the existing blade plants to allow a greater priority to disposables as well as stainless blades.

6. To ally the above manufacturing proposals with local selling companies wherever possible.

LEARNING NOTE on joint-ventures

A) Relevant to the following circumstances:

- A strong mutual interest
- Ability to cope with the inherent conflict of interest
- When 100 per cent Foreign equity is forbidden
- Markets closed to imports and/or concealed barriers to trade
- Requirement for local knowledge
- Requirement to share the risk
- Requirement to share the capital costs
- Ability to be flexible
- Concern as to expropriation/indiginization

B) The logistics

- Decide who provides what
- The company: trade marks, technology, training, marketing expertise, technical support
- The local partner: capital, local knowledge, distribution network
- Decide the equity shares and dividend policy; this depends upon such issues as the strength of the trade marks proposed, the type of technology, the amount of capital subscribed and local legislation
- Decide whether management is in proportion to the equity

- Establish local partner's intentions, (if any), as to the reselling of equity
- Decide any veto rights, any patent rights?

  C) Decide what's in the agreement

- Raw material transfer prices
- Re-export agreements
- Innovation and product development policy
- Use of trade marks and patents
- Management, who appoints the directors?
- Non-voting/voting shares
- Size of third party shareholdings
- Marketing and distribution targets
- Exit formula
- Arbitration

  D) Consider contingency, e.g. contract manufacture

- Halfway house between licensing and direct investment
- Ability to retain control of distribution
- Ability to combine with licensing

Priority Egypt

Facts and rumours

The corporate priority was to conclude an early agreement in Egypt leading to local manufacture and distribution. From the external perspective of BSR the situation appeared confusing and dominated by rumour. Information sources, none of them necessarily reliable, revealed the following:

- Still higher tariffs would be phased in over time to protect the developing local initiatives.
- A possible blacklisting by the government as a result of alleged tax and duty evasion.
- The news that an Italian disposable razor manufacturer was proposing to enter into a strategic alliance with local partners, some of whom enjoyed close government contacts. This project they discovered was to be known as the Middle East Shaving Company, or MESC.

Rumours continued to circulate which fuelled the fear that this would create a monopoly for the local manufacture of disposable razors. Any additional foreign investment in the category, it was speculated, was to be directed towards the more traditional but declining double-edged blades.

It was also rumoured that the government had an active interest in the whole industry. This could mean that the government, quite apart from encouraging local initiatives, would itself take a direct or indirect equity share in strategic alliances with foreign companies.

The government interest in this market was in part explained by the volume of government contracts for blades. These included contracts for the army and all higher educational establishments. Razor manufacturers understood very well that these young people were the prime target group for their products, as research had demonstrated many times in different markets, that shavers tend to remain loyal to the method of shaving introduced to them by their peer group in their late teens.

The candidate local partner

Shortly after the Egyptian crisis developed, the company decided to seek out a local partner with whom to establish a possible joint venture. Their contacts in Alexandria introduced them to the 'House of Haq', which was a major Egyptian trading company specialising in wholesaling and retailing. This company, who were actively seeking foreign partners, signified a willingness to negotiate an agreement with BSR.

'The House of Haq' was actively seeking co-operation or partnerships with foreign companies. Youssef Haq, the owner, is considerably wealthy and prides himself on the strength and influence of his company's business and government contacts. Haq believes that the government is anxious both to stimulate demand for steel and continue to develop local injection moulding expertise. Haq feels slighted by not being included in the disposables venture which appeared to be in part inspired by the Ministry of Planning and International Co-operation (PICO).

Haq suspects that PICO will award a major contract for disposable razors to the Italian partner in the proposed alliance. This contract, he believes, will be to provide disposable razors for a fixed five-year term to the Egyptian Army.

Privately, Haq does not believe the estimates that he has seen in the Planning and International Co-operation Ministry for the rapid penetration of the market by disposable razors. This essentially European model he believes to have been wrongly translated to Egypt. He believes that the stainless double-edged blade will remain the largest market sector for many more years. Given this scenario, BSR are the prime candidate for co-operation. Haq therefore perceives a market opportunity whilst PICO, as he put it, were looking through the wrong end of the telescope and concentrating their attention on an undeveloped market segment. Accordingly, he made contact with two companies. The two companies were British Safety Razor in the UK and American Blades in the USA. Haq is not new to manufacturing despite his concentration on wholesaling and retailing activities; he does, however, require the full support of foreign technology, given that this is his first venture in blade manufacture.

Egypt: Industry and market information

Haq obtained from PICO the following projections (Table 7.2):

Table 7.2 Breakdown of projections for razors & blades: 1994–1998 double-edged v. disposable; source: PICO

Product category estimates *Estimated unit market share % 1994-1998* *Estimated Share %*	*1994*	*1995*	*1996*	*1997*	*1998*
Carbon double-edged	10	5	5	5	5
Stainless Double-edged	70	63	58	50	45
Total	**20**	**32**	**37**	**45**	**50**
Disposable					
Of which, CDR*	0	10	15	20	22
Single-bladed	18	20	17	20	22
Double-bladed	2	2	5	5	6
Total	**100**	**100**	**100**	**100**	**100**

* Compact Disposable Razor, see section following.

Haq was also able to establish that:

1. Under State guidelines for foreign equity participation in products of this category, the maximum equity share allowable to a foreign investor is 49 per cent. This figure, however, is only allowable if the foreign company is deemed to be providing high/new technology.
2. The proposed competitive venture is being actively encouraged by PICO in order to concentrate on developing both the Egyptian and Middle Eastern markets for disposable razors and associated personal care products. It is proposed to export single-bladed disposable razors to the Arab common market, as well as supplying the Egyptian market. This venture, it is believed, will be funded 60 per cent from local private capital, 10 per cent from the government, leaving the Italian competitor a 30 per cent equity share and royalties.
3. Rumours were persisting of a government 'interest' in the industry. (The government, it was understood, would hold a veto on certain key management decisions relating to the proposed competitive venture in return for development grants.) The rumours about increased duties on finished razor and blade products continued. Local sources further suggested a complete ban on finished blades and stringent licences and quotas on components used for manufacture.

The compact disposable razor initiative

The royalties referred to above were believed to result from the Italian manufacturer's intention to license technology capable of producing a single-bladed 'compact disposable'. This was specifically designed for the developing nations of Africa and Asia, with their large populations of younger shavers. The compact disposable razor (CDR) was a potentially threatening innovation to the major blade manufacturers, as it was in effect both a single disposable razor and a low-cost version of a razor-and-blade cartridge system. The product comprised two components, the handle and a long-lasting single blade in cartridge form. The cartridge folded flat into the handle making it both safe and compact. It would therefore fit safely into pockets and army tunics.

The concern was the potential versatility of the product, in so much as it was a short step to provide refill cartridges in fives or tens as the market matured. The target might then become the relatively more expensive European systems which were based upon blade technology rather than customer convenience innovation. Experts in the industry, however, remained sceptical. There was a tendency to dismiss this so-called initiative and refer to it rather unkindly as the 'midget-cut-throat', a term which was to become the normal appellation.

The development of the Italian CDR was, however, highly regarded in the Planning and International Co-operation Ministry, as it represented innovation for developing economies, rather than the transference of existing product technology.

The future looked bleak for British Safety Razor. Their major distributor (despite his release from custody) had failed to confirm future blade orders with the London broker, given the problem that his landed cost was no longer competitive and the belief that even higher tariffs would now be phased in. He intended, therefore, to switch resources to other product categories.

Local sources continued to confirm the pending licence from the Italian multinational and the government's desire to establish export markets for both disposables and CDR's.

LEARNING NOTE on the differing perspectives to a joint venture

Negotiating strategic alliances may involve three parties with different perspectives; the Company, the Candidate Local Partner and the Government Ministry involved. In order to reconcile these differing perspectives they must first be recognised.

The company perspective:

- Seeks to operate from within major developing markets
- Wishes to avoid setting up a competitor
- Wishes to avoid attrition of other markets
- Seeks to maximise government grants
- May wish to avoid offering the latest technology
- If allowed only minority participation, will seek to know the identity of the major equity shareholdings
- Seeks to establish timing and security of dividend flows

The local partner's perspective:

- May seek the major equity share and management control
- Wishes to secure recent technology

- Wishes to secure an association with major brand names/trade marks
- Requires training and support
- May wish to pay in local currency

The national government's perspective:

- Encourage new technology
- Encourage employment
- 'Stick and carrot', grants, tax exemption v. equity constraints
- May require a re-export commitment
- Seeks hard currency but may wish to pay for purchases in local currency
- Encourage skills development and training

8
British Safety Razor B

Negotiating a Joint Venture in a Developing Economy

The case will now develop the perspective of the parties to the proposed alliance in the case material. The option is available of using this second part of the case as a negotiating exercise. The briefing material is relevent to the case, whether or not the material is used for the exercise.

The negotiating exercise

For the purposes of this exercise we will assume that the government also wishes to be represented in the negotiations and may even consider equity participation. The exercise therefore requires three parties representing the Company, the proposed Local Partner and the Host Government (Table 8.1). A discrete brief is available for each participant to the negotiations. Each party should be given the appropriate brief and have no knowledge of the other briefs apart from that contained in the body of the case.

Table 8.1 Parties to the negotiations

BSR	HAQ	Government
OIG General Manager	Youssef Haq	Official, Planning and International Co-operation
OIG Finance Manager	Amal Haq (brother and manager), consumer products	Official, Economy and Foreign Trade
OIG Marketing Manager	Commercial Director	Ministry Economist
OIG Manager, Middle East Sector	Finance Director	Official, Manpower and Vocational Training

Negotiations should proceed in the following stages or stages 1 and 3 only:

1. BSR and Haq
2. Haq and Government
3. BSR, Haq and Government

Recesses should be allowed to facilitate decision making; each group's brief should be regarded as a starting point rather than a rigid position.

The following table on developing negotiation skills, should be referred to prior to the exercise.

Table 8.2 Developing negotiating skills

What distinguishes the good negotiators from the crowd

According to research conducted by Neil Rackham and others of the Sheffield-based Huthwaite Research Group into actual negotiating performance, there are significant differences of technique between good and merely average negotiators.

No significant differences were found between the total planning time that skilled and average negotiators claimed they spent prior to actual negotiation, but there was a wide gap on other points:

- The skilled negotiatior considered twice the number of outcomes or options for action compared with the average negotiator, and three times as much attention to common ground.
- The average negotiator took a shorter term view. Only one comment in 25 met the criteria of a long-term consideration. The skilled negotiator made twice as many long-term comments.
- The researchers also asked negotiators about their objectives and recorded whether their replies referred to single point objectives (e.g. 'We aim to settle at $1.00') or to a defined range (e.g. 'We hoped to get $2 but we would settle for a minimum of $1.50'). Skilled negotiators were significantly more likely to set their objectives in terms of a range. Average negotiators, in contrast, were more likely to plan their objectives around a fixed point.
- Skilled negotiators show marked differences in their face-to-face behaviour. They avoid irritating words and phrases like 'generous offer' used by a negotiator to describe his own proposal. When the opposition puts forward a proposal, they generally avoid immediately making a counter-proposal.
- Average negotiators seem to believe that there is some special merit in quantity. Having three reasons for doing something is considered more persuasive then having only one reason. In contrast, skilled negotiators used fewer reasons to back up their arguments. They also do considerably more checking out, testing their understanding and summarising thoroughly during . . . the negotiation and reviewing it afterwards.

Over two-thirds of the skilled negotiators claimed that they always set aside some time after a negotiation to review it and consider what they had learned. Just under half of the average category made the same claim.

Source: International Management, May 1987, p. 69. Cited by Bradley, F. (1991) *International Marketing Strategy*, p. 503, Prentice-Hall.

The Briefs

The company brief

British Safety Razor were now in a very difficult position. Egypt was essential for their long-term development. Furthermore the board were pressing for a local presence in developing economies. A population in excess of 50 million could not be ignored. The company therefore were prepared to take a long-term view of any Egyptian project. The urgent need was to get a foot in the door in order to negotiate from the inside.

Under Egyptian law the maximum permitted equity share for a foreign venture of this nature was 49 per cent. In some cases, however, shares could be as low as 25 per cent if the technology base or brands offered were considered inadequate.

BSR had been tracking the Italian development of a single-bladed CDR razor for developing countries and were sufficiently concerned to advance their own programme. They had also improved the quality of their standard stainless double-edged blades which had been introduced to Egypt ten years earlier. These had proved to be a major success in competing against lower cost, lower quality, locally manufactured products. BSR's main advantages were versatility, economy, a comprehensive range of pack sizes and above all the famous international brand name.

The product/market decision

OIG were aware of the Egyptian government's commitment to the Italian development of the CDR. This they found puzzling, as it seemed premature to sub-divide the relatively small disposable sector. They agreed with Haq that there would be a significant market for the double-edged blade for some years to come. (Some people in the company still remembered when that opinion was held as a corporate tenet for the UK and Europe.)

The company, however, did not put much faith in the market projections that Haq had provided. Although it was inevitable that the disposable sector would slowly develop, they did not wish to be forced into price wars with the Italian competitor and its Egyptian partners. They preferred to concentrate upon the larger, more profitable double-edged blade market. From experience they recognised that the most effective way of competing with single-blade disposable competitors like the Italians, was to counter with twin-blade disposables. This technology they would not offer to a minority venture, given the risk that such products might be diverted to the more profitable European markets. If pushed they would be willing to provide single-blade disposable technology together with their 'Glide' international branding, but would propose minimum marketing activity for the category in view of the danger of rapidly eroding the more profitable double-edged blade sector.

After internal discussions OIG staff decided to discuss with Haq the following key issues and requirements:

● In order to build on the established demand and protect their market position, the company decided to offer its major brand of stainless double-edged blades known as 'Double A' to the proposed new venture. This referred to the existing 'imported' product which had been successful in the market to date despite the 'logistical' problems.

- The company wished to support this initiative by providing the technology to set up a double-edged blade plant.
- The company would expect to reach agreement as to marketing plans for the proposed new venture's products and have a significant input into the distribution and merchandising of individual products, to ensure that corporate marketing practices were not breached.
- The company proposed to: (a) provide technical back-up services for an introductory period of at least five years and (b) provide new models and marketing advice conditional upon an agreed marketing plan.
- The company was willing to provide at its own expense two British managers to fill the positions of Works Manager and Quality Control Manager (again for a period of five years).
- BSR would attempt to seek a 49 per cent equity share of the proposed new venture. In addition the company would attempt to limit the number of 'voting shares' to increase the possibility of retaining management control. The company would also attempt to find out the proposed ownership of the majority shareholding.
- The company proposed to pay for the equity by offering their trade mark, their technology and plant.
- Given that it would be some years before dividends would start flowing from the new company, BSR required some up-front payment as a marker of commitment from the new venture. This normally took the form of a mark-up on plant.
- Given that OIG had large export markets adjacent to Egypt in the Middle East, North Africa and the Gulf, the company was uncomfortable with any export commitment which might be requested by the government. They were especially negative towards exports of disposables. So far as double-edged blades were concerned, their objective was to hold any export commitment to a maximum of 25 per cent of sales for the first ten years of the venture. If this proved to be difficult, a second brand name would be proposed for exported products so that any unofficial exporting of 'Double A' could be monitored and controlled.
- The company, however, was keen to benefit from any tax concessions and development grants from the government in compensation for minority status.
- The company regarded contract manufacture or licensing as a fall-back position, but they believed that any premature discussion of licensing might erode the primary objective of maximising equity in the new venture.
- The company would require some form of acknowledgement of the BSR corporate identity from any new venture permitted to market its brands and trade marks.

The company was expecting problems on three fronts - the equity share, the export commitment and the 'CDR issue'. They knew they could not expect their local partner to help them on all of these issues.

BSR considered that the best hope of a reasonable equity share was to present their products as high technology together with a plant 'tailor-made' for the Egyptian market. Their impressive world-wide record with 'Double A' as 'the name on the world's finest shave' was also to be stressed.

The compact-disposable issue

The company had been developing their own CDR. This new product was sched-uled for market testing in selected South-East Asian markets (where BSR held in excess of 51 per cent of the corporate equity). This project was scheduled for April 1995. The company was therefore unwilling to offer such a 'development product' to a minority venture until the potential of the category had been established. They were also sceptical concerning the future potential of such a product in Egypt. They believed that most of the governments figures bore no relation to market realities.

Knowing the specific interest in the project in Egypt, they decided that under pressure they would offer their CDR to a local partner, provided they achieved their 49 per cent equity target. The company proposed to brand their CDR the 'Compak'. The earliest they would offer this product would be January 1996.

In conclusion the company felt that they were in a reasonably strong position given that the local partner was dependent on them for setting up and running the plant. Their keynote, however, was to be 'flexible within limits', as it was only in this way that the company could operate from inside a protected market.

The House of Haq brief

In discussing his requirements with his colleagues, Youssef Haq reached the following conclusions:

- Haq requires the major equity share together with management control of the new company to be known as Haq Razor.
- He requires a minimum of 51 per cent of their equity. Final equity shares depend upon the attitude of the Planning and International Co-operation Ministry (PICO), to the stake held by a foreign partner. Ideally he seeks 51 per cent of the equity which would allow him to sell up to 15 per cent to other local partners on a non-voting basis. (By other local partners he may be referring to friends in high places.) He strongly believes that the foreign partner must secure a minimum 40 per cent share if he is to be relied upon. Directors, he proposes, would be appointed in proportion to shareholdings (voting shares).
- Haq seeks to associate his venture with major international brand franchises. In relation to BSR he seeks the 'Double A' branding as well as the disposable branding (BSR brand their single bladed disposables 'Glide'), as a failsafe in the event of the Planning and International Co-operation Ministry projections being self-fulfilling.
- He seeks up-to-date technology.
- He expects comprehensive help in setting-up, running and training of personnel in the first five years of start-up.
- Haq does not believe that either disposables or compact-disposables will take a major share of the Egyptian market. He therefore requires the major emphasis

to be on the traditional stainless double-edged blade, which has the additional advantage of being ideal for export to developing markets. It would also avoid conflict with MESC (the disposable razor consortium).

- Haq seeks as much governmental aid as possible; in particular he is looking for tax concessions and government grants towards new plant. He therefore wishes to avoid any purchasing of second-hand plant. He intends to push hard for concessions on taxation over the initial years of the venture.
- Haq wishes to avoid any form of 'official' government investment in the venture.
- Haq requires a stream of innovation which over time would include disposables, systems and general personal care products in order to compete effectively with MESC over time.
- Haq would like to maximise exports, but understands the problems that this would give British Razor in its open markets. He insists, however, that the venture must pre-empt MESC in exporting standard double-edged blades as this provides the essential distribution base.
- Haq seeks to secure government blade contracts (for military and educational supplies), especially if he is required to make concessions to PICO.

In conclusion Haq would like British Safety Razor as a partner given that the company has been selling blades in the country for ten years and has built awareness and distribution, whereas other foreign investors would be coming in cold.

The government brief

The government's principle objective, so far as foreign investment is concerned, is to encourage local industry and employment in a situation where local unemployment is 26 per cent (and *under-employment* 45 per cent). Encouragement takes the form of:

1. Protection of local manufacturers from imports of critical foreign consumer products.(Blades are classified as critical consumer products.)
2. Encouragement of local or joint venture initiatives in the form of tax-free holidays and grants.
3. Provision of a positive climate for foreign investment.
4. Encouragement of exporting to earn hard currency.
5. Encouragement of innovation specifically related to developing economies.

The Ministry is well aware of the scepticism being expressed by some members of the blade industry on the subject of both disposables and compact-disposables. Their tests with both students and conscripts, however, demonstrate considerable potential for a compact disposable razor. These tests recently gave the go-ahead for the Italian licence and the proposed strategic alliance with the Italian partner.

The Planning and International Co-operation Ministry does not seek to grant a monopoly to MESC, given both the size and potential of the market. Rather, they wish to actively encourage a second major local initiative in conjunction with foreign technology. Ministry officials are favourably disposed towards Haq, given his success in creating opportunities for employment and foreign earnings.

Equally, the Planning and International Co-operation Ministry were willing to overlook the situation arising with BSR's Egyptian distributor, given assurances from BSR, the company's world-wide reputation and the experience of working in the country.

Bearing this in mind, PICO decided to recommend the following guidelines to the government team involved in discussions with Haq and BSR.

● The Ministry believes that the BSR/Haq venture should produce both the stainless double-edged blade and the single-bladed disposable razor. This, the government argue, will enable them to augment MESC's production as well as filling the immediate market gap for double-edged blades as a result of import controls. Suggested production split 70:30 in favour of the standard double-edged blades.
● Foreign equity participation in this case should be limited to 40 per cent, increasing to 49 per cent within three years if:
  – The plant and technology is contemporary
  – Export commitments are given for both blades and disposables
  – There is commitment to a stream of innovation
● Foreign equity payments should be in hard currency.
● Start up date mid-1996.
● A training contract will be required for local manufacturing and marketing staff.
● Use of international brand names for exports.

The Ministry recommends that if BSR/Haq can be persuaded to:

● Limit the initial foreign equity holding to 40 per cent.
● Accept a re-export commitment of 25 per cent of production, building to 35 per cent by year five.
● Bring in new plant capable of producing both blades and disposable razors.

. . . they would offer the joint venture the following concessions:

● A tax free holiday for three years.
● A rebate worth 40 per cent on the capital cost of plant installed during the first year.
● A 25 per cent rebate on the costs of training operatives during the first three years.
● A guaranteed government contract for conventional disposables in year one.
● A guaranteed government export contract for shipments of double-edged blades to Russia in year one. (Egypt has a bilateral trading agreement with the former USSR.)

Questions for Discussion

1. Tabulate and prioritise from the perspective of the global company the difficulties of operating in developing economies.
2. What do you consider to be the key success factors for successful blade marketing in Egypt?

3. Prepare a critique of the proposed OIG strategy for its major markets; what would you advise them to proceed?
4. Discuss the different contributions made by the various parties to a joint venture. What in your opinion are the ways in which co-operation rather than conflict might be achieved?
5. What lessons have BSR learned in Egypt that they might apply to another priority market?
6. Advise BRS on making the transition from International marketing to Global marketing. What would they have to do differently?
7. Discuss the ethical issues raised by this case and consider how the culture of the 'AAA' group has affected these considerations.
8. Summarise the agreement reached with your joint venture partners in the form of a draft agreement.

9
The Boston Candy Co. in Peru

The Corporation Expects . . . (January 1993 Panama City)

José Luis Fernandez was alarmed by his General Manager's ambitions for his Region. Hanging up the phone he felt for the first time (in the four years that he had been building up the South American distributor markets for Boston Candy (BC)) a distinct feeling of unease. Whilst waiting for Scott's confirmation fax (John Scott, General Manager South American Markets, S.A.M.), he realised that Scott expected him to keep in step with the major manufacturing markets within the Group. This, it now appeared, required the immediate launching of a number of new products on a pan-regional basis.

The Distributor Markets

José Luis Fernandez was a 40-year-old Venezuelan who had been the financial controller of 'Boston Candy do Brazil' for the five years prior to taking over as manager of the (non-manufacturing) distributor markets. Although he was a highly regarded financial manager, his experience of sales and marketing was limited to his current position. After receiving Scott's briefing, Fernandez remained concerned about the scale of the revenue increases required and the tight time constraints which Scott believed to be achievable. It was this latter point which worried him most, as Fernandez considered that his major priority was to achieve greater control of his existing distributors prior to any new product activity.

Scott had reminded José Luis in his subsequent fax, that distributor markets should take more advantage of the strength of Boston Candy's leading brand name, 'Fresco'. The Boston Candy distribution system, he emphasised, is ideal for the 'piggy-backing' of new products on the back of the main 'Fresco' brand. He requested that José Luis prepare proposals for the expansion of sales in distributor markets for a meeting early in January 1993 to take place at Fernandez' local HQ in Panama City. He advised that he would be accompanied by his Staff Marketing Director and his Company Manager for Brazil. José Luis knew he must now

[1] Although based upon a real business situation, information has been modified to preserve confidentiality. This case is designed to involve students in some of the factors involved with the marketing of consumer products in developing countries. The emphasis is upon a multinational company seeking to modify its distribution strategy in non-manufacturing markets as a result of global imperatives. Students have the opportunity to 'role play' the subsequent negotiation with the distributor.

concentrate on a revised strategy for his distributor markets. His thoughts were beginning to focus on the following issues:

- When to make the transition to Boston Candy sales companies, to ensure improved salesforce control and market penetration. Fernandez was actively considering the transition to selling companies in most of his markets within the next five years. This move he wished to combine with the conversion of some of the existing distributors to contract manufacture status once critical mass was within sight. What he had not anticipated was the pan-regional approach required by Scott towards the launch of BC's global products. He was in the 'chicken and egg' situation; whereas, he needed the selling infrastructure in place to achieve the sales increases, the existing sales base in his markets was as yet too small to justify the expense.

- How, then, to retain the existing distributor network whilst at the same time ensuring greater control of sales coverage, sales volumes and merchandising by the various national sales forces? The S.A.M. distributor network had been carefully built up by his predecessors and was in many instances still based upon personal understandings. Although he recognised that the network was by no means without its problems, by and large it worked well for the company. Most distributors were co-operative partners and sympathetic towards corporate requests. Appointing new distributors was at best risky and at worse impossible, given the limited number of candidates in his developing markets.

- The commercial reality was that Scott was directing an international expansion programme and that this was not the time to take on all the start-up problems of new company ventures. He began to consider the possibilities of a halfway house that might satisfy all parties. Such a solution, however, would have to be:
  a) Equally applicable to other distributor markets
  b) Lend itself to escalation to selling company status
  c) Deliver improved distribution performance across the full product range as there are still large gaps in sales coverage in many areas
  d) Enhance the ability of the existing distributor network to cope with the demands of new product distribution.

Background to Boston Candy (BC)

By 1993 Boston Candy's worldwide sales of confectionery and allied products totalled some $797m. As a result of its well-established chocolate count lines (e.g. chocolate bars), the company was a household name in the USA.

Excluding minority interests in European confectionery manufacturers, the US market contributed some 70 per cent of sales revenue and 66 per cent of profit before tax. The balance of the business was mainly accounted for by the South American markets. This situation had come about as a direct result of the 1969 acquisition of a Brazilian chewing gum manufacturer. During the 1970's the company had successfully secured direct export bases in other South American countries using local distributors. In the 1980's, as the sales volumes grew beyond expectations, local selling and manufacturing companies were established in the major markets of Argentina, Brazil, Colombia and Mexico.

This policy did not, however, apply to the smaller countries of Central and South

America where there was limited potential for direct investment. Accordingly, the company relied upon distributors for the marketing of their products. Relationships with many of these distributors were of long standing. Distributors were supplied with products from the other manufacturing locations in South America, a process co-ordinated from the distributor markets' headquarters in Panama City.

John Scott

Much of the success of the Latin American operations was credited to John Scott, the 49-year-old group general manager of S.A.M. Scott had joined Boston Candy in 1982 following a successful career in tobacco marketing in South America. He had two framed quotations in his Boston office which appeared to reflect his marketing philosophy. These quotations always made José Luis feel uncomfortable, and both sounded better in Spanish; roughly translated they read:

> This business is uncompromising; once you let a competitor pause at your gate, tomorrow they're sitting at your table; that means you out-distribute, out-merchandise and out-promote everywhere; you never overlook even the smallest store.

> It is well-known that a middleman bamboozles one party and plunders the other.

It was felt by many at Boston Candy that these two quotations reflected Scott's attempt to control the process of mass distribution as directly as possible. South America was managed by Scott at arms length from Boston. S.A.M. had been left very much to its own devices by a company that knew a lot about chocolate in the USA but little about chewing gum in South America. This was fine during the growth of the 1970's and 1980's, but the outlook was distinctly more difficult for the 1990's. Scott now found himself under increasing corporate pressure to develop additional lines to take full advantage of his strong distribution base.

'Fresco' in S.A.M.

Although S.A.M. specialised in marketing a complete range of lower-priced confectionery, 77 per cent of the sales came from the chewing gum product group. These products comprised a range of flavoured gums including fresh-breath flavours. All such products were promoted under the evocative and highly successful 'Fresco' branding (translates as Cool/Fresh). The focus for marketing activity was this successful, long-established brand name, together with strong romantic imagery. This imagery had been communicated via radio commercials so effectively that spontaneous recall of the brand in urban areas had reached 75 per cent in Rio and 69 per cent in Buenos Aires in 1992. Recall had been greatly aided by the continuous use of the 'Fresco' jingle in radio commercials targeted at young people across the continent. In Mexico and Colombia, for example, 50 per cent of the population is under 20 years of age!

Why we succeeded – Scott's view

Although he was reluctant to claim any particular marketing strategy as a panacea,

Scott did stress a number of points which he regarded as critical to get right.

In his report to the Boston Board in 1992 he was quoted as making the following points:

> As you know, exporting is largely irrelevant to mass consumption products in major markets. This means that everybody must consider local manufacturing. The difference, I guess, is that we have been doing it for 20 years. Tricks like inflation management are an old game to us. Our philosophy is to put the squeeze on costs and overheads to generate the cash to out-distribute and out-promote the competition.
>
> The key to the whole business is 'critical mass'. We have to get volume even if it means pricing way down. We always try to pitch the price to match the lowest units of local currency. It's like selling gum at the 'nickel or dime' price-break in the US. For example, in Mexico we still have to break up the five-packs hoping that somebody can afford a peso for one chew . . . and that's in downtown Mexico DF!
>
> If the price is right, getting the volume is all about in-depth distribution and merchandising coverage. That can mean that our sales vans and radio jingles are often the last markers of civilisation in any number of remote rural areas. Up-country we really rely on the 100-pack display cards which the reps. can fix up in any of the Tiendas.[2] We estimate that some 40 per cent of our total S.A.M. sales still come from rural areas. If you ignore the Tiendas you may well let someone else in . . . That's why I don't think we would have succeeded without the policy of directly selling for cash off the vans . . . next time round though, we better make sure that half of them have four-wheel drive!
>
> In the cities it's a different ball game with the emphasis on by-passing the trade by building strong consumer brand equity. In both rural and urban areas one thing remains the same . . . merchandising, merchandising, merchandising. For example, in the cities we always stress the need to get the product alongside cigarettes at the checkouts.

What Scott did not mention (as everybody knew), was that in the early days 'Fresco' almost distributed itself. Despite or because of the US association, chewing gum really caught on. It became the 'cool thing' in a part of the world where the incidence of smoking, the need for fresh breath and associating with the North American lifestyle, was becoming increasingly important for a burgeoning teenage population with its love/hate relationship with the USA. In addition the brand had associations with independence and rebellion, which research had demonstrated in the USA was strongly associated with gum consumption. Scott added the following points:

Scott's list of things to get right in S.A.M. markets

- Reliable local manufacture, given the probability of import bans on consumer goods.
- A strong brand identity and the creation of a personality for brands that empathise with the aspirations and life style of global customer groups.
- A relatively low-cost mass media with wide reach across the target markets; for example, radio.
- Pricing keyed into the lowest possible unit of currency and careful management of price changes.
- Volume built by direct selling and merchandising to all types of outlets requiring motivation and control of distribution.

---

[2] Small stores mainly in rural areas, worked by proprietors.

- Regular merchandising in all outlets requiring clear simple packaging and point of sale materials that can be used in both the smallest and largest outlets.
- Blocking of competition so that they are unable to find empty distribution channels or vacant price points to position their products against.
- Merchandising alongside allied products such as cigarettes, to take advantage of the high levels of impulse purchase.
- Control and motivation of the direct sales force, so that they are encouraged to maintain distribution pressure.
- Ensuring that prices between markets remain comparable so that these portable products are not transferred by intermediaries to more profitable regions.

LEARNING NOTE on macro-economic factors to consider in developing countries

These are normally characterised by uncertainty and dynamic change.

Economic

- Hyper-inflation
- Devaluation
- Price controls
- Foreign debt
- Unemployment
- Lack of foreign exchange
- Increasing trends towards economic integration. Examples include North American Free Trade Agreement, Andean Common Market (ANCOM), Central American Common Market, and Latin American Integration Association (LAIA)

Political

- Struggling democracies
- Insurgency
- Limitations on foreign workers
- Protection of essential industry
- Bureaucratic delays
- Strikes
- Import/export bans, quotas, taxes
- Limitations to foreign ownership
- Difficulty/Inability to repatriate profits
- Limited rural infrastructure relating to media and transport
- Population groups outside of the money economy

Social: example, demographics

- Population structures (example 50% under 20 years)
- Remaining high levels of rural population
- Drift to the cities and concentration of population

Country	Population	Population of capital city
Mexico	77m	Mexico D.F.[3] 22m
Argentina	32m	Buenos Aires 12m

Culture

- Traditional languages of Quechua, Nahuatl and Maya
- European tradition of Argentina and Chile
- Aztec/Inca cultures of Mexico and Adean countries
- Increasing literacy and education standards

Technology, impacting on . . .

- Growth in medical care
- Infrastructure; accessibility of backward regions
- Information flows; radio
- Increasing awareness of North American lifestyles
- Literacy; political awareness
- Increased movement to cities from rural areas

The Current Situation

Scott was becoming increasingly concerned with the performance of S.A.M. High growth rates in individual countries did not necessarily result in profits. His major concern was Brazil, which accounted for 45 per cent of S.A.M. sales. For the first time since acquisition the Brazilian company was losing money. One of the main contributing factors was the threat of government price control, which in the past had squeezed the already slender profit margins of Scott's operations. In addition, rumours continued to circulate of a pending major devaluation in 1994. (The company lived with the regular 'mini-devaluations'.) Scott recognised that it was imperative for S.A.M. to be less exposed to the whims of the Brazilian economy. If he was to achieve his next appointment as Group General Manager of the newly created South East Asian Group (SEAG), he had to demonstrate that S.A.M. was more than just a Brazilian operation.

After consultation with his staff Scott decided to bring forward the implementation of the parent company's request for diversification. This related to the launch of a full range of mint candy under the 'Fresco' branding. Scott referred to this as 'Project Las Mentas', which required:

1. Transferring 'off the shelf' mint candy technology from the USA and Europe to the manufacturing markets of S.A.M.
2. Sourcing the distributor markets from the Brazilian factories as:
   - New products are not subject to price control.

---

[3] By the year 2000 Mexico DF is estimated to be the largest city in the world with a population in excess of 30m. Large sections of the urban South American population will continue to live in 'ranchitos', temporary slum cities, breeding poverty, unemployment and crime.

- Minimum export problems within S.A.M. markets, given the LAIA structure (Latin American Integration Association).
- The maximisation of exports from Brazil to the non-manufacturing smaller markets gave 'Boston Candy do Brazil' greater leverage with the Price Control Board.
- New product technology in one manufacturing location to minimise start-up problems.
3. Simultaneous roll-out of the new mint product variants in all S.A.M. markets.
4. Pressure on distributor markets to find rapid solutions to current distribution weaknesses.

Accordingly, Scott instructed his manager of distributor markets, José Luis Fernandez, to prepare for major product launches supported by an improved distribution infrastructure.

Scott held the opinion that distribution in the non-manufacturing markets (mainly the Andean Group markets) was below standard. His thinking reflected the consideration that the gross domestic product of the five Andean Group countries[4] exceeded that of his second major market . . . Mexico. If he could add a second Mexico to his revenue line he was further down the road in solving a tricky situation.

Figure 9.1 Boston Candy Co. organisation

January 1993
President Domestic Division
Group General Manager – Latin America (Scott-Boston)

Manager
Distribution markets (Fernandez-Panama)

Manufacturing markets

Staff
Marketing Director (Jankowski-Boston)

Mexico   Argentina   Brazil   Colombia

Peru
Chile
Venezuela
Bolivia
Ecuador
Central America

Fernandez Prepares . . . the Current Distributor Relationship

Fernandez operated a policy of exclusive distributorships in all of his markets. Distributors took title to the goods, which might require the handling of logistics

---

[4] Bolivia, Colombia, Ecuador, Peru and Venezuela.

such as the customs declarations and payment of duty and other costs. The distributor was then responsible for generating sales of the products, delivery and taking the credit risk.

Given that some of the distributors were often limited in their resources, the ideal situation of separate sales people selling Boston products was rarely achieved. To alleviate this situation Fernandez had appointed country sales managers (CSMs), to work alongside his distributors. Most of these were also residents of the respective countries. The function of the CSMs was to train and motivate the distributor's sales force, review coverage plans, ensure attention to new products and police pricing procedures. They also acted for the company as sources of information and instruments of control.

Fernandez allowed his distributors a fixed mark up on the delivered or landed cost of the product. In this way the company had some control of the final consumer price, which was critical for this product category. Mark-ups varied from 10 to 20 per cent, depending upon the services provided by the distributor. This was in contrast to the Boston direct selling operations in the major manufacturing markets.

Fernandez did not believe that his distributors with their small numbers of sales people could cope with such an influx of new products. He needed time to encourage distributors to recruit more sales staff and correct some of the existing problems and gaps in market coverage. Nevertheless, he recognised the corporate imperative of global product launches and decided to bring forward a proposal he had been working on which might help resolve the situation. Accordingly, for the January meeting Fernandez decided to put together a presentation for Scott and his staff; this would include a recommendation to reach a new working agreement with his main distributors.

Set out below are some of the presentation charts which José Luis intended should be used to present his proposals at the Panama meeting.

Chart A

Existing distributors' weaknesses

- Distributors employ the minimum number of sales people.
- Sales efforts are confined to major urban areas.
- Distributors often handle too many lines, consequently the amount of time devoted to company products is inadequate.
- Too many gaps in distributor coverage, especially up country in the 'campo'.
- Given the expansion of the chewing gum business, distributors were running into increasing credit problems. If a client was not up to date with his payments, company shipments ceased. Consequently, our products had to compete with the credit problems created by all the lines sold by the distributor.
- Distributors' salesmen dedicated efforts to our fastest selling products in order to maximise their commission.
- Distributors' salesmen were reluctant to sell without a deal and tended to be neglectful of merchandising.
- Distributors, especially in the smaller markets, often avoided developing wholesalers as they considered them direct competitors. They preferred to maximise

retail volume where their margins are highest.
- The company's administrative and marketing requests were not efficiently or promptly attended to by the distributors.

Summary

Although distributor markets have been growing at a healthy rate (approximately 12 per cent per year, over the last five years), we have not been able to develop national distribution channels that are capable of handling major new products. This is in contrast to the S.A.M. subsidiary companies, where selling efforts are directly controlled by the company.

Chart B

Problems of establishing our own selling companies

- We intend to . . . but not until we reach critical mass.
- Need to avoid high investment in finished stocks.
- Would require long lead times for training and 'shakedown' .
- The time for a complete change is not when we are launching critical new products.
- Problems of distribution by a 'foreign' company.
- Need to retain distributor knowledge and synergy from allied products (cigarettes).
- Increased credit risks with new products.

Chart C

Objective

We require a 'halfway-house' between a conventional distributor and a sales company. This way we can better address the coverage and new product distribution priorities and share the investment with the existing distributors.

Recommendations

No fundamental changes to the basic distributors' functions of importing, taking delivery, warehousing, bearing the credit risk, delivering and the legal responsibility for doing business locally, but a significant change in the organisation and control of the distributors' sales force. Proposed is a joint operation between ourselves and our existing distributors.

- The company to take over the selling function in total.
- An exclusive sales force for Boston Candy *within* the distributor's existing organisation.
- This sales force to be hired, dismissed and supervised by our CSMs.
- Boston Candy to pay the costs of the sales force to be known as the 'Seccion Boston', an independent sales force *within* the distributor's organisation.
- This sales force would take orders to be delivered by the distributor.
- The exception would be where the sales force sells for cash up-country off the vans.

Chart D

Benefits to both parties

- A separate sales force for BC.
- Control of the selling effort.
- Additional distribution, volume and profit for both parties.
- Distributors devote their limited resources to financing stocks and delivery in key urban areas.
- BC devotes its resources to financing the selling operations and launching new products.
- Continuity of channels preserved and critical linkages with tobacco merchandising.

Chart E

The test in Peru

The distribution agreement in Peru is due for renewal this February. We propose *testing* these proposals on our Peruvian distributor 'Productos Ramirez SA'. We recognise that whatever we do in Peru must serve as a model for rapid implementation in other distributor markets.

Specifically for Peru we propose

- Four exclusive salespeople building to eight by 1995 paid for by ourselves. (This compares with the current situation of four salespeople for only 50 per cent of the time).
- The Ramirez mark-up to be reduced from 17 per cent to 7 per cent given that Boston Candy will now be financing the full cost of a larger sales force.
- Minimal additional investment required by the company, as sales force costs are funded from the reduction in distributor margin (see chart 'F').
- We will commit ourselves to a sales revenue building to $950,000 in 1995 compared with the 1993 plan of only $230,000 under the existing system.

This is justified by:

1. Four/eight full-time salespeople.
2. Additional Fresco mint products from Brazil.
3. Development of wholesalers and national coverage.
4. Extended coverage outside of Lima.
5. Direct control of the sales force by our own CSMs.

Chart F

Projected distributor margins, productos Ramirez SA, Peru

Distributor's 1994 planned transfer price to 'Seccion Boston' $451+$32 = $483,000's US; therefore 'Seccion Boston' earns $529–483 = $46,000's US; this is then used to fund sales activities (see Article 7 on page 135).

Distributor's 1995 planned transfer price to 'Seccion Boston' $813+$57 = $870,000's US; therefore 'Seccion Boston' earns $950 – 870 = $80,000's US; this is then used to fund sales activities.

$000's US (constant prices)	1993 Forecast	1994 Estimate	1995 Estimate
Revenue			
(Distrib. selling price)	230	529	950
Delivered cost	197	451	813
Distributor's margin	33	32	57
% Mark-up on landed cost	17	7	7
Selling expenses	19	Nil	Nil
Net margin	14	32	57
NM%	7	7	7

Chart G

Ramirez' ROI improves under the new system

Investment base	1993 Forecast $'s	1995 Estimate $'s
Fixed assets	4,336	1,600
Inventory @ 2 months	38,180	157,700
Receivables @ 80 days[5]	25,530	83,600
Total	68,046	242,900

[5] 50 per cent of sales for cash in 1993 which is assumed to increase to 60 per cent in 1995.

Chart H

ROI calculation

	$\dfrac{\text{Net Profit}}{\text{Sales}}$ X	$\dfrac{\text{Sales}}{\text{Investment}}$	= ROI%
Plan 1995 ($'s)	$\dfrac{57,000}{950,000}$ X	$\dfrac{950,000}{242,900}$	= 23.5%
Forecast 1993 ($'s)	$\dfrac{14,000}{230,000}$ X	$\dfrac{230,000}{68,046}$	= 20.6%

The outcome of the meeting

Scott made very few comments; after all, Fernandez had just agreed to try for considerable sales increases. The question was, how would the distributor react? Scott asked his staff marketing director for his views.

The staff perspective

Everett Jankowski was a 36-year-old Harvard MBA. He was regarded by the company as one of the inside track people passing through group HQ prior to taking a major line management assignment. Everett's principal task was to co-ordinate marketing strategy for S.A.M. As such he had 'dotted lines' to all country managers in the group. Together with the Brazilian company manager he had been the architect of 'Project Las Mentas'. He commented as follows:

> I really don't believe that the distributor will accept this degree of margin reduction and even if it's on for Peru what will happen in other distributor markets where we will have to cancel existing agreements to make this change? After all we can't afford to wait around until each separate agreement comes up for renewal! The way you have worked the ROI implies that the distributor will still be happy to bear the credit risk, even though now he has no control of the sales operation. Don't you think this is a bit like having your cake and eating it?
>
> So far as control is concerned, I have always understood that Ramirez was moving in the right direction. After all he did agree that next year a separate sales supervisor would be appointed. Agreed, we need more people in Peru to deliver this large sales increase, but we should be encouraging the distributor to appoint such exclusive salespeople himself and paying for them out of his own margin. If you follow Josés' route, what may happen is that whilst the salespeople in name report to our manager they would still look to the distributor for guidance. In view of this I don't think that at the end of the day we will achieve the projected $529,000/ $950,000 in a market like Peru unless we set up our own selling company. All in all, I am concerned that we could be de-stabilising a distributor with a good record at the critical period. In the short term we should be offering distributors more support in terms of merchandising, training and sales force incentives, in order to encourage greater penetration of the up-country areas.

Fernandez countered with the opinion that Ramirez would not have the resources or confidence in our new product potential to appoint additional salespeople. Furthermore, he believed that BC were risking too much too soon in setting up sales companies and restated his proposal for a half-way house, given the time it would take to pursue the option of selling companies. He concluded that in his opinion the distributor markets could be persuaded to try the new proposals if we took them into our full confidence and employed some of their existing people.

Scott, never one to discourage experimentation, and pleased that the sales targets were accepted by the line managers, felt that there was little to lose in using Peru as a test for the proposals. Although, like Everett he had his doubts, he acknowledged the time problem in setting up sales companies at this critical time. Accordingly, he requested that Fernandez should meet with Ramirez in Lima next week. He suggested that Everett should also attend the meeting and that a method of monitoring the test should be submitted to Boston once it had been agreed by all interested parties.

Offices of Drogueria Ramirez SA (February 1993, Lima, Peru)

On the way down to Lima José Luis briefed Everett on their Peruvian distributor. Julio and his sister Elena Ramirez had inherited the family wholesaling business in 1979. Since that time Elena and her business manager, Jorge Chipoco, had been active in expanding a small drug wholesaler into a medium-sized distributor for foreign companies. Julio, whose main passion in 1993 was preparing for the 'Camino del Inca' Trans-Andes motor rally, was in charge of the wholesaling interests, whilst Elena concentrated on the distributorships.

By 1993 the distributorships accounted for some $1,417,000 of turnover. Apart from Boston Candy, Ramirez was responsible for local sales of cigars, skin creams, toothbrushes and low-priced pens. The business had grown very rapidly and next year looked particularly exciting for them, as a European toothpaste manufacturer operating out of Mexico was considering using the company to distribute its products. Elena, however, was known to be worried about the financing of this operation.

José Luis told Everett that Ramirez employed four salespeople who worked half-time on Boston Candy. The other 50 per cent of their time was spent on the Ramirez cigar client. Three of these salespeople were based in Lima and the fourth in Arequipa. Ramirez estimated that selling costs were roughly equal for both Fresco and cigars. José Luis also mentioned that their manager in Lima was becoming increasingly concerned by the time taken up by the distributor's sales force with the tobacco client's promotion activities. There was also the concern that the 'Tiendas' only had sufficient cash to buy either cigars or gum, but not both.

Another problem that José Luis mentioned to Everett was the 'parallel trade' coming in from Mexico and Colombia. José went on to explain that 'Fresco' had been trucked in from Colombia prior to the appointment of a Peruvian distributor. In José Luis' opinion, that was why Ramirez judged it best to leave the North of the country well alone.

José Luis and Everett agreed that the presentation to Ramirez would have to be handled rather differently from the presentation to Scott. By the time they arrived in Lima they had agreed an approach, which hopefully would result in a separate sales force reporting to their own manager. They also came prepared with the revised distribution agreement.

Extracts from the proposed distributor agreement – Peru

Article 7

To cover expenses that shall be for the account of the distributor . . . and to cover his profit or consideration as distributor . . . the distributor shall keep a gross profit of 7 per cent of the delivered/landed cost of the product sold by him. The difference between the said 7 per cent and the total mark-up obtained from the sale of the products (the difference between the delivered cost or landed costs and the sale price to wholesaler/retailer or consumer), shall accrue to the benefit of the Boston

Candy Company Inc., that may use it by itself or through the distributor for the following purposes.

To pay for (a) the expenses of the sales personnel exclusively employed in the sale of the products, (b) the authorised advertising expenses of said products. They include:

1. Sales force salaries
2. Social security
3. Depreciation of salesforce vehicles
4. Travel expenses
5. Printing of price lists
6. Maintenance of vehicles
7. Salesforce stationery
8. Insurance premiums on vehicles
9. Bonuses
10. Garage for salesmen vehicles

Article 8
The distributor agrees to:

a) Import.
b) Warehousing invoicing and credit terms.
c) Delivery of orders placed by customers.
d) Provision of necessary space so that the person designated by the company may have space for a filing cabinet, a desk and a proper place for meetings with the sales force.

Article 9
In order to effectively supervise the activities of the sales force, the company shall designate a person who shall:

a) Employ and dismiss from employment the salespeople.
b) Purchase vehicles destined to be used by the salespeople.
c) Train the salespeople.
d) Determine the monthly purchases by the distributor from the different shipping points designated by the company according to the needs as related to the following:

   (i) Inventories on the date of such determination.
   (ii) Average monthly sales during a prior period of six months.
   (iii) Planned promotional activities.

Questions/Exercises

1. What are the critical success factors for distributing consumers' products in developing economies?
2. Outline the advantages and disadvantages of working with distributors in developing economies.
3. How would you react to 'Project Las Mentas' if you were in Fernandez' position?

4. Do you believe Scott has made the correct decision following the meeting in Panama? What would you have done in his situation? Are there any alternatives?
5. Do you believe that Boston Candy marketing philosophy is based upon domestic, multinational or global marketing principles?

The Negotiating Exercise

This case study now lends itself to *a role playing exercise* taking as its theme José Luis Fernandez' presentation of his proposals to the Peruvian distributor.

Negotiating teams should comprise:

Boston Candy: Fernandez, Jankowski and Boston Candy's Peruvian manager.
The Peruvian Distributor: Julio and Elena Ramirez and Jorge Chipoco.

The Boston Candy team first need to prepare their presentation charts; suggested titles for these are:

- The company's expansion plans for the Peruvian market.
- A review of the existing difficulties in the market and target areas for improvement.
- An outline of the four alternatives and their implications; no change; the distributor pays for the dedicated salespeople; an end to the current agreement and the setting up of a BC sales company; the proposed new arrangement.
- Rationale of the benefits to all parties of the new proposal.

An example of the second point appears below:

Table 9.1 Existing difficulties

The Present Situation
Unsatisfactory given:

- The split sales force
- Limited sales potential
- Distribution concentrated on Lima
- Potential for frustration and conflict between the principals
- The existing problems remain unsolved

Recesses should be allowed in order to facilitate decision making. Assume that the distributor has already been informed of the proposals by a letter from Fernandez.

Notes

What actually happened in Peru

As this case is based upon a real situation the following are the results of both the Lima meeting and the subsequent development of the business.

In March of 1993, Julio and Elena accepted, after initial reservations, the revised distribution agreement provided that the 1994/95 sales figure were achievable. This represented a request for a flat fee of $32,000 in 1994 which José agreed to for one year. They further agreed that the steady increase in business from Boston Candy was the main reason for requiring a separate sales force, paid for by the company. The strength of José Luis' recommendation was that it recognised that the distributor is trading on his own capital as an entrepreneur and therefore seeks to maximise his own return on investment. José Luis' formula of paying for the sales force immediately defused the reduction in margin issue.

Problems raised and results to mid-1995

Salesforce attention to company lines was inadequate

Elena signed the revised agreement with the additional proviso that for one year three people from her original sales force would be transferred to the 'Seccion Boston'. After six months this was seen to have been a mistake. Everett Jankowski's point that they would continue to look for guidance from the distributor proved to be correct. Within nine months, however, Elena agreed to replace two of the three and their replacements proved to be better able to work within company standards.

Sales targets

BC should achieve in excess of $1m in Peru during 1995. The sales force has been divided into urban and rural specialists.

Salespeople only pushed the fastest selling products

Quotas were established for each salesperson and for each major product. The overall result was that the 1994 plan was over achieved by 11 per cent.

Attention to administrative and marketing requests

The company now supervises directly the administrative function and implement any marketing requirements.

Developing wholesalers

Within one year, the number of wholesalers called upon increased from 15 to 30, although the problem of Colombian imports still remains.

Conclusion

The revised system allowed the company direct control of the distribution function for developing in-depth distribution of its products. It also allowed the company to establish a reasonably low mark-up for the distributor, which as volume increased (given that sales expenses did not increase in the same proportion), generated a profit for the 'Seccion Boston' after all expenses were paid.

EXTENDED LEARNING NOTE: Parallel Importing

Parallel importing (or exporting, depending on one's perspective) is a feature of many international market places. It involves the arrival of a product in a country market other than through the 'authorised' supply channels. The existence of a grey market – as it is sometimes also known – can be a major problem for the marketing organisation in the importing country. It is likely to be a major issue between the local marketing organisation and the exporting manufacturing principal.

The problem for the local organisation is that parallel importing increases the amount of competition in the market. Second, the parallel imported product may spoil their marketing strategy. For example, it may be sold at prices which are below those planned by the local marketing organisation and it may be sold in a way which damages their image – perhaps through inappropriate distribution channels and/or using unacceptable sales techniques. Third, as well as leading to customer confusion, as suggested above, customers may feel they can take the product to the organisation – for repair under warranty, for example – when it has not even supplied the product. A fourth problem is a question of adding insult to injury. The local marketing organisation may feel that their principal is not committed enough to eradicate the problem. Such perceptions may arise either because of the difficulty in combating parallel importing or perhaps because the exporter has no real incentive to curb it. This latter possibility is easily explained.

The exporter may believe that parallel importing may increase total product sales, either by widening distribution or by extra competition leading to extra promotional activity. Second, the parallel route may be through home market dealers who may pay higher prices than the authorised importer. In this case, export profitability may be increased by parallel importing. Third, the exporter may see the parallel activity as a means of controlling, motivating or providing leverage over the local importing organisation.

Notwithstanding the above, parallel importing does usually mean headaches for the exporter. First, a de-motivated authorised distributor is a time consuming problem as well as being likely to produce reduced marketing effort from the distributor. The term 'distributor' is used loosely here since the problems would apply whether the exporter had its own sales and marketing subsidiary in the importing market, or whether it used an importer/distributor and would also cause dissatisfaction to members of the authorised retail chain. Second, the exporter would lose control over the marketing channel. This may make it difficult to extend the authorised network and to persuade authorised retailers to stock the full product range. It would also frustrate marketing planning activities. Sales forecasting and budgeting would be problematic, as would be pricing. Authorised retailers may need to cut price to compete with grey market supplies thus putting price pressure on the manufacturing exporter. This leads directly to its third major problem – a potential loss of profit via reduced selling prices overall.

A fourth potential problem is image diffusion. One interesting example is provided by the manufacturers of fine fragrances such as Givenchy, Yves Saint Laurent and others. Essentially the selective distribution agreements which give them the right to refuse to supply product unless outlets meet certain criteria the perfume houses have established, have been challenged by organisations such as Superdrug and Tesco. The fragrance manufacturers claim that in order for the market to survive, the 'dream' promised by perfume has to be preserved. Much of the dream emanates not from the product itself, but from the packaging, the surroundings and atmosphere in which it is sold and the high price. Certain fragrance houses refused to authorise Superdrug and Tesco, allegedly because their premises, counters, staff and general ambience were not appropriate to maintain the dream. The retailers countered by arguing that they have equipped some stores with specialist perfumery centres staffed by specially-trained consultants and that the conditions under which they sell perfume are often much better than many existing authorised outlets. They further maintain that it is their discounted prices which is the main motive for the refusal of the fragrance houses to supply them. While discounted prices may spoil the luxury/prestige image, they will also have to be met by price reductions by authorised outlets who in turn will demand price reductions from the perfume houses. Superdrug, Tesco and many other unauthorised retail outlets are able to source some fine fragrance supplies on the grey market but may not be able to secure regular and sufficient stocks of the complete product line from this route.

A fifth problem is that grey market products may sometimes have degraded, perhaps as a result of being old stock or being sold in a market where the packaging is insufficient to maintain product quality. An example of the latter might be industrial bearings which require special protection against rusting in very humid climates. Products bought on the grey market may well have only standard packaging. Even if not degraded, products sold through unauthorised outlets may have inappropriate labelling or may lack a range of value added attributes offered by authorised channels. This may result in dissatisfaction with the brand amongst consumers unaware that they have purchased through unauthorised channels.

The size of the grey market problem varies from industry to industry and from time to time. The Monopolies and Mergers Commission estimated that grey market retailers accounted for about 16 per cent of UK sales of fine fragrances in 1992. As suggested above, the parallel trade is widespread in industrial markets as well as in consumer goods markets. Parallel importing is most likely to occur in situations where strongly branded products can be bought at different price levels in different country markets.

In some EC markets, for example, certain branded pharmaceutical products can be bought at less than half the price in other markets. The incentive to parallel export is therefore high and major problems are caused for manufacturers when highly profitable price levels in large country markets are destroyed because of parallel imports from low price small country markets. Research suggests that, in the pharmaceuticals market, a price differential of 12–18 per cent is sufficient to trigger parallel imports.

Such variations in price levels occur for a variety of reasons. First, manufacturers can extract higher prices from some markets because they are wealthier or because there is less competition or because there is less knowledge of general world prices. Second, structural factors affect price levels. Thus, in Japan, prices paid by retailers for goods bought through traditional marketing channels in Japan are high because there are often several levels in the importer/wholesaler channel and each level imposes high mark-ups. The incentive to import directly from 'non-authorised' suppliers in the exporting country is thus high. Third, a manufacturer may decide to position its product differently in different country markets. BMW, for example, has a more prestigious positioning and thus a higher price in some of its export markets than others or in its home market. This offers scope for personal parallel imports (cross-border trading) as well as opportunities for the motor trade. Fourth, currency movements can open up – or close down – windows of opportunity for parallel imports. Parallel imports can be obtained both from suppliers in the importing country and the exporting country. (In either case such suppliers are often part of the authorised network but making unauthorised sales to other wholesalers or retailers. They may do this to liquidate excess stocks or as part of an aggressive campaign to expand sales and profits.)

Given, then, that parallel imports can create major problems for manufacturing exporters, what possible responses might be available to them? Some options are listed below:

1. Reduce manufacturer-generated price differentials, e.g. increase prices to home-market authorised distributors if they are the source of parallel imports, or reduce prices to authorised importers/retailers suffering from parallel imports.
2. Promote the advantages (e.g. guaranteed product quality and continuity) of buying from authorised outlets and the disadvantages (e.g. lack of warranty) of buying from unauthorised sources.
3. Provide general support to authorised outlets, e.g. help fund sales promotions or co-operative advertising and provide distributor staff training and development programmes.
4. Interfere with grey market supplies, e.g. some fine fragrance house and also Swatch have been known to buy up the entire holdings of some unauthorised outlets' stocks of their products.
5. Allow – under controlled circumstances – some authorised distributors to supply the product to unauthorised outlets. Lloyds, the UK chemists chain, claim to have an agreement with Estée Lauder whereby customers of nominated unauthorised branches can obtain specified products via an authorised branch.
6. Request – in the interests of good long-term manufacturer-distributor relationships – that authorised outlets do not *actively* seek to supply the grey market. (Under EC legislation they may not be prevented from selling and indeed EC policy encourages parallel trading as a step towards increased competition and lower consumer prices.)
7. Differentiate the product as much as possible for different country markets. This might be achieved through labelling, packaging, exclusive designs or altered ingredients.
8. Withdraw supplies from offending authorised outlets when this is legal, as for example in the Fine Fragrance industry where the selective distribution agreements permit this.

    In order to identify the offenders, products must be identified by laser codings or some other mechanism for tracing their source. Although it will never be possible to monitor and control all grey market movements, it has been suggested that some fragrance houses, including Chanel, Calvin Klein and Guerlain, have been able to restrict parallel imports to a minimum.

9. Recognise that the existence of a parallel market may imply inefficiencies or inadequacies in the existing market supply system, e.g. a firm which transfers its product to an overseas subsidiary which then supplies distributors and retailers in that market, may find that it is the costs of supporting the subsidiary which adds sufficient to the import country price level to encourage unauthorised (and authorised) dealers to import directly from stockists in the exporting country. In this case, the exporter could streamline its subsidiary or even eliminate it and supply directly to importing dealers.

10. Do nothing and hope that the problem disappears with currency fluctuations, or is contained at a level which is tolerable.

10
Carenet

It had been a difficult night for Helen Johnson, Centre Team Leader at Carenet. The bleep had first gone about midnight, just after Helen had dropped off to sleep. What followed was a half-hour conversation with Robert, a 25-year-old man who had moderate learning difficulties, who had telephoned to say he could not get to sleep. Robert's carer, Mary Tomkins, had managed to get to sleep in the room adjacent to Robert and, rather than wake her, Robert had called the out-of-hours service for that night.

> Had Robert tried to get to sleep? No. Then how did he know he couldn't? He didn't think he would be able to. Would it be an idea to make a cup of tea and then try to settle down? It might be. What about trying that? He might do, but he still wouldn't be able to sleep.

The 3 a.m. call had been from Vera, the care assistant responsible for Bill. Bill had woken in the early hours with toothache and wanted a painkiller. Not being authorised to administer unprescribed medication, Vera had had to call Helen.

> Has this happened before? Is he seeing a dentist? Are there any contra-indications on his file?

To cap it all, arrival at the office the following morning had brought the most urgent problem. Penny, one of the seven group leaders was on a day's training course. One of her group tenants had had a flood in the bathroom, resulting in the collapse of the kitchen ceiling. The emergency services had to be summoned and immediate plans made for alternative accommodation.

It occurred to Helen that, for the moment at least, the nature of her own job had changed much less than the dramatic changes to the structure and culture of the environment in which Carenet functioned.

Carenet is a residential network, a service which is part of a County Council Social Services Department (CCSSD). It came into being when residents who had learning disabilities moved from a hostel into ordinary houses within the community and received care in their 'own houses' from staff employed by Carenet. The network was enlarged in the late 1980's and early 1990's as people began to move out of the big hospitals for the mentally handicapped and the National Health Service (NHS) paid the local authority Social Services Department to provide appropriate 'Care in the Community'.

Thus, most people receiving care within the network have lived in other residential settings (for example, hostels or hospitals). Some, however, have moved direct from their family home, often following the death of a parent.

A number of Carenet's clients receive 24-hour care because they have a high level of need in terms of help and supervision. Others may receive daily visits to help with meals, shopping, medication and housework; while a few receive help only once or twice a week, for example, to deal with money management.

Most direct care is given by care assistants and residential care workers who are organised and supervised by group leaders. Each group leader is responsible for the welfare of 8–12 service users and reports to one of two centre team leaders. The service also runs a 24-hour 'on call' system, staffed by group leaders and team leaders, to deal with emergencies.

Currently, Carenet provides accommodation – owned by housing associations or the Borough Council – for 58 clients. 40 clients have been in the network largely since its inception as a pilot scheme some ten years ago and are funded through a block budget which is more or less fixed, at least within an annual period. A further 14 clients are funded by the Health Authority on a long-term block basis. These clients were previously living in long-stay hospitals.

Since the implementation of the 1990 NHS and CC (Community Care) Act, new referrals are made to Carenet by Social Services care managers who have assessed an individual's needs and wish to 'purchase' an appropriate service from Carenet. Presently four clients are funded in this way but Carenet is only able to recruit temporary staff to provide care for them in case the funding is switched elsewhere. Carenet thus found itself in the midst of the newly-developed 'purchaser-provider' relationship. Thus a Principle Purchasing Manager, acting on behalf of the Social Services Committee of the County Council, purchased care for the 'base' client load while additional care could be purchased by care managers for specific individuals. Carenet's clients were identified as service users while Carenet itself filled the role of service provider.

The 1990 NHS & CC Act, implemented in April 1993, was the pivotal legislation in revolutionising Carenet's environment. Essentially it removed the monopolistic position of the Local Authority Social Services Department (LASSD) in the provision of statutory community care services. Henceforth the LASSDs were to act as brokers between service users and service providers, whether these providers are employed by the local authority or reside in the private (profit-making) or voluntary (not for profit) sector. Indeed, the legislation required that a minimum of 70 per cent of the special transitional grant for community care be spent with the non-local authority sector, the intention being to stimulate as rapid a growth in private and voluntary care provision as possible.

However, there was still a clear mandate to retain a good quality public service within this mixed economy. The precise balance between public and private provision and the pace of change was a decision left to each Local Authority.

The changes were associated with the diminishing belief that a large-scale public bureaucracy could solve social problems. Political and economic pressures were requiring more responsive structures, more local flexibility, more effectiveness, more efficiency and greater competitiveness.

Alongside the above issues, the notion of quality of service was catapulted to the forefront. Carenet, as part of the County Council Social Services Department, was bound by the CC's 'Quality Standard', which had introduced the following promises:

'Whenever you contact the County Council you should expect a high standard of treatment.

Individual attention
- your views listened to and taken into account
- to be told the reasons for decisions which affect you
- straightforward ways of dealing with your problems and complaints.

Clear information
- details of the services available and how to contact them
- explanations in plain language
- the name of the person you are dealing with.

Prompt attention
- a response on the spot whenever we can
- a written response to your enquiries within five working days
- if a full answer is not possible within five days, we will tell you how your enquiry will be handled, how long it is likely to take, and when you can expect a progress report.

We are also setting detailed standards which spell out exactly what you can expect from each of our services. For more information, contact the service you are interested in or your local County Council Information Point.

Our performance will be measured against this standard which is in accordance with the Audit Commission's Council-Wide Performance Indicators.'

The magnitude of the changes was reflected in a whole new language. Employees in the social services sector, schooled in the jargon of care, were now having to learn the new welfare speak which accompanied the new ethos:

'Monopolistic providers' were to become 'enablers'
'Centrally planned' services were to become 'customer led'
'Performance outcome measurement' was 'in'
'Business planning' was 'in'
Bureaucratic control was 'out', flexibility was 'in'
'Decentralised management' and 'budget devolution' were 'in'
'Bottom up' was to replace 'top down' planning
Services were to be 'targeted within available resources'

Getting the flood in Fred's house sorted out did seem a long way from the organisational and cultural change necessary to bring about the new welfare system as it was now conceived. Nevertheless, Helen had begun to think about this process and had taken steps to equip herself to deal with it. A management course had introduced her to the SWOT approach and Helen had set about her analysis, beginning with the strengths of the entire CCSSD. Helen took this as her starting point, believing that Carenet was largely representative of the strengths and weaknesses of the 'parent' organisation, as follows.

Strengths

1. A strong values base: 'The purpose of the CC is to serve the people in the county. Councillors and employees are accountable to those people. The CC will act with honesty, integrity, respect for the individual in its dealings with the public.'
2. The Quality Standard.
3. Clear customer targets, e.g. services for adults are aimed at those:
   - with a physical or sensory disability
   - with a mental health need
   - with a severe learning difficulty (Carenet's sector)
   - who abuse drugs or alcohol
   - who are HIV positive or who have aids.
4. Clear care objectives: 'To work alongside other key agencies in developing a service which is flexible, responsible to individual needs, and enables people to have as full and independent a life as possible within the community. In doing so we recognise the special needs of people with more complex disabilities and will give due regard to the needs of carers'. (Other key agencies include Housing Authorities, the Benefits Agency, Health Trusts.)
5. Policy for the development of good public relations:
   a) It is the responsibility of all employees to promote Social Services in the county in order to ensure that:
      (i) our services are understood, accessible and valued by all sections of the community
      (ii) service users are perceived as equal, valued and participating members of society, and are entitled to confidentiality at all times.
   b) All employees will contribute to this by:
      (i) developing an awareness of the views and perceptions of others
      (ii) presenting information in a clear, factual and responsive manner
      (iii) engaging with service providers and the wider community in developing understanding and pursuing common, shared goals.
6. Heavy investment in staff functional training.
7. Essentially, this is a people-centred organisation. (Change, for example, takes place following consultation and agreement rather than by dictate as in some other agencies.)

Weaknesses

1. Still largely perceived as a top-down organisation, e.g. policies and procedures are still generally handed down from County Hall.
2. The paternalistic model still exists, i.e. despite the implementation of the NHS & CC Act, it is taking time to incorporate the views of both clients and carers.
3. Both the old and the new jargon serve as barriers to communication with both clients and colleagues.

4. The realities of budget restrictions mean that the assessed and agreed needs of service users under the NHS & CC Act may not be fully met.
5. Perceived inadequate staff care policy, e.g. lack of support in the event of staff absence or work stress.
6. Punctilious performance of County Council regulations (e.g. extensive formalised staff supervision requirements) may put the organisation at a cost and flexibility disadvantage compared with private and voluntary sector competitors.

Opportunities

1. The NHS & CC Act places an obligation on the Local Authority to produce overall Community Care Plans in co-operation with Health and Housing Authorities, thus providing a mechanism for highlighting the need for community support for people with learning difficulties. This could call forth a planned commitment to the expansion of services provided by Carenet.
2. To meet specialist needs – which hitherto would have been provided by other organisations – as a result of ability to provide extra services if the purchaser has a budget. (Previously Carenet's activities were limited to a fixed number of tenants/clients and were funded in a block arrangement.)
3. Additionally, arising from above change in funding, the opportunity to provide a more flexible service package, e.g. respite care in clients' own homes.
4. Increasing use of information technology should improve efficiency and raise competitiveness, e.g. a database could be developed to provide information about staff availability to match staff to client allocation.
5. Privatisation would permit a slimmer, flexible and hence more competitive organisation, e.g. County Council employment practices could be relaxed.

Threats

1. The present Local Government Review could lead to reorganisation of the County Council, e.g. splitting into unitary authorities with different boundaries. In turn this would cause disruption, uncertainty and a break up of established relationships.
2. Continued downsizing at middle management level resulting in a loss of experience and putting more pressure on centre team leaders.

Helen was aware that, although SWOT analysis typically was presented as just a listing of areas of absolute strengths and weaknesses, strictly speaking it should be differential, i.e. strengths and weaknesses relative to competition. This had led Helen to think about the concept of competitors – did they really exist as in profit-making businesses; if so, who were they?

The Competition

There appeared to be two direct 'competitors' within the local region, one being in the voluntary not-for-profit sector, the other being in the private profit-making sector. The origins of voluntary organisations often lay with the work of charitable organisations who saw needs within the community which were not being adequately met by the public sector. Today, however, both organisations were funded by the Health Service and Social Services and made some use of properties purchased by the Health Service. Some of the staff in these organisations had approached Carenet from time to time offering their services as relief or temporary care assistants. During the course of such interviews, Helen had been able to ascertain a little about the nature of the services provided by these organisations.

Most of their clients had arrived as a result of the closure of a local hospital as part of the philosophy to place such people back into the community. Regrettably, in less enlightened days gone by, some patients had been referred to hospitals for the mentally handicapped when the true nature of their disability had not been identified. For example, the hospitals contained some deaf people who had mistakenly been thought to have had mental health disorders. Alas, whatever the origin of such patients, their period of institutionalisation had been so long that they were unable to live independent lives. Most patients, however, did have 'real' learning difficulties, many to the extent that they needed nursing care in addition to the type of care provided by Carenet.

The Health Service did refer some hospital closure patients to Carenet as well, but was increasingly using voluntary sector provision. The reason was simple – the voluntary sector offered a much cheaper alternative, a crucial factor in times of heavily constrained budgets. The price competitiveness of the voluntary sector arose as a result of several factors. First, wages paid to carers in the voluntary sector were typically 40 per cent less than those paid by Carenet. Second, the high level of supervision of carers required by CCSSD increased the overheads. Third, the number of clients sharing a voluntary home was often as many as six. Most of Carenet's tenants were in individual accommodation and the maximum number sharing was four.

Apart from this last point, there were other ways in which Carenet's offering was superior from the client's point of view. Some voluntary and private sector organisations receive a fixed contribution per client from the Health Service and DSS. Having paid for organisation expenses, only a nominal amount of money remained for the use of the client. This was provided to them as 'pocket money' but was insufficient to permit eating out, buying individual furnishings or having any real choice in terms of holidays. Limited funds meant no real independence. In contrast, Carenet clients received their full state benefits and had discretion over how to use money available to them.

'So far so good', Helen thought, 'as far as the "where are we now?" was concerned. But what of the future? Where were things heading?'

At present Carenet was free to hire more staff in response to care managers' requests for additional services for current clients and also for services for new clients. However, it appeared probable that increasing financial stringency would result in limits being set on Carenet's expenditure. This, in turn, was likely to mean that services could only be provided to new clients if services to existing clients were cut or ceased. What then, was the scope for setting marketing objectives? And were marketing objectives at all appropriate anyway? Helen began to wonder about the organisation's overall objectives and whether she was in any position to shape them.

Questions for Discussion

1. Should the notion of 'broadening the marketing concept' apply to a local authority organisation responsible for the welfare of dependent people with learning disabilities?
    a) What are the criteria by which one judges whether a particular organisational context can be/should be a valid arena for marketing principles and practice?
    b) If marketing is deemed applicable, which of its several manifestations is most relevant – marketing orientation, marketing strategy or individual marketing functions?
2. Which stockholders or publics should Carenet be concerned with and what are their respective needs?
3. Is it sensible to think in terms of marketing objectives? If so, in what terms could they be expressed?
4. In what ways could Carenet segment its customers? Who are Carenet's customers? Who could they be?
5. Are there any new product development opportunities for Carenet?
6. How can Carenet develop a sustainable competitive advantage?
7. What should Carenet's organisational mission be?
8. What should Carenet's core product be?
9. What is the scope for internal marketing?
10. Should all staff share the responsibility for PR?
11. Given that many of Carenet's clients have severe learning disabilities, how can management get feedback on the quality of the service it provides?
12. What performance criteria should be used to judge Carenet?
13. Should Carenet be part of a local authority?

11

The Mortimer Arms[1]

The Immediate Problems

The owner of the Mortimer Arms Hotel was angry. He fumed at the sheer affrontery of the bureaucrats who controlled the ratings of English Hotels. In short, the normally routine submission intended to confirm the 'Three Star' status, had not gone well. The owner was now faced with yet further expense in order just to retain the current rating.

He now knew he could no longer delay the selection of a viable strategy for the hotel. This situation had become more complex following the presentation of different alternatives by his two senior managers. He felt frustrated by all this talk of yet more changes, and wondered if there were not other alternatives, which would reconcile the differing views of his Hotel Manager and his Tavern Manager. It was not just a question of the differing views of the two managers concerned, as the staff, his external Auditors and the Town Council were now closely involved. In fact the situation was rapidly entering the public domain. Only this morning his Hotel Manager had warned that there might be a serious protest opposite the hotel in the market place if free access to Mortimer Castle and gardens was denied to the public.

The Area

The Mortimer Arms Hotel was situated in the centre of a quintessential English market town. The town, Mortimer Cross, had retained most of its distinctive character, given the conservative instincts of the local, mainly agricultural community. Apart from the ruined medieval castle, the town was known for its public school, the old Benedictine Abbey with its original fish ponds and the thriving cattle market. Mortimer Cross was surrounded by some of the finest countryside in that historic part of the UK known as the Welsh Border Country, or Welsh Marches. The area was popular for walking, riding and other country pursuits.

The Hotel

The fabric of the four-storey main hotel building had been built in 1720 against the outer north wall of the ruined fourteenth-century stronghold of Roger Mortimer,

[1] Although based upon a real business situation, all information has been modified to preserve confidentiality. This case is designed to illustrate some of the problems faced by providers of leisure services when faced by a growing but diverse customer base.

First Earl of March. (A highly colourful character; the lover of Queen Isabella; one of King Edward II's murderers and *de facto* King of England until his gruesome end.) The main hotel building incorporated the massive outer Barbican tower of the former castle.

With the expansion of the town the site of the castle gradually became the local building quarry. Accordingly, the main hotel (and much of the old town) had been built from masonry plundered from the ruins.

The fabric of the original castle had been badly damaged in the English Civil Wars of the 1640's and 1650's. In 1654, Cromwell's Major General Lambert used gunpowder to destroy the Norman Keep, to ensure that the Castle could never again be used as a centre for Royalist resistance in the West.

Today, the hotel commands a central position opposite the market place to the north, with the old castle and gardens occupying the hill to the south (area plan refers). Visitors have no difficulty in locating the Mortimer Arms as the massive Barbican tower dominates this part of the old town.

'Mortimers', as it was known locally, is owned by a minor Liberal Peer who converted the family's unwanted 'town house' and medieval ruin into a three-star hotel, a country pub and park in the early 1960's.

Figure 11.1 Map of area

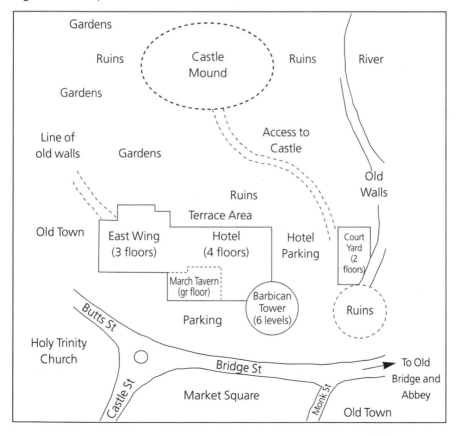

The Current Situation

Despite the location, the appeal of the area and considerable investment by the owner during the 1980's, the hotel had yet to pay its way. (Refer to the Profit and Loss Statement.) None of this had mattered in the past, as the owner had taken little direct interest in the business. He appeared to be quite content to regard the hotel as his personal hobby, even when this required meeting the demands of both the capital investment and the operating losses.

All of this was about to change, as the owner encouraged by some of his business friends in his London club, began to signal that even his pockets were not limitless. Influenced by the changes in the UK's economic philosophy during the 1980's towards efficiencies, reductions in waste and increases in productivity, he believed that the time had come for the business to pay for itself.

The Financial Situation

Table 11.1 Balance sheet

Balance Sheet (£000's) at 31-3-94	Mortimer		Prepared:	21-Jul-94
	30-3-93	30-3-94		
ASSETS	Last Yr.	Base Yr.	Yr. 1	Yr. 2
Current Assets				
Cash	55	46	0	0
Accounts Receivable	61	82	0	0
Inventory	60	54	0	0
Prepaid Expenses	3	3	0	0
Other Current Assets	5	5	0	0
Total Current Assets	184	190	0	0
Net Fixed or Plant Assets				
Land	233	225	0	0
Buildings	1,287	1,245	0	0
Equipment & Machinery	19	13	0	0
Vehicles	20	14	0	0
Other Fixed Assets	18	12	0	0
Total Net Fixed Assets	1,577	1,509	0	0
Other Assets	0	0	0	0
Total Assets	1,761	1,699	0	0
LIABILITIES & OWNERS EQUITY				
Current Liabilities				
Trade Creditors	84	74	0	0
Other Creditors	52	37	0	0

Accrued Expenses	5	12	0	0
Other Current Liabilities	4	4	0	0
Total Current Liabilities	145	127	0	0
Long Term Liabilities				
Instalment Debt Payable	0	0	0	0
Mortgage Payable	0	0	0	0
Other L-T Liabilities	70	70	0	0
Total L-T Liabilities	70	70	0	0
Total Liabilities	215	197	0	0
Owner's Equity				
Additions	171	152	0	0
Paid-in Capital	1,350	1,350	0	0
Retained Earnings	25	0	0	0
Total Owner's Equity	1,546	1,502	0	0

Table 11.2 Profit and loss statement

Income Statement £000's	Mortimer Arms		Prepared:	21-Jul-94
	30/3/93 Last Yr.	30/3/94 Base Yr.	Yr. 1	Yr. 2
Net Revenue	772	757	0	0
Bought in inc: (food, drink, housekeeping)	232	227	0	0
Gross Profit	540	530	0	0
Operating Expenses				
Wages	192	215	0	0
Salaries	41	45	0	0
Commissions	15	15	0	0
Rent/rates (to owner)	39	40	0	0
Telephone & Utilities	33	37	0	0
Insurance	12	12	0	0
Other Marketing	35	50	0	0
Maintenance & Repairs	31	36	0	0
Professional	12	14	0	0
Depreciation	69	67	0	0
Travel & Entertainment	5	6	0	0
Non-Income Taxes	0	0	0	0
Other Operating Expenses	25	20	0	0
Total Operating Expenses	509	557	0	0
Net Operating Income	32	(27)	0	0
Interest Expenses	0	0	0	0

Net Income before Income Tax	32	(27)	0	0
Income Tax	8	0	0	0
Net Income	24	(27)	0	0

Action Taken to Build Revenues

As a first measure the owner consulted his firm of auditors who specialised in private sector service organisations. They suggested and installed computerised monthly accounts for the identified revenue earning parts of the business. These highlighted the declining occupancy rates and the need to generate revenue throughout the year.

Figure 11.3 Revenue and occupancy by operations

Fiscal 1994
Total Revenues £757,000

Item	Barbican	Hotel	Courtyard	Tavern	Resid. Bar	Function Room
£000's	£75	£289	£70	£252	£51	£20
Av. occupancy	23%	60%	32%	–	–	–
Summer	–	85%	50%	–	–	–
Winter	–	35%	15%	–	–	–
Staff	6	15	5	4	3	–
(full time equivalent)						

Notes on the financial statements

- The Residents Bar revenue also includes revenue from lunches.
- Together with the £20k earned from the function room, total revenue is estimated at some £757k in the last fiscal year which is down from £772k achieved in the previous year
- Part of the Hotel/Courtyard revenues include breakfast services from the restaurant.
- Salaries include:
  Hotel Manager £20k
  Tavern Manager £20k
  Bookkeeper £12k.
- All losses are financed by the owner
- Professional costs include a £6k retainer to a freelance public relations consultant and subscriptions to professional bodies to retain listings and three star rating.
- Commissions are payments to tourist agencies for forwarding bookings. These are especially important for foreign visitors.

The auditors then introduced the owner to their associated management consultant, who went on to discuss the different nature of a service business and stressed the following service business characteristics:

- The intangibility of part of the hotel service.
- The perishability of hotel services (for example, there is little work in progress and hotel beds cannot be added to inventory and sold-off at later dates).
- Hotel beds, therefore, are a convenience of time and place and once unsold are opportunities lost for ever.
- The very wide 'product range' of the Mortimer Arms. A hotel room in the Courtyard on 1 December, for example, is a very different product from a suite in the main hotel on 1 July.
- On this basis, the minimum number of products marketed by the Mortimer Arms is the number of rooms (42) times 365 days, or 15,330 separate products.
- The need for consistency in the delivering of hotel services.
- The human element involved in this delivery process.
- The participation of the customer in the process and the essential inseparability of service consumption from service production.

Although the owner found himself somewhat at sea, especially with the last point, he took to heart the auditor's final point which was to generate revenue to increase the return on expensive assets.

When they suggested that a marketing consultant be appointed to urgently address these issues, the owner readily agreed.

An independent public relations consultant with experience of leisure marketing was therefore appointed in 1992 on a yearly rolling contract. An added benefit, it was believed, was that the consultant had a strong personal interest in English history.

The consultant's brief was to take responsibility for all the hotel's marketing communications. For the first time a separate marketing budget was established as recommended by the auditors.

In fiscal 1994 this marketing budget was employed as follows:

Table 11.4 The marketing budget

Activity	£000's
Revised corporate identity emphasising the new 'Mortimers' logo and key visual (the White Rose)	10
Local press and feature articles	2
Revised hotel literature	10
Specific advertising of Tavern events	6
Specific Barbican restaurant advertising	4
Sponsorship of folk singing for the March Tavern	3
Sponsorship of Mortimer Castle jousting	3
Free beer for Sudley Castle 'Sealed Knot' battles branded 'March bitter'	1
Sponsorship of the three counties 'Ale Walk'	3
Advertising in national guidebooks	8
Commissions to agents*	15
PR fee to freelance agent	6
Total	71

* 20 per cent of bookings.

The Situation Worsens

Despite two years of 'marketing' and the activities of the public relations consultant, the decline in the forward bookings situation continued. Of particular concern was the high level of staff turnover (the March Tavern excepted), which was having a knock-on effect on service quality. Unfortunately, the recession of the early 1990's (or so the owner said) has had a negative effect on the business over the last few years.

Although still a busy summer hotel, average occupancy rates had fallen to below 50 per cent, and the average stay to 2.5 nights. These figures appeared to reflect the transitory nature of the majority of visitors who passed through the area on the way to the Welsh coast or some other destination.

Of particular concern was that the recently refurbished Barbican restaurant was thinly occupied most nights. This prestigious dinning room situated on the first floor of the Barbican Tower had a potential of 70 'covers' (the number of diners). The average price per cover for dinner estimated from the prime records was almost £18 excluding wine.

Sadly, it appeared that the hotel was being relegated to the status of a country pub renowned for its real ale. The 'March Tavern' (once the Residents' Lounge and still incorporating the original hotel entrance), under its extrovert manager, was fast re-establishing itself as the centre of both the hotel and the local farming community. Whilst applauding the energy of the Tavern's manager, the owner regretted that the hotel, especially in winter, had now become better known for its pub, rather than for its accommodation or restaurants. The Tavern had recently begun to sell its own branded beer known as 'March Bitter'. The Tavern manager was now keen to extend the sale of this bitter to other parts of the county. In fact he was never short of ideas and now talked of franchising the 'March Tavern Concept' to other free houses.

In January 1994 after a meeting with the auditors, the owner decided to replace the current hotel manager with a young American who had been the under manager of a large hotel in Maine. The new manager, highly recommended by a member of the owner's London club, took up his position in May of that year.

The Development of the Hotel Throughout the 1980's

In the 1960's and 1970's the owner had followed a policy of minimum investment and maintained the main building as a small country hotel. The owner had expressed little interest in the running of the hotel during this period, spending most of his time either in London or Ireland. He was not too concerned with the profit motive, preferring stability to the problems of growing a competitive business. This philosophy changed during the 1980's when considerable investment was undertaken over a five-year period.

This was prompted by a number of factors:

- An awareness that UK hotel rates were now rising so fast that the potential of this unique situation was not being fully realised.
- The increased monitoring of standards encouraged by such bodies as the English Tourist Board.
- The desire to retain the existing three star rating and upgrade to four star.

- The activities of competitive hotels and restaurants.
- The desire to exploit the growth of the domestic leisure market, car ownership and foreign tourism.
- The advice of recreational and property professionals who advocated a mix of facilities to appeal to a broader leisure market in an area with limited access to spending power.
- The financial expansionist climate of the 1980's together with increasing pressure from financial professional advisors.

The owner admits, however, that some of the decisions were taken in a less than professional manner. Indeed, he still boasts of his attitude to decision making in those days. This can best be described as writing the identified alternatives on pieces of paper and screwing them into paper balls. He claimed to then throw them into the corner of his library, inviting his gun dog (Mortimer) to 'fetch'. Most people, however, knew that he could only manage one alternative at a time.

The Individual Projects and Current Status

The following major developments have taken place since the early 1980's:

1. The expansion of the Hotel, August 1983

The purchase of the adjoining building (the former town museum), now termed the East Wing. This purchase allowed the hotel to increase bedroom accommodation from 15 to 24 double rooms, together with the installation of en suite facilities to all bedrooms. The hotel was then able to offer a range of accommodation by grading all rooms in the main hotel as superior and all those in the East Wing as standard.

Currently prices per night for a double room (inclusive of English breakfast) are £69.00 and £49.00 respectively for the two types of accommodation. This comprehensive refurbishment was effected within the limitations of the main building's Grade 2 listing as a building of historic interest.

2. The restoration of the Barbican Tower, October 1986

This proved the decisive architectural development of the building, as the Tower was the only part of the original structure to have survived almost intact. The redevelopment allowed for the creation of a restaurant in a unique location and ambience. The Barbican restaurant was located on the first floor of the old Barbican tower. It was intended to be an example of fine English classical cuisine served in an elegant and relaxing atmosphere. The idea for the decor of the restaurant was inspired by 'Rules' adjacent to the Strand in London, where the owner often dined after a short stroll from his club.

The Barbican restaurant employed a small marketing budget to promote awareness amongst non-residents. The prime target group were individuals classified as 'ABs', living within one hour's travelling time of the hotel. The local business community formed a secondary target group in conjunction with the function room, which was also on the first floor of the main building.

3. The March Tavern, February 1988

The creation of the March Tavern as a distinct entity within the hotel as a dedicated area for the local community. The hotel had historically been the social centre of the old town. This was especially true of occasions like cattle market day, which attracted a wide spectrum of the area's agricultural community. As the original hotel bar was beginning to turn into something of an 'ale house' as well as becoming increasingly crowded and unruly, especially on market days, Saturday nights and after local rugby club fixtures, it was considered wise to separate the hotel guests from the local community. The Tavern is not entirely separated from the hotel as this would create difficulties for the staff. The Tavern still opens onto the main reception area and remains a source of complaint from some of the guests, alarmed by inebriated locals storming the residents bar after closing time demanding additional supplies of March bitter.

Today the March Tavern is situated in a prime position opposite the market. This is further emphasised by the fact that the Tavern includes the original imposing main entrance of the hotel as its own entrance. The Tavern has a distinct atmosphere of energy and activity. Part of the reason for this is that the Tavern Manager has attracted a number of local folk singers to perform in the evenings. The Tavern has a wide reputation for the preservation of old English country music. Performers come there from all over the country not only to sing, but also to meet other singers and song writers.

4. The main Hotel goes more up-market, April 1990

The opening of three suites on the third, forth and fifth floors of the Barbican Tower. These were termed in the best Yorkist tradition, the Neville, Montague and Woodville suites. (The castle became the centre of the Yorkist party in the West at the end of the fourteenth century.) Today they are priced at £85.00 per night per suite. Each suite comprises a double bedroom, bathroom and sitting room.

5. The refurbishment of the Hotel Bar, April 1990

In conjunction with the development of 'York' suites, the relocation and refurbishment of the Hotel Bar, to be more in keeping with the standards of a country hotel became a necessity. The refurbishment was also undertaken so that guests and visitors could be served with light bar lunches. In the past some guests had felt intimidated by the grandiose setting of the Barbican restaurant (not to mention the cost and the stately pace of the service).

This refurbishment required the relocation of the Hotel Bar from the ground floor to the first floor in order to:

● Provide additional ground floor space for the reception and the residents' lounge.
● Keep the preparation and serving of meals in one area.

- Prevent locals, drinking in the ground floor March Tavern, from 'storming' the residents bar at closing time.

6. Facilities for the business community, May 1991

The creation of a function room on the first floor of the main hotel, used by such organisations as the Rotary Group, the Country Landowners' Association, the Conservative Club and the National Farmers Union.

It was hoped that after such functions they would then be tempted into the Barbican restaurant, or at least help to spread the message. Currently, only the Country Landowners Association are regular diners in the Barbican. The remainder appeared to be happier propping up the residents' bar while enjoying a snack.

7. Facilities for passing visitors, December 1991

The conversion of the outbuildings, old kitchens and garages to the West of the main building into a motel-style development known as the 'Courtyard'. This development added a further 15 bedrooms with shower facilities; five of these rooms are single rooms. These developments were felt to be important to the business given the increasing trend towards passing trade experienced in the last few years.

Double courtyard accommodation was graded as 'economy' and priced at £39.00 per night for a double room, inclusive of breakfast taken in the main hotel. Parking was normally available to all hotel guests within the large courtyard. Traffic congestion in summer, however, was becoming worse each year, as visitors attempted to park there before visiting the castle.

Increasing Interest in the Old Castle

At present the only access to the old castle and gardens is through the hotel courtyard opposite the market square. Beyond the courtyard to the south the land rises sharply to the ruins of the old castle and the castle gardens (refer to plan of area).

The site of the old castle and its gardens is managed by a board of trustees, as the present peer's father in a public-spirited moment had felt it right that the castle and gardens should be open to the townspeople. He had wisely, however, included a right of veto for the use of his heirs and successors.

Visitors to the castle have grown dramatically in the last five years. Previously, old castle ruins were not major attractions for tourists. The current situation is now very different, as large numbers of tourists for different reasons are touring the castle and spending most of the day in the park. This has changed the previous consensus, whereby small numbers of local people quietly enjoyed their 'Castle Park'. The activities of the Town Council and the hotel's public relations manager can take some of the credit for the development of this historical tourism.

Castle-related promotional activities encouraged by the public relations manager included:

- The active encouragement of the annual open-air Shakespeare on the Castle Mound.
- The offer of an ideal setting for the County's jousting society which now organised jousts in June, July and August.
- The encouragement of historical educational visits by groups of school children.
- Lighting for the Castle ruins, paid for by the Council. These were turned on by the Lord Lieutenant of the County on the 530th anniversary of the Lancastrian siege and subsequent slaughter of the Yorkist heirs.
- Sponsorship by the Town Council to publish four historical booklets by local authors:
  a) The Wigmore Chronicler
  b) The Restoration of the Mortimer Inheritance (the life and times of the second Earl of March; at Crecy with Edward III)
  c) The Royalist Resistance in the West, 1645–1651 (From Naseby to Worcester)
  d) The Early Years of Richard Duke of Gloucester.

Her next project, which she is keen to progress with the trustees and the town council, is a 'Yorkist Heritage Trail', starting at the Castle, crossing the old river bridge and ending in the Abbey Meadows. The proposal is for the trail to be both historically interesting and replete with human interest. This project looks promising as some of the Castle's former Yorkist owners, failing to gain the sanctuary of the Abbey Church, had met a grim end in the Abbey fish ponds (still known as the 'red pools').

The Competition

The town has two other hotels all within a short walk of the Castle. Both are privately owned and operate small but relatively expensive restaurants. The difficulty in identifying the wider competition is that Mortimers seems to be competing at a number of different levels in the leisure market. The recognition of this factor should have began the process of lifting the curtain on defining the nature of the business problems.

Local competition for the hotel includes:

- Two town centre private hotels
- A country private hotel
- A country hotel, part of a major chain
- A motel on the edge of town

At present the public relations consultant is creating separate publicity programmes for the March Tavern, the Barbican Restaurant, the main hotel, the Courtyard and the castle. This, the public relations consultant maintained, has become a marketing fact of life, given the very different customer groups using each facility. For example, it would be difficult if not unwise to associate the sponsorship of the 'Three Counties' Ale Walk' (by the March Tavern), with the discrete, although limited, local media advertising for the Barbican Restaurant.

Feedback from Guests and Visitors

No formal visitor research had been undertaken, although indications of satisfaction/dissatisfaction are provided by an inspection of recent comments in the visitors' book, the suggestions book and feedback from the staff.

These comments related to the 1993/94 period.

Typical adverse comments included:
- Room service is a bad joke
- Can't find any staff . . . even to check out
- No parking near the hotel (in summer)
- Which is the main entrance?
- Can't understand why on earth you put a smoky pub in the middle of a hotel
- The constant 'muzak' is awful
- The bedrooms are too small and too noisy (courtyard)
- It took all night to get served in the restaurant
- Get yourselves a hotel manager
- The service is very poor . . . staff are under trained and over stretched
- More of a rugby club, pub, or walkers' hostel than a hotel
- Nowhere for the children to go
- It's more like a motel
- Apart from the suites the decoration is all over the place
- Like a gentlemens' club . . . Stuffy . . . No appeal for women
- The noise from that pub is dreadful
- Just like an Irish racecourse hotel the day before the Irish Derby!

On further inspection, it seemed that the majority of complaints were coming from a minority of the visitors – the foreign visitors.

Typical positive comments included:
- A lovely weekend break
- Just love the area and the town for the weekend
- A great night out
- Best food since France
- One of the friendliest and cosiest pubs we've visited
- Always enjoy stopping off here
- There's no restaurant to match it and you never have to book
- Lovely weekend break
- A walkers' paradise
- Our suite was excellent
- You feel as if you are walking into history (assumed to be a positive comment)
- Friendly and cosy
- It's quite unique
- The folks back home won't believe this (also assumed to be positive)

The Tavern Manager's Initiative

The owner, like many in the town, was impressed by the initiative and enterprise of the manager of the March Tavern. He had created a thriving profitable business from almost nothing and he often reminded the owner that the Tavern was probably subsidising the rest of the business. His appeal was quite straightforward. 'Appoint me the "Complex Manager", and I will put the business back in the black with a minimum amount of direct investment.'

The essence of his ambitious proposal was to create a 'Medieval Campus' which would offer a historical experience and inspiration to visitors for a full day. This was to be achieved by a combination of refurbishment, concessions and a joint venture with the Town Council. In addition he maintained that 'we should be building on success rather than failure'. By this latter point he meant that we should stop apologising for the success of the March Tavern in a situation where he believed the main hotel to be over-priced, pretentious and under utilised. His specific proposals which included innovative ways of passing capital investment to third parties, included:

1. The expansion of the Tavern to the whole frontage of the main building (excluding the East wing, but including the ground floor of the Barbican Tower). This would enable the Tavern to offer informal lunches and dinners at reasonable prices to both locals and visitors.
2. As far as the main hotel was concerned to:
   * Clearly separate the hotel from the Tavern
   * Restrict the hotel to the South and East of the main building
   * Offer all rooms at the £49 price point in order to re-establish the hotel as a friendly family hotel.
   The hotel would therefore carry on as it had always done, as a small friendly family hotel serving both the visitors and local community. If the Barbican restaurant would not pay for itself, prices should be reduced to a level more in keeping with the local community and the majority of visitors. If the Tavern manager's proposals were accepted the Barbican restaurant would have to be resited, given that he was proposing an alternative use for the tower.
3. Currently the courtyard site was failing to generate a satisfactory return on the land and building assets. This was all the more surprising considering the steady increase in visitors using the courtyard access to the Castle. The motel therefore should be closed and a fresh approach taken to generate returns for this site and the other under-utilised assets, the Castle and the Park.

The revised plan was very ambitious and gave the owner much food for thought. In addition to the courtyard site the proposal involved the entire Castle Park. The Tavern Manager proposed to form a business alliance with the Town Council (the majority of the castle trustees), to create a new Visitor Centre inclusive of concession exhibition, retailing and light refreshment facilities. The proposals had already received a positive response from the majority party on the Town Council who were under pressure to generate additional visitors to the town and new longer-term revenue sources. The proposed visitor centre would redevelop not only the Courtyard Motel but would also involve the restoration of two floors of the second ruined Barbican Tower adjacent to the courtyard. This would provide a retail gallery for concession units operated by local craftspeople as well as national businesses.

4. As the Centre would control access to the castle, the prime rationale for the centre would be as an access point for paying visitors to the castle and the park. Active encouragement was to be given to topical activities in the park such as exhibitions of 'life in the Castle Village'; archery demonstrations and jousting.

   The enterprise would be a joint venture between the owner, the trustees and the Council. The Council would be responsible for the majority of the development costs, whilst the owner would provide the land with the agreement of the trustees.

   The major revenue-earning activities, however, were to be generated from concession retailing activities which were projected in excess of some £700,000 per annum. These retailing operations would contribute 21.5 per cent of their net sales to the joint venture. Castle entrance receipts would go directly to the new venture on a 50:50 basis.

5. The proposals included the conversion of the Barbican Tower to a medieval museum, which with live actors, audio visual material and new interactive media technology would provide 'an interactive medieval experience'. A minority joint venture was proposed with a French technology company who had commissioned similar programmes in two French Chateaux. The Complex would provide the premises, development costs and staff (75 per cent) and the French company the installation, technology, training and programmes (25 per cent).

6. The Medieval Museum on the five floors of the Barbican Tower were to be the 'spearhead' of the Campus featuring in the literature and marking the entrance to the Castle Park.

The Tavern Manager stressed that his proposals should be considered as a 'package' as the major revenue earning units:

- The Family Hotel
- The Tavern and Tavern restaurant
- The Visitor Centre, retailing units and tea rooms
- 'Medieval Virtual Reality'

. . . would generate business for each other and would be promoted together. This he suggested was a better situation than the current separate promotion of the Tavern and the Barbican Restaurant to two different target groups.

The New Hotel Manager's Alternative

The 32-year-old New Englander appointed to this role was astonished on arrival at the wasted potential of the Mortimer Arms. He regarded the location as magnificent and the ambience quite exceptional. Almost everything about the current management of the hotel, however, he considered unstructured and unprofessional.

As a professional hotel manager he was familiar with the marketing mix applicable to a service industry.

The Hotel Manager felt that little attempt had been made to put into practice any of the basic visitor-oriented services. He found he never had to ask questions as to whether or not the basic service delivery systems were being employed, as it was so obviously foreign to both the management and the staff.

When he first met the reception staff he asked whether or not they telephoned each guest on arrival after ten minutes in their room. Their response had been a

LEARNING NOTE on the service marketing mix

The First Four P's (PRODUCT, PRICE, PLACE AND PERSUASION) plus . . .

Process

This refers to the effectiveness of the hotel delivery system. It is experienced and judged at the point of delivery, when the hotel guest comes face to face with the effectiveness or otherwise of the delivery system.

Examples: speed of the checking-out service or room service; the attitude of the reception staff; the method of answering the telephone; the length of wait in the dining room; the management of problems and complaints.

People

The management and staff involved in the delivery of the service system. One weak link, or unfriendly, rude person could put in jeopardy the efforts of everybody else. Considerations for the people element might include training, motivation, support systems, dress/uniforms and the ability to empathise with a wide range of visitors.

Physical evidence

In the same way as we may consciously or sub-consciously judge a lawyer's or doctor's competence by the appearance of their offices, reports or waiting rooms, a hotel is also assessed by its physical environment . . . but more so. Visitors will not return to an ambience if they are unhappy with the architecture, the decor, the pictures in the rooms and even the china used in the dining room. This becomes more important the higher the level the hotel aspires to position itself. The lower the level the less relevant these issues are, as expectations will have been managed down to lower levels.

blank, 'Why . . . they always call if something is wrong'.

He frequently called his friends back in Maine for an exchange of views and found himself telling them just how primitive the 'Brits' still were when it came to managing a leisure service industry. 'Even in a country of low service expectations it's a wonder the place has managed to survive as a hotel at all . . . especially as it's located in the middle of a "Beer Hall" . . . The list is endless, it seems that the place has never had a Maitre d'hôtel, nor seriously attempted to train its staff in the delivery of hotel services. It's the attention to detail that is missing. An up-market hotel is about luxury and obsession with the detail of luxury. Tea-bags rather than loose tea in England for example, is not on, nor is ordinary catering china, crystal ware and silverware for the best restaurant in the area.'

The reasons for the decline in custom (despite its location), he believed to be obvious. It had clearly never been managed, and obviously not for any clearly defined customer groups. Without a more professional approach, reputation, customer loyalty and repeat business could not be built. One of his first tasks was to look more closely at the rather inadequate hotel visitor data base.

Information about visitors was limited to their addresses and length of stay. This revealed that 50 per cent of visitors stayed for two nights or less. The majority of these came from the Midlands, The South West and London areas. Nearly all had travelled by car, most using the M5/M50 as access. These visitors stayed at the hotel on route to or from other destinations.

The exceptions were three broad types of visitors:

1. The foreign visitors who tended to book ahead for two to three nights and comprised 20 per cent of all visitors to the hotel for the period 1993/94. Foreign visitors tended to book the best rooms and make the most use of the restaurant. Their home countries in order of frequency were:
   - The USA
   - Germany
   - Australia/New Zealand
   - Japan
   - Other European.
2. The long weekend visitors, almost always English couples who also wanted the best rooms and enjoyed the restaurant. This group was the mainstay of the winter visitors staying two or three nights (20 per cent).
3. Summer holiday makers comprising of a wide variety of walkers and historical tourists, staying up to five nights (10 per cent).

Summary of the Hotel Manager's Proposals

The Hotel Manager had reacted with horror and disbelief on hearing the Tavern Manager's proposals for a theme park supported by satellite retailing and restaurant services. He decided to do all he could to force the issue into the open and wait for the inevitable groundswell of opinion to gather against raw commercialism in the centre of such a historic town. In the short term he lobbied the owner with his own proposals.

The essence of the Hotel Manager's proposals for the hotel's future are set out below:

1. Clearly define the primary and secondary target markets.
   These to be:
   - Primary . . . foreign tourists all year round.
   - Secondary . . . UK visitors, couples, AB socio-economic groups, all year round.
2. Set average length of stay targets for each target group.
   These to be:
   Primary group: four days (mix of five-day weeks and three-day midweek stays)
   Secondary: three days/extended weekends.
3. Set repeat business targets for the secondary target group.

4. Use the marketing budget to assist in achieving these objectives (using foreign media when necessary).
5. Present the hotel as an up-market exclusive hotel and submit for a four-star rating.
6. Continue to market the Barbican restaurant separately to these same target groups as well as the local community.

Implications

The implications of these proposals were what most worried the owner, as the Hotel Manager had stressed that there should be no compromise with his strategy of focusing on service delivery quality in the Hotel and Barbican Restaurant if the financial projections were to be achieved. To achieve these projections the Hotel Manager was targeting an average occupancy of 75 per cent for the main hotel and 50 per cent for the Barbican Restaurant. These objectives required:

- The closure of the Courtyard Motel and the relocation of the March Tavern to the Courtyard.
- The encouragement of activities in areas more compatible with the hotel. For example, this might include wine bar and bistro activities.
- The refurbishment of the ground floor of the main hotel to create a spacious hotel reception area, lounges and residents' bar.
- Create a luncheon terrace room overlooking the Castle Park for breakfasts, light lunches and outdoor entertaining events.
- Create a residents' cocktail bar in the unique location at the top of the Barbican Tower.
- Add a further four bedrooms in the vacated space on the first floor.
- Grade all rooms as superior.
- Convert the function room to a health centre for the exclusive use of hotel guests.
- Counter the proposals for a visitor centre on the courtyard site, by offering a new site for the town's museum in the renovated two floors of the second Barbican tower, so long as no retailing was permitted and capital was provided by the museum trustees.

To underline his point of view he always referred to the proposed Visitor Centre as the 'Retailing Centre' or 'Castle Market'. The Hotel Manager was most unhappy with the proposals originating from the Tavern manager and his contacts in local government. If these proposals were to go ahead he stressed that the effect on the hotel would be entirely negative. He had taken the time to visit similar 'Visitor Centres' and was not impressed by their business philosophy. His comments to the owner included the following observations:

1. The proposed Centre is introducing raw commercialism of the wrong kind into the heart of the hotel.
2. With the exception of the Tower, the proposed development on the courtyard site would be for a modern stone-clad and glass 'retailing centre', rather than

any real attempt to educate the visitor and preserve the amenities and tranquillity of the old castle.

3. The lay-out included tea rooms, exhibits and concession retailing units. The latter, he suggested (on the basis of other centres), would attract the worst kind of retail portfolio. This would include the normal type of tatty merchandise that the 'Great British Public' appeared to be so fond of . . . and he did not intend to target the mass market unlike the enterprising manager of the March Tavern.

Based upon his observations of the Clovelly Visitor Centre (upon which it was proposed to model this development, modified to the castle theme), the merchandise mix he suggested would include:

- Trace your own ancestors
- How to do your own brass-rubbing
- Buy yourself a title
- Cheap market stall quasi-historical novels
- Romantic historical fiction
- Plastic armour, swords and shields
- And of course, in common with the best British retailing traditions, declare Christmas to start at the end of September so that 'Castle in the snow' cards could be stocked for three months.

'Need I go on'?' he asked the owner one lunch time walking round the Courtyard.

4. As it was proposed to site the Visitor Centre astride the only public access to the Castle (to ensure that everybody paid the entrance fee), the ambience of the old Castle Park would be lost for ever. He subsequently warned of the opposition that might result, given that the Council appeared to be happy to fence off an old right of way to the south of the castle site.
5. Finally, he suggested that in these changeable times the control of the Council might yet fall to the opposition especially as boundary changes were currently in progress.

Although the hotel was not quite in the same price league as Thornbury Castle near Bristol, the new manager was highly impressed by the location and the aura of history. He was confident he could turn the business around if he was given a free hand. He had, however, one important caveat: the Tavern Manager's proposals must be resisted and the Public Relations manager must start to concentrate on the real issue of increasing the occupancy rate.

The owner now had to decide on a realistic strategy compatible with his desire for a profitable business that did not require any more regular injections of capital investment. The Tavern Manager's views of the exclusive hotel option were by now well known; he considered the new manager as quite out of touch with both the local and national trends in the English leisure market. This obvious disagreement between the two managers was now seriously affecting staff motivation.

The auditors had probed the assumptions behind the build-up of the revenue projections of both options and advised that the numbers could only be achieved if there was a clear commitment and a clear direction. Marketing leisure services, the owner had long realised, was very different from some of his other enterprises. However difficult, it was now time to act before the situation got further out of hand. He looked down at faithful 'Mortimer'. It was time to ask him to 'fetch'.

Table 11.5 The alternative revenue projections

£000's	Current Revenue	Tavern Manager	Hotel Manager
The Hotel	289	275	365
Motel	70	–	–
Barbican Rest.	75	–	135
Residents Bar	51[2]	50[3]	50[4]
Function Room	20	20	–
Terrace Restaurant	–	–	50
March Tavern	252	330	235
Tavern Meals	–	45	–
Medieval Museum	–	45[5]	–
Visitors Centre/Park	–	95[6]	–
Totals	757	860	835
Estimated Capital	–	225	200

[2] Includes lunches.
[3] Excludes lunches.
[4] 75 per cent of revenues estimated at £60k year 1.
[5] Commission on sales 21.5 of £700k/2 or £75k.
[6] Plus Park entrance fees of gate £40k/2 or £20k.

Towards a possible solution

Market segmentation, targeting and positioning

The basic problem with the Mortimer Arms is the attempt to be all things to all people. Neither of the two proposed solutions, however, will make best use of the hotel's assets and potential. In this situation the well established principles of market segmentation might usefully be applied to this case.

1. Market segmentation
A selected mode of market segmentation for the market for hotel and recreational services, might be a combination of demographic, geographic and phychographic modes. For example:

- The AB socio-economic group maybe classified as both foreign and British (FABS and BABS).
- The C1, C2 socio-economic groups are further classified by geograpy and family size, resulting in:
  LOCS . . . Locals
  MINKYS . . . 'Middle income no kids yet'
  MIKS . . . 'Middle income with kids'.

2. Market targeting

If the 'hotel products' are now entered in the left hand column, the resulting grid may be used for market sector targeting (Table 11.6).

Reading across the numbers represent estimated rankings of the appeal of each service product to the identified market sectors. These also represent distinct target groups for marketing communications.

Table 11.6 Appeal of hotel facilities

	FABS	BABS	LOCS	MINKYS	MIKS
Hotel	1	2	–	–	–
Motel	4	3	–	1	2
Restaurant	1=	1=	3	4	5
Restaurant Bar	1=	1=	3	–	–
Tavern	3=	3=	1	2	3=
Castle	1	2	3	4	5
Visitor Centre	3=	3=	5	2	1

3. Market positioning

Six dimensions of customer choice

The positioning map below plots the Mortimer Arms in relation to six perceived customer requirements. Each requirement has been expressed as a 'dimension', the parameters of which are expressed as bi-polar scales.

Figure 11.2 Six dimensions of customer choice

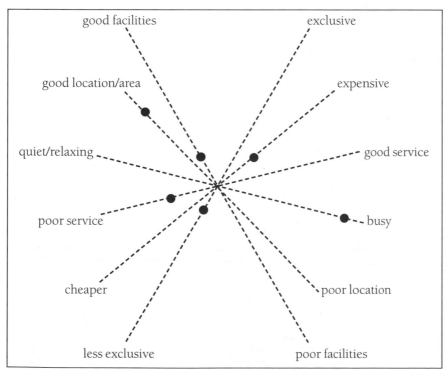

It is now assumed that the above six dimensions may be further reduced to two key dimensions which subsume all six. These are service and location. It is then possible to create a two-dimensional positioning map which plots the position of the Mortimer Arms relative to its competition. It would also be possible to plot customers' ideal requirements if these could be determined.

Figure 11.3 A two dimensional positioning map

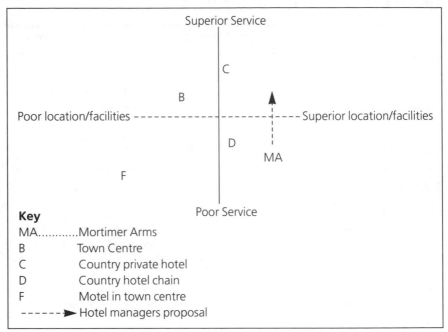

Questions for Discussion

1. Summarise the current strategic position of the Mortimer Arms.
2. Prepare a critique of the current Service Marketing Mix for the Mortimer Arms.
3. Apply the principles of Market Segmentation, Targeting and Positioning (STP), with the objective of viewing the proposals of both the Hotel Manager and the Tavern Manager in a strategic marketing perspective.
4. Propose a detailed marketing plan based upon the analysis undertaken in the preceding three questions.
5. Recommend revisions to the current service marketing mix in the light of your proposals.
6. Given what you have learnt about 'S.T.P.' attempt the mini-case, 'G'day FNQ', this refers to an Australian resort with similar problems to the Mortimer Arms.

12

G'day FNQ

On the other side of the world similar problems are being experienced by a resort complex in North Queensland, Australia. Having applied the principles of 'STP' to the Mortimer Arms, this mini-case will help you to apply the same disciplines to a different culture.

The Cassowary Beach Resort is not in fact on the beach, rather it is situated a kilometre inland and forms part of the area known as Cassowary Beach, in Far North Queensland (FNQ).

Far North Queensland has to be one of the most interesting and delightful parts of the world. It is increasingly difficult to find resorts like Cassowary Beach and its 15 kilometres of almost empty tropical beach, which have differed little since Captain Cook first took on water here. This is the area where the last stands of primeval rainforest reach the coast, or as the travel literature says, 'where the rainforest meets the reef'. Inland the distances are awesome. The rainforest gives way to the tablelands and scrub of a vast interior. The contrast between the civilization of the coast, the interior and the northern coast is dramatic. From an international perspective, this is one of the last real frontiers where four-wheel drive is the norm, real estate is cheap and hotels and travel excellent value for the dollar. The brochures stress 'the affordable Paradise' to Europeans and Japanese more used to prices twice the level.

Probably more outdoor activities are available in FNQ than in most places in the world. These activities are pursued in a distinctively Australian laid-back style. Although there is a 'go for it' outdoor activity culture, it's not taken that seriously. You can be made to feel a wimp, however, if in one week you have not scuba-dived the reef, beaten the Japanese at white-water rapids rafting, wrestled with a big 'salty' (estuarine crocodile) whilst crossing a mangrove creek (without loosing your Akubra), para-glided on to the beach for your wedding reception, or backpacked the rainforest trails by night and burnt off the leaches with a lighted cigarette before breakfast!

In contrast to what appears to be macho Aussie activities, there are also opportunities to relax at some of the finest tropical resorts in the world. Given the problem of distance, up-market tourists are normally flown in to the exclusive resort islands. These have the advantage of no 'saltys', or the far more numerous box jelly fish, which make swimming almost impossible in the rainy season on the mainland.

The area attracts a variety of different visitors.

Visitor classifications

These include such rough classifications as:
- *Foreign up-market tourists*, flown directly into landing strips on the exclusive resorts of Lizard or Dunk Island. These are mainly rich Europeans, Asians or North Americans, who expect to stay for at least one week, depending upon their desire to see other parts of the world during a typical three-week visit to South East Asia/Australasia.
- *Australian families*, escaping the winter in Melbourne, Sydney or Canberra (in the same way that residents of Boston or New York City will go to the Caribbean in January or February). Normally, they will fly into Cairns and rent a car. They would expect to stay in the same area for one or two weeks.
- *Australian families driving up north from as far south as Brisbane*; in other respects similar to those flying up.
- *Adventurers,* from all over Australia and the world attracted by the reef and the frontier atmosphere. The more adventurous will probably want to keep moving on to the wilds of Cape York and the Kakadu National Park in the Northern Territory.
- *Younger backpackers*, travelling by bus from Roadhouse to Roadhouse.
- *Package tourists*, visiting at least four different locations in two weeks. The tour operators have negotiated deals with the motel, resort and activity operators. If Australian tourists are excluded, a tourist company like 'Brits' operating in FNQ will be mainly dealing with German and Japanese tourists.

The Cassowary Beach Resort complex comprises:

- Four tropical-style residential areas located in 50 acres of rainforest. These areas are linked by under-cover flood-lit forest trails. The individual areas have distinctive names: Coral Sea, Barramundi Creek, Fernery Nest and Ulysees Falls. Each area comprises 12 self-contained, air-conditioned units with their own private patios. The relaxing tropical atmosphere is enhanced by the horseshoe lay-out of the areas which enclose landscaped pools of varying size and depth. These are planted with lush flora designed to provide not only privacy, but a natural rainforest pool ambience (as well as a croc-free zone!).
- The main hotel reception area. This includes information and booking services, a gift shop, a clothes boutique, the main hotel pool (where scuba-diving instruction is provided) and a pool-side bar.
- A formal restaurant and cocktail bar – the Rainforest Restaurant.
- The Beachcomber Bistro, a family style bistro serving food throughout the day. It is equipped with a wide screen satellite TV facility and a stage for live entertainment.

  The bistro is excellent value for the dollar and frequently crowded with locals, backpackers, German and Japanese package tourists, as well as other resort residents. The reason for this is that the local pub next door opens on to the bistro area; both the bistro and the pub are owned by the resort.
- The main pub is the focus of the Cassowary Beach community. Victoria Bitter flows almost round the clock and the pool tables are always busy. Noise levels

are high as the local radio station, 4KZ Cairns to Cardwell, is turned up high most days. At weekends the pub might be invaded by package tourists, cane-cutters, banana pickers, backpackers and barefoot 'feral' (Far North Queenslanders), all of whom guarantee a stimulating atmosphere. The local car hire company operates a 'booze bus', which drops off locals at their houses after closing time early each morning.

The resort complex is 100 metres from one of the small Cassowary Beach shopping centres. This includes an excellent Chinese restaurant and takeaway, a supermarket, a filling station, a few boutiques, Peg's Roadhouse and of course the bottle shop.

Concerns

The resort management are concerned as to the direction of the business. Their concern focuses on the increasing dependency of the business on the major tour operators who provide tour groups of 30 people or more for an average of three nights. Whilst this adversely affects margins in the busy winter season (from April onwards), it does provide a steady stream of visitors in the less popular rainy season.

The effects of the growing tour business are beginning to be felt throughout the resort. For example:

- The resort facilities are coming under increasing stress in the busy winter season . . . especially the staff on the Beachcomber Bistro, where most meals are served to the tour visitors.
- Reductions in the average length of stay.
- Language problems and misunderstandings with non-English speaking visitors.
- The rainforest accommodation is increasingly being referred to as a 'motel' (each unit has under-cover parking for cars on the outside of the horseshoe-shaped complex).
- A change in the visitor culture from Australian to overseas. This can be especially difficult when tour visitors from different cultures mingle in the pub with the locals and attempt to video FNO 'ferals' enjoying themselves.
- A decline in the more up-market independent visitors (both Australian and overseas), who prefer the more expensive, quality dedicated resorts on the coast or islands. The large tour coaches parked outside the reception area do not set the right tone for these visitors.
- These trends are having a knock-on effect. For example, numbers are rapidly declining in the Rainforest Restaurant and rapidly increasing in the Beachcomber Bistro. Additional income from resort-arranged tours and scuba-diving courses is declining, as tour operators began to deal directly with the providers.
- Independent visitors are beginning to drive down to the beach and dine at the smaller but more exclusive new Castaways resort.

The management consider that future growth in tourism will come from South East Asia. At present, however, the balance appears to be wrong and is generating too many problems.

Can you help? (The following targeting matrix may be useful (Figure 12.1).)

Figure 12.1 Cassowary beach resort: Targeting matrix

Facilities / Demographic Group	Rainforest Restaurant	Beachcomber Bistro	Hotel Units	Main Hotel Service	Bar
Foreign Packed Tours					
Australian Winter Escapers					
Rich Australians					
Rich Foreign Tourists					
Weekenders					
Backpackers					
Locals					

13
Carlsberg Ice Beer[1]

The beginning was really in 1991 with the intention to form Carlsberg-Tetley Brewing Ltd as a 50/50 joint venture between the brewing interests of Danish owned Carlsberg A/S and those of British-owned Allied-Lyons plc. The 1980s had been the decade of pan-European alliances and the logic of Carlsberg-Tetley as a joint venture in the UK market was clear. Allied had great strengths in ale with six breweries and a wide brand portfolio including national and regional ales. From a geographical point of view it was strongest in the North and Midlands. Allied also had strengths in directly delivered free trade outlets, and a tied estate of some 4,400 pubs (though this would later be reduced as a result of the so-called Beer Orders). By contrast, Carlsberg in the UK was a business based around a single brewery (additional supplies of Carlsberg were also being brewed under contract by Courage) with distribution generally arranged through third parties, mainly other brewers and wholesalers. However, Carlsberg had a tremendous UK reputation and a worldwide lager strength with over 60 breweries in 40 countries, which in the UK was focused solely on the Carlsberg brand and whose largest penetration had been achieved in the South of England.

Product and distribution complementarity was not the only logic behind the venture. Although standing in third place in the overall UK beer market, Allied's market share was well behind the leaders. Carlsberg and Tetley combined, however, would produce a third force able to challenge Bass and Courage for leadership.

The retail beer market can be divided into the on-trade (approximately 80 per cent) and the off- (or take-home) trade. An on-trade outlet is licensed to sell alcohol for consumption on and off the premises. The main on-trade outlets are public houses of which some are tied to the supply of particular beers through ownership by brewers, some are owned but controlled at arm's length (free on-trade) and others are independent (free trade). Other on-trade outlets include clubs and restaurants. The main off-trade outlets include specialist off-licences (multiples and independents) and multiple and independent grocers.

Having been delayed, pending an investigation by the Monopolies and Mergers Commission, Carlsberg-Tetley finally got together in January 1993 with a brand portfolio which included the best-selling bitter brand in the UK (Tetley) and a range of lagers which were either owned or brewed under licence.

The main lagers were:

- Carlsberg Pilsner, 3.4 per cent ABV, the fastest growing major draught standard

[1] This case was written in collaboration with Liz Morgan.

Table 13.1 Major brewers' shares of total United Kingdom final beer sales by type of beer and type of outlet, 1991 (%).

| | By type of beer | | | By type of outlet | | |
	Total	Ale	Lager	Tied on-trade	Free on-trade*	Off-trade
Allied	13	13	13	15	13	10
Carlsberg	1	0	2	0	2	1
	14	13	15	15	15	11
Bass	22	20	24	22	24	18
Courage/Grand Met	19	17	21	19	18	22
Whitbread	12	13	11	13	11	11
S&N	11	12	9	7	12	14
All national brewers and Carlsberg	78	75	80	75	80	76
All national brewers	77	75	78	76	78	75

Source: Allied/Carlsberg estimates and major brewers.
* Includes sales to independents.

lager in the UK on trade, supported by the famous 'Probably' campaign.
● Carlsberg Export, 4.7 per cent ABV, number two draught premium lager in the independent trade.
● Carlsberg Special Brew, 9 per cent ABV, the leading superstrength lager in the UK.
● Castlemaine XXXX, 3.9 per cent ABV, fastest growing major draught standard in free pubs, award winning advertising campaign.
● Skol, 3.4 per cent ABV, number two in the off-trade.
● Swan Light, 0.9 per cent ABV, number two selling low alcohol lager in the UK.
● Lowenbrau, 5.0 per cent ABV, leading German draught premium lager in UK.

Carlsberg-Tetley now felt it could claim a leading brand in every sector of the market. However, there was a general feeling that while performance had been solid, it had not been exciting. With the Carlsberg brand itself this had largely been deliberate. Carlsberg had steered clear of radical innovations in the beer market (such as Dry Beer) in order to avoid diluting its credentials as the custodian of traditional, quality lager beer values. Nevertheless management sensed that Carlsberg-Tetley had not had a great story to stir the trade and the public since the launch of Castlemaine XXXX in 1984.

Additionally, it was recognised that the Carlsberg-Tetley presence in the Premium Packaged Lager (PPL) segment was not as strong as desired. PPL was now equivalent to 10 per cent of the total beer market and growing at a rate of 7 per cent year on year. This contrasted with the premium draught lager sector which accounted for only 5 per cent of the market and was growing at only 1 per cent per annum and standard draught lager at 25 per cent of the total market, the largest sector, but declining by 5 per cent year on year. Increasingly PPL drinkers were looking for an ABV per cent above 5 per cent and were looking for ever increasing quality and distinctiveness.

The Ice Sector

The Ice Beer Process was developed by Labatt and introduced in Canada in April 1993. The process involves freezing all the beer at –4°C and then gently removing the ice crystals. The result was said to be a 'uniquely balanced smooth tasting beer' and an ABV per cent of 5.6.

Labatt's were not to be alone in the market for long. Molson introduced their own beer in Canada in 1993 but using a different process. Their beer was 'super-chilled' rather than frozen leading to an ABV per cent of 5 and, purportedly, not quite able to replicate the same degree of smoothness and balance.

In July 1993 intelligence from Canada suggested that ice beer had rapidly gained as much as 8 per cent of the total beer market, equally divided between Labatt and Molson. However the impression within the on and off-trade was that there was a 'definite possibility' that ice could be another short-lived fad like 'dry'. In the short term, however, Labatt had other worries. In August they filed an injunction against Molson's use of the term 'ice-brewed'. They issued the following press release:

> We have a responsibility to our shareholders, to our employees, and to our consumers to put a stop to false and misleading claims by Molson. We are also taking this step to protect the $25 million investment we have made in developing the exclusive ice brewing process which gives us this unique product.
>
> We created the Ice Beer category and Labatt Ice Beer™ is the only legitimate entry. However, in recent weeks Molson has deliberately attempted to create confusion in the minds of consumers by re-labelling several conventionally-brewed brands as 'ice-brewed'. If it's not Labatt, it's not Ice Brewed™.
>
> Labatt Ice Beer uses exclusive equipment and a proprietary technology developed in the Labatt experimental brewery in London, Ontario. The company has applied for patents on the technology, and is in discussions with brewers around the world regarding potential licensing agreements.

One such brewer was Carlsberg-Tetley, who already had good trading relationships with Labatt in the UK and had helped establish Labatt Ice Beer in the on-trade through their extensive distribution network. Carlsberg-Tetley thus had early recognition of the response to Labatt Ice Beer and results were coming in of launches in other countries. In Australia Ice Beer from Carlton and United Breweries captured over 10 per cent of the beer market within four months. Share in Canada had by the end of 1993 risen to 12 per cent of the beer market. In the USA ice beer had a 4 per cent share. Perhaps most impressive of all was Labatt's sales of two million cans in six months in Japan, making it the leading imported beer there.

The questions facing Carlsberg-Tetley seemed to be:

- Would ice beer become a long-term sustainable opportunity or would it be a short-term fad?
- Would the introduction of an ice beer under the Carlsberg brand endanger its position as a serious brewer?
- Was there room for another ice brew market entrant?
- What would be the impact on Labatt ice sales if Carlsberg-Tetley introduced its own brand?

- If Carlsberg-Tetley did introduce an ice brew should it use the Labatt process?

The last question was the easiest. Although Carlsberg-Tetley would have to pay royalties to Labatt, they would gain a number of benefits. First they would be able to offer a 'genuine' ice brew. This would provide one point of differentiation against most competitors as well as preserving Carlsberg's genuine credentials. Second it would maintain and build good relationships with Labatt. Third the Labatt process could be easily accommodated in Carlsberg-Tetley's Wrexham brewery.

The other Labatt issue was only slightly more problematic. While there would clearly be some element of competition between Carlsberg and Labatt, it was generally felt that a Carlsberg brew using the same process would boost the total sector to the benefit of both brewers. A further point on which Carlsberg-Tetley were relatively happy was that there would be sufficient scope for differentiation of Carlsberg from Labatt. Different recipes and ingredients in addition to the benefits of the Labatt process would result in product variation. The scope for differentiation through packaging and promotion was also thought to be considerable.

In terms of the third question, American experience suggested that the number of entrants would increase. Within 12 months of Labatt's launch in North America, there were 30 ice brands on the market. Carlsberg-Tetley formed the view that if they could be satisfied on the first two questions then an early launch in the UK market would give them a measure of protection against subsequent followers. 'Early' really meant 'second'.

Debate within Carlsberg-Tetley focused on these questions and associated issues. While some saw ice as just another fad, there was also the possibility, at the other extreme, that with its perceived quality advantages the ice brew could develop into a mainstream process. A parallel dichotomy existed in respect of the Carlsberg brand. On the one hand, without a new sub-brand for 20 years, it had avoided being associated with gimmicks. On the other hand, without any innovation for 20 years, was the brand in need of some regeneration? Carlsberg-Tetley decided to submit the issues to research.

Preliminary research had led Carlsberg-Tetley to the conclusion that ice beer could have strong potential but only if managed carefully, and further, that it could play a role in enhancing the Carlsberg brand credentials within the PPL sector and in revitalising the brand in general – but again, subject to careful handling. Accordingly further qualitative research was commissioned to increase understanding of the emerging ice beer opportunity within the PPL sector.

Project rapide

Ten focus groups were held in London and Manchester covering the following drinkers of more than six bottles/pints per week of premium lager.

- Labatt Ice trialists, aged 20–25
- Carlsberg loyalists, aged 25–40
- Carlsberg rejectors, aged 18–25
- PPL/PDL (defined as most often drinkers of Budweiser, Beck's, Molson Dry, Rolling Rock, Oranjeboom, Grolsch, Coors, etc.), aged 18–25 and 25–35.

Discussion topics included drinking behaviour and attitudes, recent innovations, brand imagery, awareness and expectations of the ice beer concept, reactions to Carlsberg Ice Beer and alternative packaging graphics.

Ice trialists had so far tended to be 'serial experimenters' and 'promiscuous' within the PPL category. Research suggested their approval, if not enthusiasm, towards product performance. It also appeared that the product story was not well understood and that the product concept of 'balance' had not yet been grasped. Perceptions of current packaging were not favourable, adding to the problems of visibility caused by limited distribution. Trialists had rarely repeat purchased. In short, ice beer was not yet established.

Non-ice trialists showed immediate curiosity as to the reason for the development, but on balance expected it to be more of a sales gimmick than an enhanced product until they tested the product itself. However they did associate innovation with the PPL sector.

Among respondents in general there was an expectation that an ice beer would emerge from a brewer with one or all of the following characteristics:

- record of innovation, PPL credentials, brewing excellence
- affinity with a cold climate
- a need to enter the PPL sector

Figure 13.1

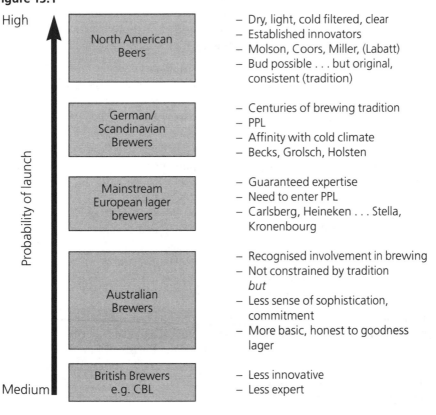

High

North American Beers
- Dry, light, cold filtered, clear
- Established innovators
- Molson, Coors, Miller, (Labatt)
- Bud possible . . . but original, consistent (tradition)

German/ Scandinavian Brewers
- Centuries of brewing tradition
- PPL
- Affinity with cold climate
- Becks, Grolsch, Holsten

Mainstream European lager brewers
- Guaranteed expertise
- Need to enter PPL
- Carlsberg, Heineken . . . Stella, Kronenbourg

Australian Brewers
- Recognised involvement in brewing
- Not constrained by tradition
  but
- Less sense of sophistication, commitment
- More basic, honest to goodness lager

British Brewers e.g. CBL
- Less innovative
- Less expert

Probability of launch

Medium

Reaction to the notion of Carlsberg introducing an ice beer was generally one of modest surprise but not real resistance. Amongst existing Carlsberg drinkers 'hard core' loyalists were perplexed by the proposal, while those who included Carlsberg within a wider repertoire were more open-minded. Further reflection led to the view that Carlsberg must consider ice beer to be a genuine innovation in brewing technology because it would not risk its reputation for a 'quick buck'.

Carlsberg-Tetley management felt that Project Rapide research had been sufficiently encouraging to move ahead with further product research and development, and consideration of positioning concepts. It seemed that Ice Beer could potentially complement the existing Carlsberg range and result in a portfolio that was clearly targeted at distinct types of drinkers (and perhaps, drinking occasions) and yet remain consistent with Carlsberg's overall desired positioning as 'The best quality sessionable lager, brewed with experience and expertise'. The management pondered on the possibilities:

Carlsberg Pilsner brewed for......................................

Carlsberg Export brewed for ....

Carlsberg Special Brew brewed for ....

Carlsberg Ice Beer brewed for ....

Beyond this, the ultimate opportunity lay in the possibility that Carlsberg's association with brewing excellence could bring further endorsement to ice beers while the introduction of ice beer could lead to a re-discovery of Carlsberg. Clearly the realisation of this potential symbiosis depended on how effectively Carlsberg-Tetley implemented the positioning strategy. The key issues seemed to be:

1. How to identify and describe the target drinkers.
2. How to convey the taste and drinking benefits produced by ice brewing.
3. How to add an appropriate emotional dimension to the functional benefits.
4. How to use a more measured and less brash tone of voice than existing ice brands so as to convey more self-confidence.
5. How to manage the branding process so that Carlsberg values are linked to ice beer without the Carlsberg name swamping the identity of ice beer.
6. How to package and advertise the product in line with the considerations above.
7. How to price.
8. Where to distribute.

Two further general decisions needed to be addressed:

9. What taste formulation to settle on.
10. How much investment to put behind the launch.

In terms of consumer segmentation, Carlsberg-Tetley management had been searching for a more appropriate basis than demographics. The pressure to find a solution had hitherto not been so great since the Carlsberg brand, albeit with a leaning towards lighter and older users, had traditionally appealed to a wide range of users. In fact, research had shown that Carlsberg was second and third choice amongst a wide variety of drinkers.

It was now becoming clear, however, that to achieve preference more attention needed to be paid to tighter segmentation and to better understanding consumer needs and wants. One approach under consideration, based on TGI data, led to the view that 'Good Time Men' was the market of principal interest to Carlsberg (Figure 13.2), with the possibility that 'Good Time Boys' (Figure 13.3) might be the right target for Carlsberg Ice Beer. Whilst 'Good Time Men' could be considered as 'Good Time Boys' who had grown up, there was also a degree of cross-over. TGI data showed that such profiles applied to above-average consumers of lager from all ages and social grades.

Figure 13.2

WHAT THEY READ	ASPIRATIONS	WHAT THEY WEAR
Time Out	Golf GTi	Timberland
Car Week	MG	Kickers
Loaded	Convertibles	Levis
Q		
NEWSPAPERS Classic & Sports Car		
The Guardian Mojo		
The Independent Today		

Good Time Men

FILMS	TV	SPORT
The Crying Game	Whose Line is it Anyway	Rugby
Much Ado About Nothing	Red Dwarf	Motor Racing
Philadelphia	Absolutely	Cricket
Unforgiven	Northern Exposure	Snooker
RADIO	Channel 4 News	Football
GLR	Southbank Show	
JFM	Cutting Edge	
Virgin	American Football	

Figure 13.3

WHAT THEY READ	ASPIRATIONS	WHAT THEY WEAR
Vox	Motorbikes	Fila
GQ	Jeeps	Stussy
Performance Car	Harley Davidsons	Lonsdale
Penthouse	Porsche	Diesel Jeans
Sky		Caterpillar
Viz		
90 Minutes		

Good Time Boys

NEWSPAPERS
Daily Mirror
The Sun

FILMS		TV	SPORT
True Lies	**RADIO**	Big Breakfast	Football
Sliver	Capital FM	Games Master	Horse Racing
Wayne's World	Kiss FM	Vic Reeve's Big Night Out	
	Faze FM	Beavis & Butthead	
		Spitting Image	
		Men Behaving Badly	
		Beverly Hills 90210	
		The Word	

A second approach was based on the degree to which consumers exhibited different degrees of dependence on beer as a vehicle for self-expression (Figure 13.4).

With the target consumer in mind, the Carlsberg-Tetley team began to develop a tentative marketing plan for a possible launch of Carlsberg Ice and its subsequent development. The basic brand proposition which was emerging was: 'Only

Figure 13.4

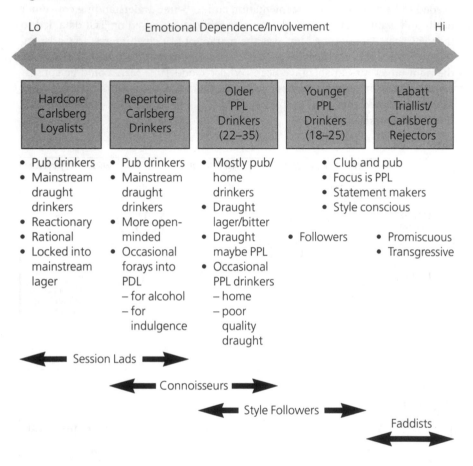

Carlsberg achieves the desired balance between the distinctiveness of ice beer and the heritage, authority and confidence of an international brewer's reputation'. Was this strong enough to motivate consumer and trade?

Project Rapide packaging research had shown clear preference for one of the packaging alternatives – a 330 ml. long-neck amber bottle with screen-printed white and silver graphics. But was it sufficiently distinctive and was the graphic balance between Carlsberg and ice beer about right to make it 'clearly Carlsberg but distinctively ice beer'?

Initial thoughts on pricing suggested a premium to Labatt Ice. This might help support a long-term objective to become a mainstream PPL competing with Beck's and Budweiser, but would it make it difficult to secure initial distribution? Maybe not, if distribution were deliberately built slowly, targeting initially only leading-edge brasseries, café bars, wine bars and night clubs.

Meanwhile additional product research based on refined formulations was looking even more favourable. A total of 138 male PPL drinkers aged 18–30 produced the following responses. The beer was better than expected said 64 per cent;

82 per cent claimed they would definitely/probably buy; and 21 per cent said it was better than their usual brand.

Within a fortnight, however, Fosters Ice Beer was launched in June, making it the second UK ice contender and re-focusing attention on Carlsberg's approach to promotional activity. Estimates suggested that a combined total of £7.5 million was being spent on product launch by Fosters and Labatt. Would Carlsberg need to spend similarly to be noticed or would the visibility created by Labatt and Fosters create sufficient interest for consumers to actively seek out other brands to try?

The die was cast for the moment. The trade press was alerted on 4 July and a full briefing of the Carlsberg selling team would take place on 1 August. Support material would be available to the trade from mid-August. Carlsberg Ice Beer had arrived but the debate was by no means over. The first indications of success or otherwise would not appear until October when distribution, rate of sale, repeat purchase and response to promotional campaigns would be subject to their first evaluation. Had Carlsberg brewed up a hot prospect or would the icy future be a bleak one?

Questions for Discussion

1. How critical was it for Carlsberg to be first or second into the UK market with an ice beer product?
2. How important was it for Carlsberg-Tetley to have a significant presence in each product sector?
3. Do you see an increasing number of ice beer market entrants as contributing to a growing of the whole sector or as reducing the prospects of profitable sales for each competitor?
4. If one of the motives behind launching Carlsberg Ice Beer was to revitalise the brand, what alternative strategies could Carlsberg-Tetley have considered?
5. What were the risks in stretching the Carlsberg brand across the ice beer product? How real are the risks and what can be done to minimise them?
6. Which of the models discussed in Chapter 3 can best be used to explain Carlsberg Ice Beers' desired brand positioning?
7. Given that the Carlsberg brand generally appealed to a wide range of consumers why was it felt necessary to develop a more targeted approach for Ice Beer?
8. Which of the two segmentations being explored by Carlsberg-Tetley appears more helpful in terms of formulating and implementing marketing strategy?
9. What are the advantages and disadvantages of Carlsberg Ice Beer's relatively modest launch compared to a higher profile campaign?
10. What factors will determine the success of the ice beer sector in total? Which of the competitors is more likely to be successful, and why?
11. Will consumers come to perceive ice beers as a distinct product category? What factors inform your prediction?

14

Montpellier Spa Water[1]

It was the summer of 1994 when the public analyst confirmed the preliminary findings on the Cotswold bore hole. This significant reserve of water was pronounced suitable for all domestic purposes, including drinking. More importantly, the source below privately-owned farmland near Cheltenham, qualified under European directives as 'Natural Mineral Water'.

European directives state that natural mineral water (for example, Brecon, Highland Spring, Spa and Evian) must be extracted from the ground untreated, except for basic processing and filtration *and bottled at source*. This is in contrast to:

- Naturally carbonated natural mineral water (for example, Perrier, Badoit and Vichy), which is sparkling at source. The carbon dioxide can be removed before it is bottled and then re-introduced, providing that the final product contains less rather than more CO_2 (than it would have contained in the natural state).
- Carbonated natural mineral water (for example, Malvern, Highland Spring and Brecon), which is the sparkling version of natural mineral water with added CO_2.
- Spring Water. Although most spring waters have sought re-classification as natural mineral waters, products such as Ashbourne Natural Water need only comply with regulations on the quality of water for human consumption. This product classification has the advantage that they can be bottled away from the source.

The year before, Amelie Andersson had finally secured the rights to use the 'Montpellier Spa'[2] identity in the UK. In the meantime her leisure enterprises, in both her native Sweden and the UK, comprising health farms, sports centres and dedicated restaurants, had prospered to the point when she was seriously considering an attractive offer equivalent to £20m and a part-time management contract from a major European catering company. The time could be right to sell out the Swedish-controlled business and move on to her next European business challenge: the manufacture and distribution of a natural mineral water with the aim of establishing a viable position in the UK's £250m market.

In her own business links with the UK, Amelie had become aware of a number of factors impacting upon the market for mineral water, which might offer

[1] The data included in this case material has been modified for student learning purposes and should not therefore be used for research purposes.
[2] This did not extend to the European Union given French opposition to the implication that Montpellier referred to the town in the South of France.

opportunities to entrepreneurs such as herself. These may be summarised under two headings. The first was the more sophisticated 'continental' lifestyle of the upwardly mobile, which over time also affected the less prosperous. These trends were evidenced by the increasing incidence of foreign travel, wine consumption, eating out and the expectation of higher service standards. The second factor was the increasing concern with the natural environment as expressed by the trend towards more natural, purer products. In relation to tap water these concerns were reinforced by real concern about water pollution which was focused upon:

- The carcinogenic hazards of excessive nitrates (mainly from fertilisers) and the disinfecting process at water treatment plants.
- Lead from old pipes and the possible effects of lead poisoning.
- The build-up of aluminium which is frequently used to improve the translucence of water. Alum is often added as part of the cleaning process for reservoirs. This in turn may be linked to the occurrence of Alzheimer's disease as well as being significant for people with kidney failure.
- The build-up of Trihalomethanes, another possible carcinogenic, as a result of water treated with chlorine.

There is a conflict between the interests of shareholders and the interests of improved water. Private water may not mean healthier water, as the water companies can save investment by letting the water quality deteriorate. This is even more alarming as the quality of drinking water at the start point for privatisation was low by European standards. In December 1985, for example, the Department of the Environment acknowledged that most Water Authorities were supplying water below agreed European standards. If it were not for the threat of European legal action, improving the quality of the UK's water might well be a 'pipe dream'.

The quality and safety of drinking water in the UK varies by region, depending upon the sources and the incidence of re-cycling. Cleanest water in general terms is found in the West and North of the country, where the incidence of ground and reservoir water is highest. The lowest quality is to be found in London and the South East, where there is higher dependence upon a combination of surface water, rivers and re-cycling. (In urban areas such as London, tap water may be drawn in part from water that has been re-cycled up to eight times.) In these sources there is greater risk from nitrate contamination.

The UK market

Although per capita consumption of mineral water remains one of the lowest in the European Union, the UK market has seen dramatic growth in the 1980's (see Table 14.1).

The life cycle of the mineral water market appears to comprise a number of distinct phases identifiable with classic market life-cycle theory:

1. The advent of primary demand manifest as an expanding discrete sector of the wider soft drinks market.

Table 14.1

Total volume in m/lts. (amended from Euromonitor)	
1986	+20%
1987	+36%
1988	+43%
1989	+30%

2. Market development and the 'first window of opportunity'. This stage has been characterised by the domination of the major European suppliers. Given that the European product mix includes 'natural mineral water', these suppliers are required to bottle at source and incur heavy distribution costs before their products can be distributed by national UK distribution networks.
3. Market fragmentation and the development of new sectors. Examples include catering and bulk mineral water supply, the development of the hotel sector, the development of 'flavoured' variants and the take-off of the supermarket own-label sector. At the same time this stage was characterised by the advent of local competition, 'without the trace of a foreign accent'. The entry of these mainly 'spring waters', was characterised by aggressive competition from large numbers of local competitors (perhaps encouraged by the demise of Perrier).
4. The 'shakeout', as the weakest competitors bow out, having suffered serious losses consequent upon volume shortfalls and price competition.
5. The second phase of market growth and second strategic window of opportunity. This is the current situation which Amelie believes can be exploited if her timing and marketing strategy is appropriate.

The difficulty is to find a way into this highly competitive market where the only markers of differentiation appear to be the shape of the bottle and the colour of the label. Although market opportunities may become more apparent from segmentation studies, there appears to be no consensus as to modes of segmentation. It is quite acceptable to segment the market on a number of different criteria.

The following are examples of acceptable candidate modes of segmentation:

- By product type (as established by legal directives: Natural Mineral Water; Spring Water; Naturally Carbonated Natural Mineral Water; Carbonated Natural Mineral Water)
- By region (given the importance of variations in the local water quality and purity)
- By customer lifestyle
- By trade sector
- By health concern
- By taste
- By price

The UK market differs from continental markets in terms of product type. In value terms the UK market segments 70 per cent in favour of sparkling variants, whereas the opposite is true of the continental situation where 'still' water predominates. On a volume basis, however, a 50:50 split between the two product types is more realistic. The forward trend appears to be the growth of the still sector, fuelled by the supermarkets in the belief that the UK will follow a similar market structure to the European model. Growth, therefore, may be concentrated in the least profitable segment of the market . . . own-label mainly 'still' products.

The UK market is also characterised by the polarisation between a limited number of major manufacturers and the supermarket own-label brands. Numerous smaller manufacturers are 'stuck in the middle', fighting for second brand listings in national food chains. The dominance of the own-label brands refers to an estimated 50 per cent volume share of the 'still' sector and some 40 per cent of the sparkling sector. These figures would be higher if the base was revised to solus supermarket outlets. This suggests that there is little room for major branded products outside of Perrier in the sparkling sector and Evian in the still sector, who are estimated to hold 30 per cent and 12 per cent value shares respectively of the total market. This compares to a supermarket total value share of some 28 per cent, which leaves only a 30 per cent value share for all other brands. The prospect of new entries being squeezed between the major nationally advertised brands and the own-label sector is not attractive, especially when the unit price analysis is considered. This is set out below:

Amelie remained optimistic, as she believed that most of the major distributors

Table 14.2 Where the money goes

% of VAT exclusive RSP; (retail selling price) and MSP; (manufacturers selling price)		
Item	Sparkling 1.5lt.	Still 1.5lt.
Vat exclusive RSP	100	100
Retail margin @ 27% on return	27	27
Manufacturer's selling price (MSP)	73	73
Manufacturer's profit	15	10
Bottle/Cap	31	37
Label/Packaging	9	8
Processing	18	20
Marketing	12	8
Distribution	15	17

and supermarket chains were looking through the wrong end of the telescope, as they sought to apply mass merchandising techniques to a highly individual market and had yet to address the real environmental and consumer concerns.

Consumer data indicates that some 35 per cent of adults had drunk mineral water during 1993, up from 22 per cent in 1985. Of these, heavy users, classified as those who drink mineral water more than twice a week, comprised some 31 per cent of total drinkers. These frequent drinkers were concentrated in London and the South East and in AB socio-economic groups. (Source: BMRB Amended.) Significantly 40 per cent of all value mineral water sales occur in Greater London. Whilst Amelie recognised that 'Southern Yuppies' had pioneered the market in the

1980's, the way forward was with ordinary people, mainly women, who had serious environmental concerns. The question was one of *ethical marketing*: how best to raise the level of concern, without appearing irresponsible; and how best to capitalise upon this in terms of marketing strategy.

Distribution Channels

If the market is segmented by distribution channel it may appear to be less contested. Broadly the market may be divided into the 'take-home' market, 70 per cent of total value, and the 'drink-out' market comprising the balance. Taking the analysis a stage further, resulting distribution channels and opportunity areas may include:

- Branded products through supermarkets.
- Manufacture of own-label products.
- Branded products through off-licences.
- Branded products to hotel and catering organisations.
- Bulk products to hotels and catering organisations.
- Branded products to on-licences (public houses and bars).
- Bulk product to institutions both private and public.
- Specialist products to hospitals and health organisations.

Physical distribution for a product category that might require bottling at source is a significant added expense in this market. Much depends upon building strategic alliances, in order to source a distribution network with access to the required channel coverage. Perrier, for example, established its position with the help of a distribution deal with Britvic, which gave them access to Britvic's network of 250,000 retail outlets. When the benzene scare broke, other products served by the Britvic distribution network (Buxton and Ballygowan) were well-placed to fill the void. Other distribution companies include the BSN group (Evian); A.G. Barr (Highland Spring); Food Brokers (Ramlosa); and Cranbie Eustace (Spa and Brecon).

Entry to non-food distribution channels is normally based upon the same formula of strategic alliances. In this case the distributors are more specialised. Examples might include Grand Metropolitan Brewing for pubs and clubs; Matthew Clark & Sons Ltd for the licensed trade; the cash and carry wholesalers and catering wholesalers for the vast and fragmented catering market. Serious penetration of the catering sector might, however, depend upon an alliance with one of the big two catering companies, Compass (Grand Metropolitan) or Gardner Merchant (Trusthouse Forte). Second league catering companies such as Sutcliffe or ARA Services could also be approached for more specialist distribution. The appeal of the catering sector for the smaller manufacturer is that success might be achieved more quickly than in the retail market, as a limited number of direct customers are targeted who will require a product made to precise specifications.

Trade margins vary considerably by distribution channel (for example, the estimated margin on return for the 'take-home' channel is 27 per cent and 72.5 per cent for the 'drink-out' channel). There is a considerable difference therefore between market sector values at retail value and market values at manufacturers' value (MSP/RSP factor). Drink-out channels are generally characterised by the very high prices per litre compared to comparatively low prices for similar or identical products on the supermarket shelf. This rarely benefits the manufacturer who is expected to supply to the institutional trade at similar prices to those obtained by supermarket groups. Coming to terms with this market, therefore, is being realistic about the power of intermediaries to dictate terms.

Your Tasks

In the form of a management report prepare a proposal which addresses the following issues:

1. Determine appropriate marketing objectives for the launch of Montpellier Spa.
2. Formulate an outline marketing plan with a three-year time horizon.
3. Establish the key issues of implementation which would require critical attention.
4. Determine how the success or failure of your proposals will be measured.

You are free to make whatever assumptions may be necessary to support your proposals, provided that they are consistent with the body of information presented in the case material.

In addition:

5. Discuss the implications of market life cycle theory on market entry decisions.
6. Recommend strategies for manufacturers to limit the ability of distribution channels to dictate terms.
7. Consider the importance of lifestyle segmentation in deciding marketing strategy.

15
Roses Grow On You

The Crisis

In the autumn of 1990 John Scarman faced the deepest crisis of his business life. In the seven years since he founded Roses du Temps Passé (RTP) there had been some very close shaves; but these had been weathered, and the growth of the company had in fact been very much in line with the original Business Plan he developed in 1983. This was different. The Business Plan had projected a turnover for 1991 of some £225,000. In the second half of 1990, order intake within the UK had virtually disappeared and John's most realistic forecasts for 1991 now suggested a sales level of only £50,000. How ironic, but also fortunate, John reflected, that he had only just received joint first prize in the Staffordshire European Awards for export achievements by small businesses. Fortunate, because there had been a £2,000 cash prize.

The medium-term future looked very bleak, with John beginning to question the very strategies that had led to RTP's foundation and success. The immediate prospect, however, was even worse. RTP had entered into a contract with a Leicestershire grower to purchase 100,000 roses per annum at a fixed price. There seemed to be no prospect of either selling the roses or of being able to pay for them.

As he grappled with the problem, John's mind began to wander back to when it all started.

Beginnings

John's early career could not have seemed further removed from his present predicament as a rose-grower in deepest agricultural Staffordshire. And yet, it was some of this early experience which was to sow the seeds of future ideas.

Having joined EMI as a management trainee, John was soon appointed as Personal Assistant to the International Managing Director. As such, much of his time was spent working on licensing and franchising deals for music and musical equipment for a variety of smaller overseas markets. The perks of the job included attendance at Beatles' recording sessions in Abbey Road. Later appointments included EMI General Manager in Kenya and Marketing Manager in Nigeria.

In his mid-20's, family reasons prompted a return to the UK and John joined a London-based confirming house. A deep love of the country and of natural history meant this was a less than satisfactory way of life and prompted the sort of step that perhaps only those suited to the risks of self-employment might take. A personal advert in *The Times* offered the young international executive's services as a private gardener. Private gardening at prestigious homes in Gloucestershire and Hampshire provided both enjoyment and learning and prepared John for his subsequent appointment as Head Gardener at Weston Park, a stately home with extensive gardens in the south of Staffordshire.

Working at Weston brought John into contact with those who practised the 'old fashioned gardening ways' and taught him 'skills which had been lost in most communities'. Most horticultural colleges' curricula, by contrast, assumed that the majority of students would ply their trade in local authority Parks Departments. The move to Weston Park required a new home and the Scarman family rented a cottage and three acres within the grounds of Woodlands House in nearby Stretton. The cottage and land were to feature prominently in the business-to-be. After several years at Weston Park, John became Nursery Manager at David Austin Roses. David Austin was high amongst the list of top rose-breeders in the UK and was perhaps the ideal place to learn the business.

The Concept

Representing David Austin Roses at a London flower show in 1982, John was intrigued by a conversation with a stand visitor from Tours in the French Loire Valley. Adrianne Niesburg had rued the absence in France of old-fashioned roses – the very ones which had emanated from France and been so popular in the period after Napoleon. The germ of an idea took hold and after further correspondence with Adrianne, John visited Tours in the summer of 1983. Both he and Adrianne felt that, not only had the old roses been forgotten, but that roses in general were not being marketed seriously in France. Although Adrianne had no business experience, the two began to formulate a new product concept.

They believed that France's interest in its 'glorious historical past' allied to a specially selected range of fragrant roses would provide a consumer proposition which would fire the imagination. John smiled at the prospect of the restoration of this lost French art by an English rose-grower. It would be in the best traditions of selling coals to Newcastle . . . if it came off. The successful establishment of the concept appeared to rest heavily on the brand name. It had to convey - simply, succinctly and memorably - the intended positioning in the market place. 'Roses du temps Passé' was born.

In the meantime John had already agreed with David Austin that, as a means of supplementing his income, he would be free to grow some roses for export at his home. Following the initial meeting with Adrianne in London he had thus planted a balanced collection of 5,000 roses, specifically with France in mind. He had also begun to research and write the catalogue which would be central to the presentation of the concept. Not only would this need to feature high quality photographs and general information relating to growing conditions and maintenance, but it would have to provide the historical background and heritage of each variety. Long days were filled with heavy gardening and delicate photographic work. Long evenings were spent on reading and writing.

The first edition of the catalogue featured 90 varieties in contrast to the 200 or so varieties offered by David Austin and the 700 total number of rose varieties. It was thus entitled *A Selective Guide to Old Roses* and John was hopeful that this more focused approach would simplify matters for the consumer as well as differentiate himself from a conventional rose-grower.

The catalogue itself was seen as more than the main promotional tool. It was also an integral part of the product. Not only did it define RTP's product concept, but it allowed the reader into a world of history, fragrance and form previously only accessible to the few 'cognescenti'. The outside front cover set the scene with a delicate 1798 painting of Rose de Meaux while the inside front cover featured a colour photograph of a magnificent rose border at Woodlands house, with the following copy on the facing page:

> The Old Cottage Garden roses were, curiously, nearly all French in origin. They were preserved in Cottage Gardens during the time that the Victorian Gardeners were competing with each other growing ever larger and brighter English Hybrids.
>
> Thanks to people like Gertrude Jekyll and Vita Sackville West, who had a great appreciation of the charm and delicacy of these plants, and their many uses, we are able to recreate some of the joys of the earlier gardens.
>
> The charm of these roses is that they can be planted as they used to be; with herbaceous plants, herbs and lavenders. Fortunately, well over a thousand varieties survived, and the collection in the catalogue represents a selection of the most reliable and interesting of these fascinating plants.

Each rose in the catalogue was accompanied by a colour photograph plus a description of the plant in terms of origin, fragrance and any other notable factors. This contrasted with the dry product descriptions without photographs typical of most rose catalogues of the time. The catalogue also contained guidance on planting schemes, pruning, budding and other aspects of cultivation and maintenance.

As catalogue preparation proceeded, it became clear that Adrianne was not going to be able to do the required job in France. Her initial prompting and enthusiasm would not translate into the necessary skills and commitment. This would not be the first time that apparent good fortune and convenience were not tempered with a sufficient degree of realism.

Events nearer to home were also about to take a new turn. Having joined David Austin, John had envisaged that he would progress to the point where he would be offered equity participation. This possibility receded early in 1984 when another family member decided to join the business. The die was cast sooner than expected. John and David parted on amicable terms and the redundancy money permitted the catalogue to be printed. With this alone accounting for some £1,000 for 2,000 copies, John joined the then Training and Enterprise Allowance Scheme which provided a £40 weekly allowance for start-up businesses.

The initial assumptions about the French market were that it would take at least ten years to establish a new name in the rose industry. Since nearly all names were based on a person or a location, it had been decided to use a different approach which encapsulated the product concept in an imaginative and romantic way. With Adrianne, and France, out of the picture, John had the catalogue printed in English, retaining the Rose du Temps Passé name. Since there was no direct translation, John was concerned over its comprehensibility and acceptability in the UK.

Nevertheless RTP was registered as a partnership, with share capital and functions divided equally between John and wife Teresa.

The first task was to plant a further 6,000 roses. The second was to sell the initial 5,000 which would become available for market in the autumn. The first problem was a cash flow crisis, which was temporarily resolved with a £1,000 bank overdraft. The cash shortage was also a severe constraint on promotional activities. Partly through force of circumstances and partly through scepticism as to the benefits of advertising, marketing communications and promotional activities were restricted to attempts to secure press coverage.

Media interest was negligible. With hindsight John reflected that he must have failed to define sufficiently accurately the essence of the business and had not been able to convey its 'newness' to the extent that editors were inspired to write about it. By the end of October, the roses were ready but the orders were not. The bank wanted to call in the overdraft. The new venture might not survive its first year. Immediate action was needed.

John's response was to design an innovative gift voucher featuring card with rose, and showing catalogue details. The donor could pre-pay allowing the recipient to order roses up to this value direct from RTP. Press releases were written majoring on the new gift voucher concept rather than the rose concept. The media response this time was different and instant. Editorials appeared in the *Financial Times*, *The Times* and the *Daily Telegraph* in the same week. The whole rose stock was sold and at an average price of £4.00 retail, turnover in the first year of operation was £24,000.

The lesson on the value of media coverage was not lost. Principally in an attempt to develop a more planned approach to public relations activities, the decision was made to exhibit at the Chelsea Flower Show in 1985. John believed that Chelsea would allow him to build close relationships with the media and would provide the opportunity to meet with customers. He felt that this was important for a direct mail business like his. Although Woodlands House offered a facility for personal callers, this was not on the scale of what competitors such as David Austin and Peter Beales could offer through their extensive nurseries and their wholesaling and retailing activities. Finally, John's desire to be taken seriously within the industry suggested that the visibility and prestige offered by Chelsea would be indispensable.

Exhibiting at Chelsea is by invitation from the Royal Horticultural Society. The space is free of charge, but the other costs are high. Stand design and construction and the transport of exhibition material, plus the cost of ten days' accommodation in London are major direct expenses for a cash-starved small business. Perhaps even more damaging are the opportunity costs – the time which cannot be spent on growing, marketing and running the business. The attention and detail necessary for Chelsea were highly time-consuming. On top of this were the costs and problems associated with forcing roses into bloom approximately one month early. The only way in which exhibiting so early in RTP's development was possible was by sharing a stand. Collaboration was the only means of overcoming the shortage of time, money and plants to show. The partner was Jane Fearnley-Whittingstall, a garden designer whose commissions had included an exhibit sponsored at Chelsea by Christies, the auctioneers. A by-product of this collaboration was a developing interest in the principles and practice of garden design, an interest which would prove crucial in the years to come.

Another by-product of Chelsea '85 was the chance to meet the French media. This was to result in a half page article in *Le Figaro* magazine. The impending appearance of this article redirected John's attention back to France. The catalogue was translated into French and the classified columns of a French gardening magazine, *L' Ami du Jardin*, were used to advertise for an agent. The only respondent with a background in horticulture was a Monsieur Maugar, a nurseryman from Brittany specialising in herbaceous plants. Maugar visited Stretton and the return visit revealed a smallish operation, dealing mainly with passing trade but with some garden design and maintenance.

The arrangements which were negotiated were intended to provide an economical and simple entré into France for RTP. RTP would arrange promotion from the UK which would result in direct orders to Maugar. Maugar would collect payment and send order requirements to RTP who would then consolidate the individually-packed, bare-rooted dormant roses. Shipment would be made by road to Maugar using only one set of export documents and sanitary certificates to cover the whole consignment. Maugar would then post to individual customers. Once delivered, Maugar would remit 70 per cent of the rose sales value to RTP. The business would be as profitable as UK domestic market sales because the French average retail price was fixed at the equivalent of £5. This compared with £4 charged in the UK, a level which was set to be 10 per cent below David Austin and Peter Beales. In addition, the cost of postage to individual customers was borne by Maugar while RTP only shipped in bulk.

The response to the *Le Figaro* editorial was also huge and once again rose stocks were cleared out. And also once again, export business which had been the initial focus of RTP and then abandoned, was back on track. The French operation was mentioned in a three-page colour article produced by the Royal Horticultural Society for its prestigious journal *The Garden*. This produced an enquiry from an Italian nursery, Vivaio Anna Peyron. Vivaio was a reasonably large operation but without roses in its portfolio. Visits were made each way, but the outcome represented a major change of direction from the French model.

John Scarman's confidence had grown during the early part of 1985. Chelsea had gone well, as had the succession of press releases and articles. RTP felt sufficiently bullish to plant 15,000 roses but the still small turnover (up to £32,000 in 1985) along with the increase in stock, were continuing to perpetuate cash flow problems. Vivaio, in contrast, had no such difficulties and they were keen to fully exploit what they saw as a new opportunity in the Italian market. A franchise agreement appeared to meet the needs of both parties. In return for a one-off fee of £10,000 RTP granted the exclusive Italian rights to use the RTP catalogue (Vivaio paid for translation and printing costs) and also trained Vivaio to grow. Further, RTP provided 4,000 understocks, which John delivered in person having packed them into two suitcases for the flight from London to Milan. The final element in the franchise package was a 5 per cent royalty paid annually against sales revenue plus 2½ per cent to cover technical assistance.

But the course of exporting rarely runs smoothly. RTP's freight forwarder experienced difficulty in delivering a consignment to France. On telephoning RTP for instructions, they were asked to break down the consignment and despatch to individual customers themselves. Monsieur Maugar had gone bankrupt and disappeared, thankfully without owing any money to RTP. The freight forwarder and his wife took on the agency. When one door closes . . .

In 1986, RTP's planting programme increased to 25,000. A Chelsea stand was again shared with Jane Fearnley-Whittingstall. The design included a rose tunnel constructed from metal arches. The tunnel was sold off-the-stand to Sara Ferguson's mother, thus sparking off a new product development. Marketed under the RTP brand name for direct sales to the public, the arches and pergolas were manufactured to order by a local metal engineer. Apart from the usual launch press releases, the only promotion behind 'Arches' consisted of inserting a leaflet into copies of the rose catalogue.

Arch sales proved disappointing. John hypothesised that prospective customers had a clear notion of what constituted 'the price for an arch' and that this notion had been formed with reference to the price of wooden arches universally available at garden centres. A 20 per cent price premium might not be seen to represent value for money.

Promotional activities in 1986 continued to major on press editorial. For example, a half-page feature in the *Sunday Times* specifically on climbing roses produced a huge response. Copy and photographs were both supplied by John. RTP maintained files on all key journalists and made a point of providing each with a new story every year. Equally a record was kept of all sources of catalogue requests. It was using this system which confirmed John's suspicions about the value of media advertising compared with press editorials.

RTP experimented with a three-month advertising campaign in the gardening section of the *Daily Telegraph*. The copy offered a free catalogue and response was large. However, conversion rate into orders was minimal. In contrast, respondents to press editorial had to pay £1 to obtain the catalogue and they produced a conversation rate of one in four. The difference was attributed to the ability of editorial to effectively qualify the prospect for the product and the implied endorsement by horticultural journalists.

Press editorial was thus the principal method of promotion. In turn, those who had purchased were added to a customer database which, by the end of 1986, had risen to 3,000 entries. The database listed only purchasers and not enquiries, and so was regarded by RTP as a prime source of 'hot' prospects for future sales. RTP estimated that 30 per cent of customers would buy again, at least once. RTP began to use the database to mailshot customers, particularly with end of season special offers.

The year of 1986 was one of increasing economic prosperity. The impact on RTP's business appeared to be two fold. First the housing market was buoyant and the increasing number of house moves resulted in a larger demand for whole planning schemes. RTP's catalogue offered free-of-charge designs and planting schemes, which were sketched out on the kitchen table over an evening glass of wine. John had a free hand to specify the number and variety of roses. The temptation to over supply and to suggest poorer sellers had to be resisted in order to maintain the high reputation which was the bedrock of referral and recommendation. RTP estimated that about 30 per cent of their order book at this time consisted of schemes with a considerable proportion of individual order values of £500 compared with the previous average of £25. The second factor was that the largest increases in prosperity (and reductions in taxation) were sponsored by people matching RTP's customer profile. A selective product profile and RTP's marketing approach - based on press editorial in quality media, a tasteful and informative catalogue, exhibition at Chelsea and good personal relations with key designers, journalists and customers - had attracted a wealthy clientele. Although not a major part of RTP's marketing communications mix, some personal relationships had been built through personal callers to Stretton. The latest revision of the catalogue incorporated a garden design by Jane Fearnley-Whittingstall which John had replicated at Stretton as an added visitor attraction. The garden had cost £3,000 to construct which represented a sizeable investment given the lack of feel for how much business resulted directly - or subsequently - from personal callers.

Turnover for 1986 more than doubled to £75,000, although this figure did include the one-off franchise payment from Vivaio. RTP rented an additional 10-acre field allowing 60,000 roses to be planted.

1987 saw a promotional innovation. RTP approached IPC magazines proposing a readers' offer based on four old roses for £19. Such readers' offers provide benefits for all parties. For the reader, the price represents a 20 per cent discount off the normal retail price. For the magazine the potential for extra sales is added to the certainty of a profit from the venture. (The magazine typically takes 40 per cent of the offer price.) RTP receives only about 60 per cent of the discounted magazine price but benefits in a variety of ways. First, experience allows the magazine to predict fairly accurately what take-up will be. With a lead time of approximately one year this allows RTP to grow specifically for the offer. The fixed combination of four roses produces huge savings in picking and packing, typically 20 seconds packing time compared with three and a half minutes. Secondly, all promotional costs are borne by the magazine and, in particular, no catalogue cost is involved. Thirdly, the RTP name is placed before the gardening public although the actual customer list remains the property of the magazine and is not available for future use by RTP. The first readers' offer appeared in *Homes and Gardens* resulting in sales of 3,000 packs against a forecast of 2,500.

By 1990 RTP were involved in three readers' offers a year with IPC magazines through *Homes and Gardens*, *Ideal Home* and *Country Homes and Interiors*.

Throughout 1987 RTP's interest in a new venture had been growing. Partly to try and reduce dependence on mail order business, partly to increase profitability and partly because of a love of the subject, John had been researching the opportunities for rose oil.

John had started breeding roses specifically for oil production almost as soon as he was established at Stretton and by this time he had a specimen which was approaching the required characteristics. He now needed access to the perfumers, access to a suitable growing and distribution site and access to finance. The first task was underway.

The second two tasks suggested the need for a joint venture partner. To produce roses on a sufficient scale for distillation, and sufficiently cheaply, required land availability, climatic conditions and labour costs markedly different from those in the UK. Western Europe, perhaps making use of contacts and expertise in France and Italy, was too costly. Bulgaria was eliminated because of the presumed difficulty of entering into an arrangement with an Eastern bloc grower. Turkey was eliminated because desk research had revealed that traditional farming methods had caused significant problems with rose sickness.

Further desk research suggested that Morocco was a country which met the key criteria. The right combination of climate and altitude was available near the foothills of the Atlas mountains. There was an existing rose industry which implied the presence of propagation and harvesting skills. There were low labour costs. There were also low visit costs via holiday packages from the UK. There was a well-developed commercial and managerial infrastructure. Finally the current political and commercial climate was welcoming to the development of joint venture business. RTP felt that the rose oil project would be particularly attractive to potential host countries like Morocco since it would be geared to producing for export.

Although subject to negotiation with any prospective partners, John envisaged that RTP would provide initial stocks of the exclusive cultivar (code-named 'Woodlands'), technical knowledge and training and would also be responsible for the sale of the resultant oil to the perfume houses. The host partner would provide land and labour for volume propagation and would also purchase and operate the distillation plant. Both partners would share in profits equally, with RTP paying an agreed price for the oil in accordance with quality.

Accordingly, a visit was made during Autumn 1988 in order to confirm the horticultural suitability of Morocco and to seek potential joint venture partners. With the help particularly of the British Moroccan Society, a number of visits were made to the horticultural farmers in the Agadir and Marrakech areas, many of whom concentrated on the growing of fruit and cut flowers.

John's rough calculations reflected the quantity and quality of roses he saw.

Planting density	70,000 roses per hectare
Yield (based on 50 flowers per annum per plant with average weight of 4 grammes)	14 tonnes per hectare
Less allowance for harvesting slippage	4 tonnes per hectare
= Minimum output	10 tonnes per hectare
Oil yield (based on 1kg of rose oil from 4 tons of flowers)	2.5 kg
Sales value (2.5 kg **x** £2,500)	£7,500
Less costs of packing and preparation	£2,500
Gross profit	£5,000

It seemed that the relatively high profitability would be attractive to Moroccan rose-growers whose cut flowers were having to be sold at depressed prices because of production gluts. In the event, a number of growers were interested but appeared to want much larger scale operations than John had in mind. He feared that he would lose control of the venture and having made available the Woodlands cultivator, would then be at the mercy of any partner. The venture was put on ice for the time being.

Meanwhile turnover and production in the UK had continued to increase steadily. 1987 marked RTP's solo debut at Chelsea, Jane having decided not to show. RTP's stand featured an old wall smothered in old roses. The stand in the following year in 1988 was designed by a friend, Brian Glover, who was museum manager at Stratford for the Royal Shakespeare Society. His theme was the 'War of the Roses' and the show was a tremendous success. Turnover rose to £95,000 and 100,000 roses were planted. It was also through Brian Glover that Scarman met Leoni, an import agent based in Hockenheim. She handled a wide variety of products including pub signs, but nothing in the horticultural line.

Leoni, however, sensed potential on the German market for the RTP concept and arranged for a German photographer to take pictures of the garden at Stretton and for an article on the Scarmans. This was published in 1989 in two German magazines - *Architektur und Wohnen* and *Krauter und Ruben*. The latter's literal English translation of 'Cabbages and Turnips' may not at first sight have appeared to be the right vehicle for fragrant old roses but it was, in fact, a journal with 'clout' in the market place which reflected the importance of the 'green' movement in Germany. The response was staggering. A total of 10,000 roses were sold immediately in a market that John had expected to be difficult to penetrate.

The relationship with Leoni was formalised, but yet again on a different basis. Roses would be marketed under the RTP brand name with Leoni acting as a distributor. An export price, fixed initially at £2.25 per rose, recognised that Leoni would undertake all marketing activities within Germany. The RTP catalogue is used with overprinting in German, paid for by Leoni.

Turnover in 1989 rose to £125,000 but the planting progression at Stretton was halted. Although turnover had grown continuously from 1984 to 1989 John felt that the rate of increase was slowing and he was having to work harder to achieve it. Promotional spend, for example, was increasing as a proportion of sales, particularly in relation to an increasing number of mailshots. He was beginning to suspect that RTP was operating in a niche market which was showing signs of saturation. Concern over this, combined with the worries of employing staff and the recognition that costs were too high, led to re-assessment of operations strategy. Rose-growing at Stretton was too labour-intensive and picking and packing were too slow. Not only that, they accounted for far too much of John and Teresa's own time. An additional factor was the financial strain of funding the growth in planting which was needed to support the increase in sales. This was particularly acute because of the 18 months between planting and sale. (RTP had, however, resisted the temptation to inflate profitability by over-valuing rose stocks, which they showed in the accounts at cost.) The decision was thus made to sub-contract growing to a professional wholesale grower in Leicestershire. RTP committed to take 100,000 roses per annum of a given assortment at an agreed price, provided they were of first class quality.

The intention was to turn RTP from a 'manufacturing' company into a marketing organisation and at the same time to re-establish control over managerial and administrative tasks. Two full-time agricultural workers' jobs were shed and John took over duties previously carried out by a part-time clerical assistant. 'Leaner and fitter' were the watchwords of the time.

The sales in 1990 were to be met from the final crop at Stretton and the year started propitiously. Export sales were now running at 50 per cent of total turnover, an achievement which was recognised with joint first prize in the Staffordshire European Awards. But the reality of the UK recession hit shortly afterwards at Chelsea. Stand sales were down by 30 per cent compared with 1989 and worse was to come. Recession cut disposable income and checked house moves. The gardens of existing clients were full. To cap it all, the huge losses suffered by Lloyds names inflicted blows on many of RTP's best clients.

The Response

John and Teresa reflected on the ironical possibility that the very basis of their success had also proved to be the instrument of their downfall. Faced with a saturated niche market, the RTP name and concept would probably not appeal to wider audiences. The price of exclusivity was to be paid by the seller as well as the buyer. The way forward seemed to require a re-thinking of the whole concept.

Noting the popularity of such books as *The Country Diary of an Edwardian Lady,* the Scarmans felt that the future lay in repositioning their offering to appeal to the apparently universal desire to get closer to nature. Linking this to the wave of nostalgia which was sweeping through the UK, they juggled with a new concept based around the cottage garden. The idea was refined and finally emerged as the provision of cottage garden borders – off the shelf.

Old roses would still be featured prominently but the number of varieties offered would be reduced to around 30. Foxgloves, pinks, violets and other 'cottagey' plants would be added. A new catalogue would be needed and John set about writing the text and designing border layouts while Simon Buckingham, Teresa's brother, provided the illustrations. Unfortunately, existing rose turnover virtually disappeared and with new catalogue costs estimated at £20,000, the venture had to be abandoned. The work was not completely lost, however, as the catalogue turned into a book, *Create a Cottage Garden*, written by Kathleen Brown and illustrated by Simon Buckingham. John has the rights to text and illustrations. To reflect the new intended direction, RTP became Cottage Garden Roses. In the meantime, strategic initiatives were coming to fruition on the international front.

As a result of a visit to Stretton by relatives, the story of Barney Gasston was brought to the Scarmans' attention. Barney had been managing a cut-flower and rose business in Kenya, but had recently sold up in order to establish a farm for the harvesting of roses for the extraction of rose oil. A meeting was arranged and John travelled to Tanzania with a view to acting as consultant to Barney. The deal subsequently struck was that in exchange for allowing the newly formed 'Damascene Essential Oils' the rights to Woodlands Rose, John would receive 20 per cent of the equity. Barney would hold 80 per cent of the shares and a loan of $25,000 US was obtained from the World Bank by the Finance Director, the third member of the team. John was also to be paid £175 per day plus expenses to cover consultancy fees.

The first crop was planted in 1991 in order to provide a stock bank and by the end of 1993, 50,000 plants were available for harvesting. Barney's workers have been trained in propagation techniques and a distillation unit installed. The first samples of commercial oil are ready for presentation to the perfumers.

Back at home, survival, not launching into the glamorous and international world of perfume, was still the order of the day.

What was needed immediately was an income-generating activity with no over-heads. The notion of a Garden School seemed to fit the bill. The old RTP mailing list had grown to some 6,000 clients. A mailshot was devised explaining the name change and inviting clients to a series of groups at Stretton. For £35 per head the visit lasted from 11 am to 3 pm and included lunch and a rose-pruning demon-stration. Clients are also able to enrol in a club and receive four bulletins a year at a cost of £10 per bulletin.

Garden School visits averaged 25 to 30 participants and initially ran at the rate of 12 a year. Again, signs of saturation appeared but the Schools led to some requests for John to undertake pruning in clients' gardens. Realising the potential in this area John broadened the scope of this activity to include garden assessment, re-laying and maintenance plus new designs for complete gardens. At £165 per day plus expenses John is fully booked from October to March and in July and August.

Whilst the mailing list plus referrals are the main methods used to obtain clients, these have also led to another channel of communication. Clients from the mailing list have used John to give lectures at charity fund-raising events, thus allowing free publicity to a wider audience. Needless to say this has sparked off an interest in the possibilities of income generation through lectures. John is currently writing a book on *Pruning Old Fashion Roses* to build credibility to gain access into the high fee paying US lecture circuit.

Another income-generating activity has been the provision of dinner, bed and breakfast at Stretton at £50 per person. So far this has only been offered to the German clients and a German leaflet is available.

The transition from a product-based business towards a service business has thus been substantial. However, the old RTP product range is still available through Cottage Garden Roses, of which Teresa is now the sole proprietor. Production has moved back to Stretton but will be restricted to 10,000 plants per annum. A new employee has been taken on to help both Teresa and also John in his horticultural consultancy.

Questions for Discussion

1. In what ways could you attempt to segment the gardening and/or rose buying public?
2. How can a small business (particularly one where the 'production to sale' cycle is so long) going for growth cope with the dangers of over trading?
3. Was the original RTP product concept strong enough? Could it have been adapted over time? If so, in what ways?
4. Would you describe RTP as being product-oriented, customer-oriented, marketing-oriented or other?
5. What alternative growth vectors were available to RTP? What criteria would you use to evaluate these?
6. What alternatives were there to RTP's 'go-it-alone' growth strategy?

7. What were the advantages of RTP's direct marketing strategy? Were there any viable alternatives?
8. What were the advantages and disadvantages of RTP's public relations-dominated approach to marketing communications?
9. What sort of life cycle could you plot for the development of RTP over time?
10. What organisational change could/should RTP have planned for?
11. What business domain did RTP believe it was in? What other domains could it have perceived itself to have been in?
12. What were RTP's core competencies?
13. Evaluate the different approaches used by RTP in its international market entry strategy.

16
SilverWorks Product Design Limited

Background

The SilverWorks business was established in the early 1960's by a product designer who had built a personal reputation for excellence in industrial and craft design. Industrial contacts in Sheffield, linkages with livery companies and referrals from the Craft and Design Councils followed. The design company received six prestigious design awards following the success of the philosophy of translating classic industrial houseware design into contemporary specialist silver pieces.

Today the SilverWorks business comprises the design of awards, one-off commissions in highly prestigious sterling silver and the design/manufacturer of limited editions. This specialist business has important international dimensions. The reputation of the designer and the requirements of the commissioning client, are very much in the international domain.

SilverWorks' clients have included English Cathedrals, The Royal Family, livery companies, Downing Street, Oxford and Cambridge colleges and international sports associations. In addition, third party commissions for European houseware manufacturers provide prestigious links with Italian, French and German contemporary and classical designs.

SilverWorks have been working with precious metals since the early 1960's and have, overtime, acquired a bank of knowledge and expertise as well as a small committed highly-skilled labour force.

Invention and Application

The SilverWorks design unit is characterised by a fully integrated Design and Pilot Manufacturing Process. This process includes the following steps:

- Deciding the brief
- Researching the project
- Providing initial designs
- Forging consensus with the client
- Creating three-dimensional models
- Working with the 'real materials'
- The technical input
- Pilot production

In short, the company is providing a unique link by demonstrating how innovation can be commercialised as well as designed (invention and application).

Despite the distinctive industry positioning and the commitment of a small team the business is experiencing profitability problems. Relevant considerations include:

- Operating at/below critical mass in relation to the associated people overheads has resulted in a loss on a fully-absorbed basis.
- The rapidly rising costs of bought-in precious metals which are estimated to be in excess of 50 per cent of net sales value.
- A single distribution channel of 'one-off' commissions which restricts contribution margin.
- Inability to reap the full benefit of the experience curve, given the one-off nature of the commission business.

The business appears to be trading off its former reputation. This situation is unlikely to last much longer unless positive action is taken to rebuild the client base. Consequently, in recent years this design group has experienced problems as a result of a combination of falling volumes, low prices for third party commissions, high bought-in costs and the overheads required to retain a dedicated specialist team. Any further decline in revenues might result in the loss of specialist staff. Given the craft skills and training required for the design and production of silver-based products, such a loss of the skill base would be irreversible in the medium term. What is required is a reassessment of the design team's strategic direction.

SilverWorks SWOT analysis

Strengths
- An established reputation in craft design.
- The reputation and experience of the founder who has worked in the design world from the 1960's through to the 1990's.
- A reputation amongst the existing client base for excellence, dedication and innovation.
- The ability to operate a fully integrated design service from the initial concept through to the pilot manufacturing process.
- A specialist group of dedicated designers.
- Specific experience of designing and working with precious metals resulting in the manufacture of highly prestigious products for a wide range of organisations.

Weaknesses
- Over dependence upon one or two major clients.
- The lack of critical mass and the forecast losses for the business.
- The one-off nature of the business for prestigious commissions.
- High raw material costs.
- Increasing complexity resulting in a longer cycle from receipt of order to final delivery.

Opportunities
- The opportunity to deal directly with final customers for silver products rather than with intermediaries.

- The opportunity to market a series of silver products, rather than one-off items.
- The opportunity to secure royalties rather than design fees (or as well as design fees) from silver/industrial-based businesses.
- The opportunity to market the credentials of the business to a wider international target group.

Threats

- The loss of one major client to competition or a client's decision to set-up their own in-house product design unit.
- The continuing high level of bought-in costs in the silver unit adversely impacting on profits.
- The inability to market effectively a craft/silver-based business.

Elements of a revised strategy

The SilverWorks team set themselves three objectives, two of which related to non-traditional business approaches. They were especially concerned as to how these objectives could be implemented and supported by marketing communications. The three objectives related to:

1. Rebuilding the ad hoc commission business for one-off specialist pieces

The problem remained that business would not flow in, unless a dedicated effort was made to contact past and potential clients on a regular basis. In addition, different marketing approaches would have to be developed for both direct and indirect clients (through intermediaries). This would require the efforts of a well connected person who could both empathise with the requirements of specialist organisations and evangelise the uniqueness of the SilverWorks approach to the design and manufacture of precious articles.

As well as this 'selling' effort, SilverWorks would need to reassert itself amongst its peer group and opinion leaders, influential in this specialist design field relating to precious articles. This would probably require building upon or re-establishing contacts with design opinion leaders supported by a carefully targeted public relations campaign.

2. Attempting to secure royalties by designing for major international manufacturers of housewares

SilverWorks did not wish to rely solely on the existing ad hoc commission-based business. Although they felt this route should remain the 'bedrock' of the Silver business, they believed it should be complimented by other sources of revenue. Their concern was that (even after efforts to recreate the success formula of the past), the business might still be locked into an ad hoc, high-cost operation, with little opportunity to capitalise on the sunk design expenses.

As SilverWorks had considerable experience of working with metals other than silver, they perceived an opportunity to sell their houseware product design and manufacturing skills to major international organisations.

The ad hoc nature of the silver commissions business would then be balanced by designing for third party volume houseware manufacturers which would introduce more financial stability into the business. In addition, the business would have the opportunity to expand outside of the limitations of precious metals and work with such materials as stainless steel and aluminium alloys.

There remained an important caveat: to associate only with the more prestigious manufacturers, to ensure that the 'design integrity' of SilverWorks was not compromised. To date SilverWorks had two contacts in Germany who were expressing a positive interest.

This alternative would require marketing efforts to be complimented by a marketing communications mix targeting, for example, the prestigious European hollowware, tableware and kitchenware manufacturers, who are seeking external innovation both in design and application.

3. Attempting to market 'limited editions' by direct response

SilverWorks was also considering taking responsibility for the marketing of its products direct to a wider group of end users. This offered an opportunity to enhance margins, as full advantage could be taken of selling at the full retail price. There was also the perceived advantage of generating volume by creating a series of products or limited editions. SilverWorks had noted with interest the collectors' clubs and direct response marketing methods of the more down-market 'Mints' and other collectors' companies. Some of the unresolved questions, however, were:

- Whether or not the concept could translate to an up-market limited edition business, where the selling price per article was likely to be hundreds of pounds, rather than tens of pounds.
- Given that the target group would be international, would the concept have international appeal?

SilverWorks was therefore considering re-building its business by marketing directly to private collectors both in the UK and overseas (as well as continuing to seek specialist ad hoc commissions from a variety of public and private organisations), if design integrity could be reconciled with the poor image of direct response marketing. The very expression 'direct response' was, however, painful to the current culture and tradition of unique prestigious commissions.

Nevertheless, this channel of distribution was attractive for the following reasons:

- The scale of the operation is controllable; a business can be built at a pace dictated by the company.
- There are no intermediaries.
- The full product range can be included as from day one.
- A unique loyalty can be created by building up a specific mailing list for high value items and converting these over time to a collectors club.
- Even allowing for credit, this is basically a cash business.
- The full retail price may be charged.
- For high value items, marketing costs are modest compared with lower value items.

SilverWorks' limited research into this distribution channel suggested the following 'guidelines' if they were to succeed.

Key factors for the success of a direct response experiment

- Specialise in a particular area and build a continuing relationship with the direct response customer.
- Market collectable products that can be presented as a series in order to maximise the initial marketing and advertising expenditure.
- Build the customer relationship subsequent to advertising by direct mail shots, information sheets and visits to the SilverWorks design studios and production unit.
- Use advertising and brochures to 'paint a picture' and 'tell a story'. Pan European collectors' publications would be considered as well as UK-specific publications as vehicles for generating responses.
- If possible, generate unique designs.
- Offer products that are unique and cannot be obtained through any other channel of distribution. Products should be presented as genuine limited editions, numbered and authenticated by certificate. For example, museum reproductions would carry numbered certificates of authenticity signed by the designer/museum concerned.
- Make products topical to current lifestyles and/or events.
- Link with other organisations; this may involve offering royalties to a museum or society in return for using their name or sponsorship.
- Offer credit/extended payment for high value items. Investigate international legal liability, including the equivalent of such bodies as NOPS in the UK (National Newspaper Mail Order Protection Scheme).
- Offer viewing facilities at exhibitions.
- Creatively exploit emotive themes.
- Company/product name to be compatible with high quality products.

Direct response models

The following three tables (Tables 16.1, 16.2 and 16.3) set out two examples of limited edition marketing. These are:

a) An edition of six silver goblets sold at prices of £398/2,025; one/set of six.

b) A limited edition of two specialist reproduction candlesticks sold at a price of £350/650 one/pair.

Your Tasks

1. Formulate the detailed marketing communications mix to support the three marketing objectives proposed by the design team. This will require:
   - A consideration of the various elements in the communications mix
   - Clear communications objectives for each part of the mix

Table 16.1 SilverWorks direct response. Model based on one insertion (in reality only used for test purposes, as in practise an on-going media campaign would be required for a number of different items).

	Example (a) (Goblets) Specialist Press	Example (b) (Candlesticks) High Circulation National Magazines
Publication	Decanter and The Collector	Country Life
Period	Monthlies	Monthly
Circulation	20/30,000 ABC	42,000 ABC*
Item	Series of six goblets	Series of two candlesticks
Price per item	£398.00	£350.00
Response rate	0.002%	0.001%
Number of orders	100	42
Cost of space per ½ page colour	£1,107/£967	£3,416
Potential 'Series' revenue for two/six #	£95,850	£21,000

* Audit Bureau of Circulation
\# See next table below

Table 16.2 The direct response marketing of limited editions – the series potential

a) A limited edition of six silver goblets – (Base 100 responses)

	Pack of 1	of 2	of 3	of 4	of 5	of 6	Total
% Purchasing	20	50	–	20	–	10	100
Units	20	100	–	80	–	60	260
Orders	20	50	–	20	–	10	100
Price/pack	£398	£785	–	£1,420	–	£2,025	–
Total Revenue	£7,950	£39,250	–	£28,400	–	£20,250	£95,850

b) Reproduction museum candlesticks – (Base 42 responses)

	of 1	of 2					Total
% Purchasing	50	50					100
Units	21	42					63
Orders	21	21					42
Price/pack	£350	£650					–
Total Revenue	£7,350	£13,650					£21,000

- ● The recognition that different target groups normally require distinct communication mixes.
2. Critically review the direct response proposals including:
   - ● Your recommendations whether or not to go ahead/for modifications
   - ● The likely difficulties of implementation
   - ● A proposed media schedule for the direct response advertising. This refers to

Table 16.3 Direct response marketing of limited editions P&L projections

	(a) Goblets	(b) Candlesticks
Total no. of items	260	63
Total Revenue inc. VAT £000's	96	21
Total Revenue ex.VAT £000's	82	18
Gross Margins at 70%/75%*	57	13
Advertising space cost	3	2
Production costs	1	1
Post & Packaging at £10 per item	2	1
Handling charges	1	1
Literature brochures and Photography	4	4
Credit Card fees at 1.5% of VAT Inclusive revenue	1	–
Total marketing expenses	12	9
Profit contributions	45	4
Profit contributions %	55	22

* After: materials, packaging, polishing, assay and design.

   the number, frequency and type of publications you would recommend to SilverWorks.
3. Having arrived at your own conclusions, critically review the proposed SilverWorks communications plan (see page 210).

LEARNING NOTE on the marketing communications mix

As marketing communications are so often the visible part of the 'marketing iceberg', many non-practitioners sometimes confuse parts of the marketing communications mix with the overall marketing function. This is understandable, as advertising and personal selling, for example, may be more visible to the observer than the building blocks of marketing strategy. In short the process of market segmentation, targeting, positioning within a segment and the selection of a marketing mix as a vehicle for competitive positioning, should precede the communications decisions. This is indicated in the continuum below:

● analysing markets
● segmenting markets
● targeting market segments
● positioning products or services against competition
● deciding the marketing mix
● deciding the communications mix.

The marketing communications mix decision relates to the choice (or relative emphasis) of the various communication vehicles:

- press publicity
- lobbying
- event creation and management
- other public relations activities
- design and corporate identity
- exhibitions
- theme advertising
- scheme advertising
- direct response advertising
- direct mail
- personal selling
- after-sales service
- sales promotions.

One of the criteria to employ when choosing between these alternative communications vehicles is to establish the critical point in the communication process. The communication process may be summarised as a spectrum through which the target customer may progress or regress. The choice of communications vehicles and their mix may therefore depend upon where in the spectrum the prime target groups are currently positioned. This simplified spectrum is set out below:

Communication stage	Suggested relevant communications vehicle
Unawareness	
Awareness	Advertising/Personal selling
Positive attitude	Public relations
Relevance	Design values
Conviction/desire	Personal selling
Action/purchase	Sales promotion
Repeat purchase	Selling/sales promotion

This process is obviously complex, given the difficulty of determining where in the spectrum the various target groups are positioned. For example, SilverWorks services may be well known in the industry, but may be considered to be of little relevance to customers' needs.

What may be equally difficult is the integration between these various communications vehicles. All too often an organisation's communictions suffer from imbalance. For example, the salesforce, the public relations company and the media advertising may be communicating from differing perspectives and differing objectives.

The starting point for deciding the SilverWorks communications mix should be the target group you have selected. In this context you will need to decide:

- What is known about the target group: their attitudes, opinions, buying patterns? It would help to clearly profile the primary and secondary target groups.
- What are your communication objectives? You will need specific objectives for each part of the communication mix; no objectives, no outcomes!
- What response is required from the target group? What action do you expect them to take as a result of your communications?
- What emphasis should be given to different elements of the mix, to media advertising, to personal selling, to public relations, to exhibitions, to packaging and to literature?
- How will you co-ordinate all parts of the marketing communications mix, ensuring that areas of possible imbalance and conflict are minimised?

And in the specific context of media communications:

- What proportion of your target group do you need to reach in order to achieve your objectives?
- How often will you need to repeat your message to achieve your objectives?
- How will you buy your media and decide your creative theme?
- Will your choice of media and creative theme be compatible with the SilverWorks image and reputation?

The SilverWorks Marketing Communications Plan

To meet the first objective

SilverWorks recognise that their first objective of reviving the commissions business depends largely on direct selling efforts. The efforts of the founder now have to be duplicated by another equally motivated individual. In addition, direct selling needs to be complemented with a supporting marketing communications mix. Currently under consideration are:

Exhibitions
It is proposed to take part in the specialist exhibitions sponsored by such organisations as the Design Council, the Craft Council, livery companies and other dedicated specialist organisations. Such exhibitions have more in common with private art gallery showings that the mainstream exhibition world.

Direct mail
A supportive direct mail programme is being considered to support the direct

selling efforts. The objective of the programme is to form strong links with both direct commission clients and intermediaries who can refer business to SilverWorks. It is considered that this programme should target the following customer groups:

● The design associations; for example, the Design Council.
● Industry and trade associations who commission awards.
● Specific organisations commissioning articles of beauty in precious metal; for example, livery companies, guilds, cathedrals and colleges.
● Sports associations and organisations.
● Large corporations requiring presentations.

Before the campaign can be actioned, SilverWorks consider that they need to create a database of intermediaries and direct clients. This database would include all previous clients and would be supplemented by researching new groupings matching the above categories.

The objective of the direct mail campaign is to secure appointments to present the credentials of the company. Guidelines for an effective direct mail programme are believed to include the following:

● The direct mail pack should include a one-page letter plus a corporate 'flyer' (a simple folded two-page A4 sheet). A corporate brochure is subsequently mailed in response to enquiries.
● Mailings should be restricted to the above list of intermediaries/direct clients.
● One specific individual should be responsible for the direct mail plan, working to monthly targets.
● Follow-up telephone calls should be made.
● The number of mailings should not exceed the ability of the organisation to follow them up.
● The covering letter will be as specific as possible to the prospect's perceived needs.
● On a 10 per cent strike rate for presentation appointments, a minimum 240 mailings should be made per annum or 20 letters per month, hopefully resulting in one client gain per month.

Public relations

SilverWorks are also giving consideration to a supporting public relations campaign with the following objectives:

● Present SilverWorks as a unique company which designs *and* makes to order unique high value items.
● Generate awareness of SilverWorks amongst prospective client companies and opinion leaders within the design industry.
● Present the SilverWorks craft design group as leaders in the field, as evidenced by referrals from the Design Council and the stream of design awards.
● The overall objective is to secure recommendation via 'word of mouth' based upon the knowledge and awareness of the SilverWorks operation.

Public relations is considered well-suited to promoting the SilverWorks craft/silver design group, given the distinctiveness and wide interest in *objet d'art*. SilverWorks are working on commissions which the specialist press might welcome as the basis of feature articles in their publications. As research has demonstrated that clients tend to choose product design consultancies on the basis of 'word of mouth' reputation, SilverWorks considered it vital that their reputation should be enhanced by media exposure targeted at both prospective clients and opinion leaders. Features of the PR campaign under consideration are:

An on-going press relations programme

This will target the specialist press. Target media will include the marketing and promotional magazines, the silver and craft industry specialist press, specific end-user press and publications covering the design industry. This on-going press campaign will require the preparation of press kits to include at least two brief articles on the SilverWorks product design philosophy and creative approach, as well as specimen case histories of prestigious commissions. As far as possible, press releases will be actioned in conjunction with previous and current clients in order to maximise impact and take up by the media; for example, the involvement with the International Sports Federation will help spearhead a marketing campaign to other sports associations and organisations. Press releases will also highlight the in-house design and batch manufacturing skills.

Special feature articles

Exclusive stories will be offered to the specialist press; these might relate to:

● Specific case histories and prestigious client contracts on a problem/solution result format.
● Interviews with the design team discussing such activities as the re-creation of original Victorian industrial houseware designs. The credibility of the company would be further enhanced by stressing the design awards received by the company for craft work.

Specific events inclusive of exhibitions, seminars and press parties

As the relationship with the press is slowly re-built, the press will be invited to a specific exhibition of the craft design group's work, so that specific commissions could be discussed and press kits passed to the specialist press. At least two such exhibitions/press parties will be considered per year and a theme created for each. These themes will relate to activities such as the contemporary expression of Victorian Designs, or to the specialist limited editions currently being progressed. These 'press parties' would also be used to entertain existing clients in order to build on goodwill, which might then result in further media articles. The first step, however, is for SilverWorks to concentrate on basic press relations and generate support material inclusive of press kits and specific craft brochures.

The direct selling efforts of the SilverWorks manager

Most of the above communication activities are designed to support personal selling efforts. In many ways the term 'selling' is unsuitable in this context, as business has been built on the basis of reputation and the delivery of a unique service. Without sustained effort, however, goodwill decreases over time. The above activities, it is hoped, may result in 'pushing at an open door'. The alternative scenario, summarising the old maxim, is less than pleasant for the person at the sharp end:

> I don't know you, I don't know your company and I don't know your products, now what do you want?

To meet the second objective

Although much of the activity designed to restore the historic business base would also relate directly to the second objective, SilverWorks recognise that the international dimension requires additional direct selling skills. These skills require an individual with an international design reputation who is willing to act as a roving European design consultant. They are considering supporting this individual with:

- A selected Pan-European direct advertising campaign in specialist housewares/product design and collectors' media.
- A public relations campaign targeting European design opinion leaders, especially those in Italy and Germany.
- An extension of the design exhibitions to embrace the international dimension.

To meet the direct response objective

So far as the third objective is concerned, SilverWorks are sufficiently interested to test their model. The problem they have is the selection of the media. Which publications would provide the best coverage of the target group?

Readership profiles

The next step in progressing the development of a possible direct response business is to review candidate publications for direct response advertising. In evaluating media candidates the company believes that it should consider the following points:

- Profiles of each candidate publication.
- Cost of the media in relation to circulation and readership.
- The quality of each publication given the nature of SilverWorks' limited edition products.
- The timing or 'copy dates' of the publications (as advertising material is required in advance of the publication dates).
- Payment terms required by the media/media buyer.

Once candidate publications were available, a full media schedule could be created, setting out the timing and costs involved in mounting a campaign. An example of a media schedule is included at the end of the case. The media schedule would also be used to estimate the response rate prior to committing to the full programme.

SilverWorks decided to approach a 'Media Buyer' rather than a full-service advertising agency given both their own creative skills and the more specialist media buying requirements.

LEARNING NOTES on buying creative services

There are three distinct areas of expertise involved in the purchase of advertising. These are:

● The creative concept or inspiration for the advertising message.
● The creative execution or production of the commercial or press advertisement.
● The buying of the media or the booking of the space and production and control of the media schedule.

The client has the choice between buying media from a 'full service advertising agency' or going 'à la carte'.

The Full Service Agency

In common with many other agency-lead businesses, advertising agencies would like you to believe that their services involve no cost to the client company.

Full service advertising agencies historically worked on a 15 per cent commission from the media owners. Agencies purchasing on behalf of their clients a nominal £100 of media, were subsequently invoiced by the media owners for £85, whilst agency clients were charged the full £100 (or 17.5 per cent on the net £85). This lead to the convention of agencies marking up other client services by the customary 17.5 per cent. The exception to this rule was the convention that initial creative work actioned by a full service agency resulting in media advertising was not charged for (on the basis that the client had already paid by being charged the full rate). Note that creative work does not refer to the production of TV commercials or press ad., which is normally a significant expense.

This system, which remained intact in the UK until the mid-1970's, tended to under-reward smaller agencies, working on complex smaller budgets (which often comprised large amounts of non-media related material, such as literature and exhibitions).

In contrast the system over-rewarded the large agencies, who often earned high margins on national TV budgets. This was especially true when:

● Creative was rarely modified between campaigns.
● Commercials were rolled out from regional to national coverage.
● The creative was provided by a multinational company so that efforts were focused only on media buying.

The system was gradually broken in the 1970's by the general trend towards deregulation, the more competitive agency environment in the USA, as well as pressure from major UK advertisers seeking better value than the closed shop was willing or able to provide.

Change was only achieved in the face of opposition from the monopoly providers, the major advertising agencies, who insisted that quality would suffer if 'outsiders' entered the industry, or if their margins declined. Some well-established agencies did their best to oppose any recognition by the media owners of 'media buying independents'. This effectively delayed change in the industry until the alliance between astute, progressive advertisers and independent media buyers generated economies as a result of competition.

A La Carte

As with a menu the client may now select any combination of advertising service providers. This means that the choice is any combination of the following:

- A full service advertising agency for the three major elements referred to earlier. If the client is in a strong negotiating position (significant media expenditure), a fee basis is normally agreed. For example, the agency might agree to rebate all commissions from the media owners in exchange for a 10 per cent fee levied on the gross advertising budget. Conversely, if the client is in a weak position the fee paid by the client may well exceed that which would have been generated by the commission system.
- A creative 'hot shop' for the creative and paid for on a fee basis.
- A Production House for print advertising production.
- A TV/Cinema Production House for the 'execution' of the creative.
- A specialist Media Independent who purchases only the media. As such the independent media buyer is 'recognised' by the media owners and receives the full commission; part of this commission is then rebated to the client, depending upon the media buyer's charges. The client will probably use this rebate to fund the creative part of the process.
- An advertising agency may be retained on a fee basis for one or more of the major elements.
- A public relations company rather than the client company co-ordinating the three major elements of creative services.

Conclusion

Media independents have not replaced the conventional advertising agencies. They have, however, made their point by introducing much needed competition (and lower charges) into the industry and helped to narrow the gap between media owners and media customers. Today, for example, it is common for a media independent to have a number of smaller advertising agencies on their client lists.

Recommendations of the SilverWorks Media Buyer

The media buyer assessed some 22 media options and the following summarises their recommendations in terms of those publications that they believe will be most effective in reaching the target group.

The target group

The basis for selecting these publications was that they should be read by the 'right people'. Demographically, the target group is to be: A B C1s, age group 45-plus, with a high disposable income and a high interest in *objet d'art* and quality ornamental items.

The resulting media list includes publications targeted at such people.

Media list

The Spectator

Circulation 43,888. The profile of readers is affluent, sophisticated and professional men and women who enjoy good living and support luxury buying habits. They generally shop with store cards (23 per cent have Harrods cards) and credit cards (31 per cent use Amex), and when surveyed, 61 per cent stated that they looked at advertisements in *The Spectator.*

The demographic profile of the readers is as follows: 79 per cent are male, 69 per cent live in the South of England, 54 per cent are aged over 45 years; 59 per cent are classed as ABs. Editorial in the publication covers foreign affairs, politics, non-political articles and book/art reviews.

The Collector

Claims to be the number one publication for private collectors, antiques dealers, interior designers and their agents. *The Collector* has a circulation of 20,000, mainly distributed through art dealers, centres, markets, fairs and salesrooms. The circulation also has a large number of subscribers who are a select and interested audience. Again, these people are affluent (ABs) with a high interest in fine art and antiques.

Decanter

Circulation 20,000 (UK) plus 13,500 (overseas). *Decanter* is read by consumers and by the wine trade. In the UK 13,500 consumer and 6,500 trade copies are circulated. It is widely regarded as the best wine magazine in the world. The profile of the average reader is predominantly male (92 per cent), with 61 per cent classed as AB in socio-economic terms. Some 30 per cent of readers earn in excess of £50,000 per annum.

House & Garden (incorporating Wine and Food magazine)

Circulation 142,851; total readership 1,419,000. A total of 65 per cent of the readers of *House & Garden* are women. Again the majority of readers (64 per cent) are in the upper socio-economic groups, and 52 per cent are aged 45 or over. Editorial in *House & Garden* reports on the finest interiors, decoration, cuisine, art and antiques and travel world-wide, appealing to readers who, according to a NOP survey, live in houses valued at approximately £166,000 (average), and one quarter live in houses valued at over £200,000.

Specifically, the interest in art and antiques in the readership is extremely high; for example, 17.3 per cent of readers are known to collect silver for interest, whilst 25 per cent collect silver for investment.

Country Life

Circulation 42,066. The circulation is predominantly in the UK (36,228) with just 5,838 copies circulated overseas. *Country Life* is well established as a leading commentator on architecture, gardening, collecting and wildlife. A quality publication in every sense, appealing to men and women equally. Again the readership is exclusive: 39 per cent are classed as AB, and 33 per cent as C1s; some 60 per cent of readers live in London or the South East; 52 per cent are aged 45 years plus.

The Field

Circulation 30,675, with a total readership of 383,000. *The Field* is the leading journal on rural sports, amusements and occupations and is aimed specifically at 'the country gentleman'. It is natural, therefore, that the readership is of the higher level: some 68 per cent are ABs and 61 per cent of readers are aged over 45 years.

Sunday Times Magazine

The circulation of the *Sunday Times (Magazine)* is 1,218,440, with a readership of 3,527,000, split 53 per cent men: 47 per cent women. Reaching a more diverse audience than other publications profiled above, the *Sunday Times Magazine* is the number one 'Sunday' magazine. The predominantly ABC1 readers (80 per cent) are recorded as spending a large proportion of their time on their Sunday reading. Readers of the *Sunday Times* newspaper and its associated supplements are 38 per cent aged 45 or more, and are well educated with 32 per cent possessing university degrees.

Table 16.4 Draft media schedule

Publication	Size	Colour	Position	Cost	No. inserts	Total	Dates
Country Life	½ page (143x98)	4 col.	Premium	£3,416	2	£6,832	2 Sept '93 28 Oct '93
House & Garden (inc wine & food)	¼ page (137x98)	4 col.	R.o.P.	£2,847	2	£5,694	Oct '93 Nov '93
The Field	½ page (132x203)	4 col.	R.o.P.	£2,115	2	£4,230	Sept '93 Oct '93
The Collector	1 page (196x135)	4 col.	R.o.P.	£967	2	£1,934	Oct/Nov '93 Dec/Jan '93/4
Decanter	½ page (135x185)	4 col.	R.o.P.	£1,107	2	£2,214	Oct '93 Nov '93
The Spectator	½ page (125x190)	4 col.	R.o.P.	£2,713	2	£5,426	Sept '93 Oct '93
Sunday Times Magazine	¼ page (142x114)	4 col.	R.o.P.	£7,274	2	£14,548	Sept '93 Oct '93
						£40,878	

Source: Total Media.

17
Benetton – Feeling Off Colour?

One of the highest profile success stories of the 1980's was the Italian fashion firm Benetton. Starting from nothing in 1955, world-wide sales had reached around 250 million dollars at the start of the decade and almost 2 billion by 1990. Pigeon-holing Benetton is difficult. Is it a manufacturer, designer or retailer? Does it grow and internationalise via a franchise system or not? Does Benetton really aim to meet the needs of the global mass market through its system of 'industrial fashion' or is it catering only for high-income-level consumers? Is Benetton's advertising strategy drawing the world's attention to key global issues or is it cynically using controversial images to generate publicity for Benetton whether good or bad?

Benetton's success has been grounded in the development and exploitation of a business strategy which confers competitive advantage through its own value chain system and superior value to its end-user customers. It is also, perhaps until recently, thought to have conferred competitive advantage on its retailers.

In terms of its value chain activities, Werner Ketelhohn claims that Benetton 'derives its strength from the simultaneous pursuit of two contradictory objectives – economies of scale and manufacturing flexibility – through a negotiated strategy'. Thus purchasing of raw materials is handled centrally to achieve economies of scale, making Benetton the world's largest buyer of wool. Also undertaken in-house are state of the art processes for creating colours and for computer-aided design. However, while these core competencies are nurtured in-house, flexibility is achieved by sub-contracting manufacture to a network of some 700 independent or partially-owned suppliers. Changes in fashion can be rapidly accommodated. At the same time, Benetton's commitment to providing such contractors with full order books and guaranteed costs of materials and prices for manufactured goods allowed them to minimise marketing and finance costs, thus keeping the guaranteed prices low.

For end-user customers in the 1980's Benetton provided medium-priced, contemporary, brightly coloured and co-ordinated casual wear in natural fibres. The Benetton brand also offered them the chance to make highly visible yet suitable personal statements in an image-conscious era.

For the retailer too, the Benetton brand was highly desirable and, allied to Benetton's investment in communication and distribution technology, provided a powerful incentive to join the Benetton family. Benetton claimed to be able to re-stock any store anywhere in the world in 15 days.

In the same way that Benetton networks in its 'upstream' activities, it also does so in its 'downstream' activities. Although widely regarded as the 'franchising king', Luciano Benetton and other senior management have denied this. Chief Executive Officer Aldo Palmeri stated in 1993:

> It is completely different from franchising. It is a partnership.

By the end of the 1980's, the Benetton network included some 1,600 retail shops in Italy, 2,400 in the remainder of Western Europe, 800 in the Americas, plus others in the Far East and East Europe.

Benetton retailers are store-owning independent entrepreneurs who are required to finance their own investment in furniture and displays. They are also required to shop-fit according to standard designs laid down by Benetton, including the use and location of the green and white logo, the distance of window displays from the glass and the number of colours used. They need also to follow Benetton guidelines on price mark-ups and on sales promotions. They are committed to achieving certain minimum sales levels and are not permitted to return unsold merchandise. Finally, they are only permitted to sell Benetton clothes. The store owners do not pay any royalties to Benetton.

The downstream network is completed by some 80 'agents' who are usually store-owners but also supervise groups of stores. They are responsible for motivating retailers and also ensuring that the retailers adhere to Benetton style and culture. They agree new store openings including location and merchandise assortment.

Sometimes such location decisions have resulted in as many as three or four shops in close proximity. This has provided Benetton with a measure of security in that the failure of one shop can be offset by the success of others, and has also provided motivation through 'internal' competition. Conflict between stores, however, was partly mitigated by the opportunity offered by over 7,000 product items to permit different collections in different shops.

Agents also had a role to play in discussing with Benetton HQ matters relating to new collections, price levels and competition. Agents' remuneration consisted of a 4 per cent commission on the value of goods shipped plus the opportunity to invest in, and take profits from, the retail outlets.

The agency system was seen as key to Benetton's success. The agents are seen as the commercial department of Benetton but with the independence, incentive and closeness to the customer which comes from being outside the company. On top of this, the system allowed Benetton to globalise without the need to invest huge amounts in distribution. The degree of control offered by the system also allowed Benetton to build and protect its brand image in its specialised store environment.

The first signs that perhaps not all was well in this seemingly idyllic system occurred in the US where the number of Benetton outlets fell during a time of rapid expansion elsewhere in the world. One major reason cited was the trend for Benetton advertising to become increasingly shocking. Apparently this alienated American consumers.

The Benetton poster campaign was designed in-house by art director Olivero Toscani who had been hired in the mid-1980's. Amongst many others, the adverts depicted:

- A man on the point of death from AIDS.
- A white (apparently angelic-looking child) with a black child (apparently with devil-like horns).
- A duck smothered in an oil slick in the aftermath of the Gulf War.
- A military cemetery.
- A Mafia widow weeping over her husband's corpse.
- A portrait of the Queen as a black lady.
- A photograph of Luciano Benetton himself – naked.
- A photograph of a dead Croatian soldier.

In explaining his use of images – culled from news pictures – that people tend to shy away from, Toscani seemed to present two angles. He has said that he wants to use advertising to change society. He has also said that he wants to devise campaigns with very little investment but which everyone will talk about. He has further said that the intention is not to shock, but just to be different.

Aldo Palmeri has expressed Benetton's viewpoint in a different way:

> It is totally crazy to say we use advertising to increase sales. We are a global company. We need to understand the problems of the people wherever they live. We use advertising to demonstrate our capacity to be close to the needs of the people.

Others have commented that, in Third World markets such as Cuba, Benetton is not targeting the 'average' consumer but is aiming at the wealthy élite and the tourist trade where that exists.

Palmeri's explanation for the closure of some 300 shops in the USA seemed to imply that the Benetton proposition, rather than its advertising, lay at the heart of the problem: 'The American customer is very different. They take care about a dollar difference in price'.

Following the USA, the next anxiety for Benetton arose in Germany in 1995 where some retailers refused to pay for unsold stocks. They claimed that sales volumes were down some 30 per cent compared with two years previously and attributed this to the nature of the advertising. Some 50 retailers had even taken the step of suing Benetton. A recent survey of Benetton retailers in the UK contributed to the debate. Amongst verbatim comments from respondents, the following appeared to be typical:

> Some of the images were too strong and had the effect of alienating us from our customers . . . a lot of customers refused to look at the products.

> There is no relationship, no team spirit. The franchise takes all the risk. Benetton takes none.

> Benetton totally ignores the retailers.

Questions for Discussion

1. How has Benetton been able to build a global brand so successfully?
2. Benetton appears to have several competitive advantages. How sustainable are these? What are the core competencies which nourish them?
3. The 'network company' concept has many benefits. What – if any – are the disadvantages?

4. Is Benetton a franchisor?
5. Is the relationship between Benetton and its retailers based on an equal sharing of power and responsibility?
6. Is Benetton targeting the same consumer segment in each different country market?
7. Is Benetton offering the same brand proposition in each country market but targeted at different segments?
8. Is it possible to have a standardised global marketing communications campaign when reactions to Benetton's poster campaign appear to vary so much between cultures?
9. Can the creative approach adopted in Benetton's advertising be justified?
10. Is the Benetton creative approach beginning to suffer from 'strategic wear-out' or is the overall consumer brand proposition beginning to suffer from wear-out?
11 How can Benetton repair/retain loyalty from its consumers and its retailers?

18
Bearing the Brunt

The Mighty Widget Company (MW) manufactures a comprehensive range of bearings which are sold both through industrial distributors and direct to end-users. The end-users are mainly Original Equipment Manufacturers (OEM's) but many also buy bearings to replace worn-out bearings in their own plant and machinery. Some customers buy both for the above reasons and in order to sell some bearings as spares to customers who buy their OE products. As a result of a series of 'clashes' between MWC salesmen and its distributors, MWC has decided to appoint a Distribution Markets Manager. The Manager's objectives include the need to make policy recommendations geared to resolving the problems whilst safeguarding the interests of both parties. As an immediate problem the Manager also needs to make recommendations for dealing with the particular situation at Southampton Manufacturing Company, a medium-sized producer (OEM) of industrial pumps.

Background

In the 1950's and 1960's the market for bearings grew strongly and the main problem for manufacturers was limited factory capacity. Some manufacturers had regional depots which maintained limited stocks of the most popular bearings (and also a few specialised bearings which might be peculiar to a particular industry or customer in a region). Salespeople used their local regional depots as their 'office base'.

There were few distributors, and those which did exist were small and tended to be single outlets or have no more than three or four outlets restricted to a region (for example, the Midlands or East Anglia).

When the occasional salesperson left a manufacturer to set up on his own as a distributor, his former company was fairly happy to supply him. Even when such distributors took some manufacturers' accounts (usually because the service they offered on replacement bearings needed urgently was better) there was no real problem because there was plenty of business for everyone.

Times began to change in the 1970's. World economic growth slowed and bearings also reached the maturity stage in their product life-cycle (at least in developed world markets). Together with the increase in manufacturing capacity which now came on stream, there was a dramatic increase in competition and consequent reduction in margins for manufacturers. As manufacturers' profitability fell they sold off their regional depots to cut costs. Service levels therefore continued to worsen for some customers despite more production capacity. Distributors both grew in size and increased in number. By the end of the 1970's a few distributors were actually bigger than some of the manufacturers. (The largest distributor had 80 salespeople.) The basic pattern of distributorships therefore emerged as follows. There were five or six large distributors (20–70 branches) which operated throughout the UK. There were some 15–20 'second line' distributors who typically had three or four branches in one region. Finally there were around 100 single-branch distributors.

The decline of the manufacturers in the 1970's worsened sharply as the recession of the early 1980's bit. Manufacturers competed fiercely with one another and also on occasions with their distributors. Sales and marketing management found itself faced with a number of conflicting problems. On the one hand it felt it needed to increase penetration in many direct accounts. On the other hand it was facing increasing distrust and hostility from some of its distributors who felt this action was often at their expense rather than at the expense of competing manufacturers. Some MWC managers feared that one or two of the largest distributors might decide to retaliate by replacing MWC as the main supplier for some or even all product lines. Other managers felt that this was highly improbable considering that MWC were a major force in the world market and therefore felt that all distributors should be delighted to associate themselves with MWC. They also tended to feel that even if one or two distributors stopped buying from them they could be replaced by others since there were no exclusive distributorships in the bearings industry. No distributors had sole rights in any territory and large distributors tended to deal with many bearing manufacturers, although they usually regarded themselves as 'official' distributors for one, two or three of the main competitive manufacturers.

Sales Meeting

At one of its monthly sales meetings, members of the 20-strong regional accounts sales force were discussing an approach from one of their major national distributors, M & E, to their Sales Manager asking MWC to withdraw their quotation to Southampton Manufacturing Co. This would leave M & E as the sole offerer of MWC bearings to compete against other manufacturers and distributors. An extract of the conversation went something like the following :

'*Well, I think we would be crazy not to compete with M & E at Southampton Manufacturing Co. For one thing they might be offering our bearings this time but you know as well as I do, they will offer whoever's bearings will give them most profit. Next time they'll be pushing the competition into Southampton. They've got no concept of loyalty at all.*' John Hemmings was furious at the proposal that he should give M & E a free hand in trying to get the business. '*Anyway, Southampton themselves would rather deal direct with us. The only reason M & E got the enquiry was because it has a few seals and belts on it and M & E can supply those as well.*'

'What's the price level?' asked David Lowe.

'*Well that's another thing*', added John, '*We've been selling to Southampton at a level of 190 while we sell to M & E at 180. We make more money when we sell direct.*'

'What level are M & E quoting to Southampton?' continued David.

'At around 220. I should think they probably won't get the business anyway at that level and if we pull out, it'll go to competition.'

'I agree . . . it's mad,' Jim Mountford joined in. 'These distributors are just parasites, they want a mark up of 30 per cent for what? M & E won't buy from us until they get the order from Southampton. We might as well sell direct to Southampton, get paid more for it and increase our chances of staying in a job.'

'Exactly,' Bill Allen joined in. 'As far as I'm concerned, if M & E, or any of our other distributors, start selling to any accounts I'm interested in, then I deal with them the same as any other competitor.'

'What about the accounts you don't want?' asked David. 'Do you help the distributors there?'

'No, I don't even pass leads on to them,' replied Bill. 'There's no point. If you give a lead to M & E, then that is not fair to the other distributors in the area. They're all at one another's throats.'

'I agree,' added Jim. 'We've got a real case of the tail wagging the dog in this industry. These distributors get on to management – dictating price levels, saying what accounts they want, etc., etc. The reason we've got into this situation is because we've let distributors get too strong over the last few years. The more we support them, the stronger they get and the more bargaining power they use against us. They should stick to looking after the needs of the customers who are too small for us to supply economically.'

Questions for Discussion

1. What perceptions of the distributors are held by MWC salespersons?
2. How have such perceptions developed?
3. What are the ideal characteristics of distributors from a manufacturers point-of-view?
4. What are the ideal characteristics of manufacturers from a distributor's point-of-view?
5. What are the main areas of dissatisfaction that a distributor might experience with manufacturers?
6. Does MWC need distributors? If so, what should their role be?
7. What specific policy recommendations can you suggest in respect of:
   – allocation of distributor franchises?
   – appointment of individual distributors?
   – allocation of end-user accounts between manufacturer and distributors?
   – distributor motivation?
8. In what ways could the immediate situation at Southampton be resolved?

19

Kowloon Oils and Essences (KOE)

This Hong Kong-based partnership was established by Michael Yuan and Qian Qiechen in 1989. The partners operate a small specialised international commodity brokerage from both Hong Kong and Kuala Lumpur. Close contacts with farm co-operatives in mainland China and Indonesia, allied to skills in developing customised databases, enabled the partners to influence the brokerage and trading of specialist oils and natural commodities. These included Tea Tree Oil, Vetivert Oil and Sassafras Oil (to name only three from a range of some 200 products regularly traded by the brokerage). As a result of family connections they opened a buying office in Kuala Lumpur (KL) in 1992. Michael always refers to the office in KL as the 'spying' office, given that the rationale for its existence included the contacts with Indonesia (the historic Spice Islands).

Given the nature of their chosen niche market, competition was limited to a small number of specialist brokers who were normally the subsidiaries of finance houses in London and New York with access to greater financial resources. None of these organisations, however, were dedicated to the trading of natural essential oils and essences, nor could they rival the knowledge base that the partnership had built up not only in South East Asia but across the developing world.

Brokers and Dealers

The partnership acts mainly as *brokers* in the specialised international Essential Oils and Essences market. They are 'market makers', who do not hold stock, but trade on 'back to back' deals, whereby each transaction is comprised of a contract to buy and a contract to sell. The partners were attracted by both the low entry barriers and the low funding requirements. As the sale and purchase occur, 'back to back' funding is not normally a significant consideration. The expertise required to enter the market relates more to the availability of information and contacts in a wide range of international markets. As brokers, KOE's commissions fluctuated between 2 and 5 per cent, depending upon the volume potential of the product. (Low volume, specialised products generated higher margins and attracted less competition.)

By contrast a *dealer* generally takes possession of the goods (before identifying a buyer), and as principal, finances the stockholdings. KOE has recently complimented its brokerage activity with dealerships. This trend has resulted from privileged information (from contacts in China and Indonesia), which allows KOE the opportunity to purchase, for example, more than 70 per cent of the world's supply of specialist crops. The ability to 'corner' a market and generate monopoly prices has begun to concentrate the minds of the partners.

KOE now found themselves in the position of being able to dominate the market for such specialist essential oils (taking examples from most letters of the alphabet) as:

Absinthe Oil	*Olibanum Oil*
Bay Oil	*Pimento Leaf Oil*
Cedarleaf Oil	*Rosemary Oil*
Gingergrass Oil	*Sandalwood Oil*
Ho Leaf Oil	*Tagetes Oil*
Juniperberry Oil	*Valerian Oil*
Lemongrass Oil	*Verbena Oil*
Myrtle Oil	*Wormwood Oil*
Nutmeg Oil	*Ylang Ylang*

The end-users for these products are mainly the international consumer goods processing companies requiring flavours and fragrances. The larger of these end-user companies are serviced by dedicated aroma chemical manufacturers and the fragrance houses, who often attempt to integrate backwards to the raw material sources. Natural products with significant volume potential (such as citrus fruit extracts, menthol and peppermint) are normally sold directly to the producers of food or beverages. The lower volume natural products are characterised by large numbers of manufacturers, traders and specialised brokers.

Definitions

Natural Essential Oils are volatile materials of vegetable origin that are isolated from particular flowers and plants mainly by steam distillation or solvent extraction. Such natural oils suffer from uncertainty of supply and physical instability. All of this leads to a highly volatile market characterised by price fluctuations, tariff complications and competition from synthetic competition based upon the petro-chemical industry.

Aroma Chemicals. In order to produce commercial quantities, aroma chemicals are based upon petro-chemical technology using natural raw materials and/or synthetic equivalents. Given the instability of natural raw materials the synthetic industry continues to grow. Another growth driver is the almost unlimited possibility open to perfumers and flavourists, to find new combinations and create original flavour and fragrance compounds using aroma chemical research. A useful analogy may be the fragrance market itself. For example, concentrated perfume is rarely purchased at point of sale; more often it is a question of the level of concentration of the fragrance in a cologne spray which is the commercially important factor. Equally, the natural ingredient may not be present in any form, as the flavour or fragrance may be 100 per cent synthetic and imperceptible to the final consumer.

Financial Performance

The commission base is some US $13.550.000 of transactions, which generate some $405,000 of revenue. Until recently the brokerage had enjoyed steady growth from a standing start. In the last year, however, commission revenues have slumped by some 35 per cent. This trend appears to be common to the major trading markets of the USA, Europe and South East Asia. Competitors attribute the decline to the recession in the developed world (where the majority of end-user manufacturers are located). KOE believe that the positive aspect of this decline is that competitive brokerages will be even less interested in this niche market.

Despite the global dimensions of international brokerage activities, this international niche market is highly introverted, as a significant number of transactions take place between brokers before the products move along the chain towards the end-user. This gives rise to the distinctive nature of this business, as KOE's competitors are, unusually, also their suppliers and customers. Nevertheless, business is conducted in an atmosphere of secrecy, given the importance of market knowledge. An analysis of KOE's sales by customers shows that some 39 per cent of last year's transactions took place with five of the major international brokerages in Hong Kong, New York and London.

Profits from dealing, as distinct from brokerage activities, are expanding. In the last year dealing activities had expanded to account for some 26 per cent of total partnership net margin (from 10 per cent in the previous year). To date such trading activities have been confined to South East Asia and are dependent on environmental conditions and privileged information.

The Existing Competitive Advantage

KOE's domination of the market for specific natural oils and essences is based upon:

- Niche market brokerage concentration.
- Their policy of concentrating upon specific low-volume, high-margin raw materials (especially those which have no synthetic alternatives).
- Superior access to information in a secretive industry often unwilling to identify sources of information.
- Their linkages with larger commodity brokers in the Hong Kong market.
- Personal contacts with mainland China and Indonesia.
- Their ability to fund stockholdings when opportunities identified themselves.

The Industry and Market

1. The industry is still characterised by low levels of information created by language barriers, unidentified sources and intentional secrecy. The market place is relatively unsophisticated and information flows are incomplete. This creates an opportunity for the broker who is able to access supplies and satisfy demand. Information is only valuable if it is held exclusively by a broker, as this provides power over the market place. KOE's competitors have found it almost impossible to rival the partnership's information relating to South East Asia and specifically China.

2. As most products originate in developing countries, transactions are vulnerable to foreign exchange gains and losses, as well as dependent upon unpredictable environmental and political factors.
3. Social change continues to have a major impact on the industry, given that the demand for flavours, fragrances, essential oils and essences is derived demand, depending upon trends in consumer product markets (for example, shampoos and deodorants). One example of this is the increasing trend towards natural ingredients.
4. KOE attempt to specialise in those products that are relatively price inelastic. In the case of some natural products, this may result from an inability to produce synthetic alternatives. Natural products may be supply-inelastic due to the inflexibility of the growing seasons for particular crops. This creates price volatility, as any shift in demand cannot be satisfied in the short term. This situation provides an opportunity to corner the market and maximise profits by acting as a dealer rather than as a broker.
5. Despite the trend towards natural products, scientific advances are providing an ever-increasing number of substitute synthetic products. These are frequently produced in bulk and are price competitive.
6. The industry is characterised by a long exchange chain, from the raw crop in a developing economy to the industrial manufacturer of food, pharmaceuticals or fragrances in the developed world (from the grower through to the end user). These exchange chains are typically more complex in developing countries where most of the primary products are produced. The exceptions are the vertically integrated consumer goods or aroma chemical companies.

The Exchange Chain

KOE had now become the centre of a complex exchange chain. At one end of the chain is the grower and the foreign merchant for the specialist raw material; at the other end of the chain is the end-user, who is normally an overseas-based processor. Examples of two such chains are summarised below in Figure 19.1.

Figure 19.1 The exchange chain

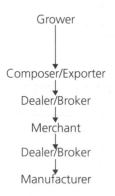

Grower → Merchant → Compounder → Domestic broker → Foreign broker → Dealer → Process industry → End-user

Grower → Composer/Exporter → Dealer/Broker → Merchant → Dealer/Broker → Manufacturer

As there is an additional mark-up at each stage of the chain, an increase in the number of intermediaries in the chain is likely to erode the profit element within each stage. Conversely, the further up or down the chain a broker can operate, the greater the profit potential. Typical margins would be 2 to 5 per cent for brokers and 5 to 25 per cent for dealers and merchants. The situation that KOE is now faced with, is that as the total mark-up within the chain may be as little as 30 per cent (with the dealer/merchant extracting the lion's share), the key requirement is to reduce the number of transactions. This is now becoming possible as global communication becomes a reality.

The Large End-Users

The industry is characterised by the polarisation between the large and smaller end-users. A few large multinational companies operate closely with the major end-users (cutting out brokers and middlemen). Included in this category are such well-known organisations as Proctor and Gamble, Colgate Palmolive, Lever Brothers and Coca Cola. These companies create and manufacture in-house (partially or totally) their own fragrance compounds and limit external purchases to aroma chemicals, essential oils and other natural products. In this context they are major customers for the international fragrance houses.

The major international fragrance houses such as IFF, Givaudan, Haarmann and Reimer, Firmenich and Dragoco have long recognised the need to service and support end-users' requirements by investing in creative talent and flavour and fragrance expertise. This reflects the almost unlimited possibilities open to perfumers and flavourists to find new combinations and create original flavour and fragrance compounds using aroma chemical research. Such high-impact aroma chemicals are often low-volume/high-priced products and therefore the domain of the specialist fragrance companies.

The Smaller End-Users

At the other end of the scale are a large number of small and medium-sized organisations operating across the exchange chain and across a number of niche markets. Such organisations are more likely to be dependent on brokers to identify and source their specialist requirements for relatively small quantities.

Problems and Opportunities

The partnership could rationalise the decline in revenues as a product of the recession of the mid-1990's in the developed world. This in turn was depressing commodity prices in developing economies. The partners considered this to be only part of the story. They believe the market is undergoing a more fundamental structural change. Whilst the specialist broker for natural essences is facing a continuing shrinkage of his business, there is a positive trend away from synthetics towards natural essences. This seemingly paradoxical situation appears to have come about as the two ends of the exchange chain (end-user manufacturing companies and growers) increasingly seek to bypass the centre (the activities of the brokers and merchants).

This market discontinuity is perceived by Michael and Quian as an opportunity to reconfigure their core competencies. The partners recognise that they have more to gain by embracing change rather than resisting it. They perceive that their expertise could lay the foundation for a significant international trading company, provided that they are able to articulate a viable strategic plan. This is required to establish credibility with financiers in Hong Kong, as bank borrowings will be essential to support their vision of a global business. Fortunately, both partners are ambitious and share a common aim to use the current business as a stepping stone towards a more tangible and more significant global business.

The elements of a possible forward plan to achieve this ambition are now beginning to fall into place. These include:

- The opportunity to move the operation from the centre of the exchange chain towards the supply and demand ends.
- Increasingly offer a specialist sourcing service (rather than a brokerage), to specific end-users, based upon the ability to source specialist essential oils and essences world-wide, fully exploiting the trend towards natural flavours and essences.
- End-users to be targeted would be operating in niche markets where compounds have low to moderate volume but high value in use. These compounds would represent only a small fraction of the customers' total costs.
- Emphasise the trading activities (which require the funding of stockholdings) rather than the brokerage expertise, and develop complementary expertise as suppliers to specialist end-users anywhere in the world.
- Continue the specialisation in natural essences of low volume and high margin and act as stocking agents for identified specialist crops.
- Escalate the number of direct contacts with growers, merchants and traders in developing economies in order to seek agency agreements for identified specialist crops.
- Apply this policy to China as a primary objective.
- The recruitment of a network of international agents to negotiate agency purchase agreements with suppliers.
- Turn themselves into international account managers by targeting specific end-user processors/manufacturers in North America, Europe and South East Asia.

It was this last point which was worrying the partners most. The problem was how to identify those processing companies whose needs were not being serviced by the major chemical companies and fragrance houses.

What is not in doubt is the need to move from their current niche before their revenues decline still further.

Your Tasks

Accepting the strategy proposed by Michael and Qian, your task is to recommend a marketing plan to implement and control the new direction indicated by the partners. You will need to:

1. Identify the key marketing issues that have to be addressed, and attempt to prioritise these issues.
2. Propose solutions to the key issues identified in 1 above.
3. Structure a strategic marketing plan which places the emphasis on implementation and action.
4. Detail outline marketing programmes.

Guidelines for the Kowloon Oils and Essences Questions

Taking into account:

- What is the optimum balance between broking and trading activities? Are they mutually supportive?
- Should they concentrate on identifying the suppliers or on identifying the customers?
- What is the time frame for strategic change, how fast should they move?
- What additional resources are required?
- Should they form additional strategic alliances?
- How should the partners identify global client-processing companies?
- What specific service will they offer and how will they deliver this service?
- How will they ensure regular communication and coverage of global clients?
- How will they maintain and extend their superior information base?

20

Philips Electrical Kettles

By J.M. Thölke

The Company and its Market[1]

Philips DAP is a division of Philips Electronics Inc. Philips Electronics Inc. consists of 12 different divisions. The headquarters of all divisions are situated in The Netherlands, while the factories for production are spread all over the world. Philips Electronics Inc. is represented in 60 different countries by national sales organisations (NSOs). In 1994, it employed over 250,000 people. The turnover rose in 1994 to 61.0 bn Dutch guilders, while the financial director published the net profit as being 2.1 bn guilders.

Philips DAP employs about 7,700 people of which 2,900 are in The Netherlands and about 250 at the headquarters in Groningen. Within Philips Electronic Inc., the division is one of the most consistent. Even in the most turbulent years, DAP provided a small but positive share of the total profit. The total turnover of DAP in 1994 was about 3 bn guilders.

In accordance with its name, Philips DAP has two business units, one for small electric domestic appliances and one for personal care products. The business unit of Domestic Appliances is divided into two sections, Kitchen Products and Home Comfort Products. Both sections contain several 'article groups'.

Article groups combine related products. The article group 'beverage', for instance, combines, among other beverage products, electrical kettles and coffee machines. In Philips terms, the latter are called 'product groups', since electrical kettles can be divided again into conventional steel kettles and plastic jugs. Each article group is supervised by an article group manager and each product group has at least one product manager. Those product groups are developed and managed by separate, multi-disciplinary article teams. The management functions involved in the development of electrical kettles, like marketing, consumer research and design, are based in the area of Groningen. The actual place of manufacturing is in the British town of Hastings, on the south coast of England.

Product development at Philips DAP

The development of new products is the task of the article team. The article team is responsible for the realisation of the business strategy in the product. This includes

[1] Besides internal reports of DAP, the following sources were used in this section: *Kernes, M.* (1995), Metamorphosis of a National Symbol, in: *NRC Handelsblad* (14.4.95), 11–12. *Levine, J.B.* (1993), Has Philips found its wizard? *Business Week*, 6 Sept. 50–51. *McAusland, R.* (1988), Designing for a Giant. *Industrial Design*, Jan/Feb, 1988, 6–59.

tactical decisions, such as, the choice of features. The product manager is the official leader of the team. He has to report to his superior, the article group manager. The team consists of managers of the same hierarchical level. Next to the product manager, three parties build the core of the article team: a designer, the head of development and production, and a member of the British sales organisation. The designer co-operates with the product manager, but he is not integrated into the same hierarchy. His function is subordinated to the design manager of the business unit who reports directly to the corporate industrial design department of Philips Eindhoven. Design therefore has a rather independent (and therefore a relatively powerful) consulting task within the team.

Next to the core members of the article team, several other specialists (market research, logistics, quality control, etc.) join the article team whenever their advice is required. The core group recently decided to include the purchasing manager as a permanent member of the article team, since relations with suppliers became increasingly important for the development of electrical kettles.

About two or three times each year the strategies of the various article groups of the business unit are co-ordinated in a 'product policy meeting'. In those meetings the article group manager and the product manager report to the business unit manager.

History

The electrical kettle is a typical British product and therefore British manufacturers dominated the market for a long time. Philips has concentrated on the business since the 1970's. At that time, the firm offered kettles with a relatively weak market position. In the early 1980's a British designer sold Philips a more advanced jug concept. The Dutch manufacturer improved the concept slightly. As electrical kettles gained more importance on the continent, in the early 1990's, DAP decided to put more effort into this market. The design department became more important during the reorganisation, as stressed earlier, and the products created were obliged to have a typical 'Philips look'.

The Product

When experts in the industry talk about an electrical kettle or a jug they talk about a plastic jug. Those jugs enable us to boil water more rapidly than conventional non-electric water kettles and they are independent of hot plates. Next to boiling water with a cooking pan, the electrical kettle is in Europe the most common tool to prepare hot water. Figure 20.1 shows the high-end model of the Philips kettles, introduced as the 'Filter-Line' kettle.

The electrical kettle is not a product that appears to be overloaded with features. On first sight one even has to think about what features a kettle possibly could have and they do not come to mind easily. The managers judge the importance of features as relatively small compared with styling, ergonomics and emotional appeal.

The increase in features might be accelerated due to the replacement of mechanical functions with electronics. For instance, the steam chamber that worked until now with a bimetal device will be replaced by steam sensors.

Figure 20.1 The HD 4391 electrical kettle

The filter, a success story

Until the introduction of the 'filterline' jug, Philips played a negligible role in the market. However, by adding a filter to the known concept of an electrical kettle, the company conquered a major market share in the UK. The filterline kettle was introduced in autumn 1992. Philips' market shares rose from 1.1 per cent of the corded and cordless versions, to 9 per cent (corded) and 18.9 per cent (cordless) respectively. Total market share (including filterless kettles) rose from 6.6 per cent to 16.4 per cent, which shows that the filterless kettle models profited from the success of filterline.

The invention of the feature

In products like the jug, scale was always a problem, especially in England were the water generally has a low quality. The scale settles around the open heating element. If the element gets hot, the metal expands and the scale breaks off into the water and finally into the cup of tea. The R&D manager explains:

> The more scale there is in the water, the bigger is the chance that the heating element blows up. Of course we write in the product's instruction that one has to descale the jug occasionally, but in practice this does not often happen. Then the products come back broken and the discussion starts – who is responsible, the user, the manufacturer, the retailer, the supplier of the heating element?

One solution to prevent at least the scale from getting into the drink, was filtering the water in the kettle. The idea was discussed vaguely, but the responsible people (R&D and product management) put the idea aside with the argument, 'It does not solve the consumer problem'. The discussion about the filter feature came back in the years 1989–90. Those years were extraordinarily dry, and in England, the water was extremely poor. Next to the 'normal' scale, other dirt particles floated in the water. This caused many jugs to collapse and the number of jugs returning to the factory rose. The R&D manager continued:

> Consumers are powerful in the UK . . . If you are not happy with the performance of your new product you just bring it back and get the money.

The dirty water was a real problem to the customer. The tea water was too off-putting to drink without filtering it first. Retailers reported those market signals to the national sales organisation (NSO). At that time, smaller manufacturers started to offer loose water filters to overcome that problem. One of Philips biggest competitors decided to promote those loose filters together with their electrical kettles, according to the product manager, and Philips was forced to react:

> O.K., then we said that we needed a filter in our jug that improves the quality of the water to such an extent, that most of the dirt and the scale stays out of the customer's cup of tea.

The choice to develop such a filter was still very controversial and the idea had already hung around for two years before it was finally approved. It was a top management problem, as the product manager explains:

> Because of bad management, the filter idea was for a long time neglected. Management suppressed the idea because they were not ready to fight the actual problems up front.

Opposition came especially from the technical people in the development team. It was difficult to put such a filter in the jug design and one doubted that this feature would be successful in countries other than the UK. The technical staff (R&D) wondered if it would be possible to communicate the advantage to the customer since a filter keeps scale out of the tea but the water still destroys the heating element:

> The only problem we solve, is that the consumer does not get so much scale in the cup. One perceives the water as even more dirty, because the particles stay in the jug.

But there were also rumours that competition was working on the same idea. Under the push of the British NSO and product marketing, prototypes were created and the tests with consumers indicated a major success. So the filter was incorporated into a jug concept that was almost ready for production. A former marketing manager remembered:

> The filter idea came in a late stage of development. Caused by the technical problems, we decided to put one single person on the filter project to develop the best solution possible. At that time we also decided to postpone the introduction of the new product for the development of that feature.

The development of the feature and the necessary changes in design proved to be worth the efforts. The product manager said:

> Honestly, we could have never foreseen what a success it was finally. I don't think that there are examples of such a movement in any other business. At that time it did not go very well with Philips jugs, actually with nobody in the market. We achieved with the filter an increase of the whole market of 25 per cent of what it was before and that in as competitive a market as the UK.

This success came as a surprise. After six to 12 months, all of the bigger competitors had copied the idea of the filter. The product manager continued:

> You could easily see how they had to hurry with copying the feature. You see that they put filters in models that were never designed to carry a filter.

Competitors preferred bizarre solutions and sub-optimal performance to a product without a filter.

Problems and Key Topics

The following section explores the factors that turn the decision about new product features into a difficult task.

Division of responsibilities

In the company's past it was often top management that put the team under pressure, whenever competition introduced a new feature. Today, it is the official rule within DAP, that the article team has full responsibility over tactical decisions. However, the unco-ordinated involvement of top management is still a difficult topic. On the one hand it motivates, on the other hand it can hinder the process; if management promotes single features for other than strategic reasons, the team members get frustrated and the process loses efficiency.

Lack of control

The control of a proper translation of market needs into a technical specification is a major problem in the development process. The more specific the knowledge of a discipline, the more freedom there is to manipulate the marketing briefing.

Evaluation of a product advantage

A clear product advantage is the most stressed success factor of a new product. Marketing is supposed to focus upon the consumer need, while examples of the past showed that market research does not produce valid results and often hinders innovations. The senior product manager claims:

> You cannot ask consumers directly [if they want a feature], they have a limited view . . .'

It is a difficult task to anticipate a feature's value before the market has actually shown its advantage. Acceptance at the retail and user-level cannot be predicted for certain by marketing instruments. Concerning innovations, the managers are sceptical towards market research activities. Research, for instance, reports the feature 'tiredness of the customer'. However, contradictory to research findings, consumers that are in the purchase situation prefer products with many features to products with few features. As the designer said:

> One is still educated in such a way as to think *more* resembles *better*!

This statement of the designer contrasts the opinions of R&D and product marketing respectively:

> Before, we thought we have to offer [. . .] more and more [. . .], but [now we know that] this is not true.

According to the marketer it is the retailer who seeks for 'more', while the consumer asks for 'better' . . .

retail has a shorter scope than the consumer has. . .

In the eyes of the marketer, consumers are not interested in more features. The perceived irrationality of the consumer, who asks for simple products and in spite of that buys complex products, enlarges the manager's frustrations with market research.

The art of selecting product features

Ideas for new features can originate anywhere in the organisation. The product manager explained:

It is dangerous if there is [a strict division between] the research laboratory that has the task to find inventions and other people who get paid to sell the [inventions]. [. . .] In many cases it works, though [feature innovations] can originate everywhere in the organisation. It is an art to grab those ideas and push them through. This is [just as important as] spending money on research, since you need to know what to look for.

A strict division between research and the rest of the company is dangerous, since they are the people who are in contact with the market and who know about consumer needs. Features are not exclusively invented by professional researchers. New ideas can come, for instance, from outside the company (retailers and suppliers) or from inside the company (research, article team, etc.). Many ideas for new features exist in the company for years before they get 'discovered'. The quest for new product ideas and their recognition is described by the product manager as an art. This art of organisational knowledge has two dimensions: one has to recognise the idea and one has to have the power to push it through. The manager evaluates this 'art' as equally important as, for instance, the company's research efforts.

The rules of the market

Features of a product hardly fade out anymore. Retail and consumers expect the product extras as standard and therefore the basic product is constantly growing. If this process goes on, electrical kettles could enter the same dead-end road as many items in the consumer electronics and telecommunication industry have. Take for example the programmable video recorder. First, the feature was introduced to gain advantage, now it often hinders the ease of use of the product. Second, price erosion occurs when new features become standardised too quickly. Products with too many features are a typical symptom of a mature market with high competition. In the mature market, retail and supply become more dominant and threaten the manufacturer's profit.

Speed to market

This is an essential factor for new product success. Kettles are developed according to certain deadlines that are co-ordinated with the national sales organisations and retailers of different countries. New seasons, trade fairs and the publishing of product catalogues are major causes behind those time limitations.

The tendency to speed up product development cycles has the consequence that products get onto the shelves with a higher risk of sub-optimality. The pressures of time and money encourage mis-communications early in the process and narrow down the flexibility to discuss solutions later on.

How the company deals with the problems

According to the R&D manager, in the past decision problems such as that with the filter were common practice, but nowadays it is 'unthinkable', due to the clear strategic goals and the professionalism of the article team.

The company appeared to evolve from a reactive and technology-focused organisation, to an innovative firm that seeks to provide products that make life for the consumer more convenient. The new 'official' philosophy of the Philips division is represented by the company's strategic intent:

> DAP will be perceived as the best company, because we deliver best on the core consumer need through better product performance. DAP improves the lives of consumers.

The reorganisation within DAP led to a few changes to past practice. The main improvement is the focus upon a single, clearly communicated core consumer need. The consumer need is defined in the company strategy and serves as a guideline for product decisions. So the R&D manager claimed:

> Now, we want to find core consumer needs and focus upon them. If we orientate ourselves constantly on the developments of the competitors, like it happened in the past, then we would lose our own strategic direction within a few years.

Furthermore:

> Now we do feature development in line with the strategy. As long as we follow [the strategy] top management is not going to say: 'guys, the strategy has changed, let's do something else now!' [. . .] In the past, this happened a lot. Especially in the period when we reacted on competition all the time. [. . .] We have now such an atmosphere within DAP, that nobody would accept that anymore.[. . .] Five or six years ago we mainly imitated features. [. . .] Now we try to innovate, driven by a consumer need. [. . .]

Today, new features evolve due to a concentration on the core consumer need while in the past improvements often were results of coincidence. In the past, one did not innovate according to a given strategy, but because of competition. Then, top management involvement was common practice; now the article team has more responsibility of its own. The clear strategy gave structure to the decision process and imitation was replaced by innovation.

The strategy is described by naming the ten most important steps that lead to the evaluation, the selection, the development and the marketing of product features.

1. A strategy with a core consumer need.

First the core consumer need is defined in the strategy. The selection of the core consumer need is a task of top management and is based on market information combined with a vision of future developments. Top management also translates the core consumer need into a keyword (e.g. cleanability, safety, usability, etc.) that serves as a guideline for further product decisions. The R&D manager explained:

> We talk with [the Business Unit Manager] about consumer needs. Those consumer needs built the basis of our product strategy. [. . .] Safety is an example of such a core consumer need. 'How' we implement this consumer need and 'what' features we choose, does not interest him that much. He only checks if those features are in line with the strategy we agreed upon.

A core consumer need such as 'safety' is not selected for a single product category but for several article groups .

2. The team approach.

Later, an interdisciplinary team is responsible for the development of the new product or product line. An efficient team approach and a highly structured development process are strong points of the development at DAP. The team consists of technical and commercial experts and a facilitator, who is the formal leader of the project. Other professionals, who do not belong to the core team, assist whenever needed.

The feature decision is determined by a reactive and a proactive dimension. The reactive choice focuses on 'what is', while the proactive choice is directed on 'what could be':

> We make a product that will be placed in a certain market environment. [The new product] must fit in the existing 'feature picture' of the market [. . .]. That is first, the *reactive choice*. Secondly, very important is the *proactive choice*: [. . .] can I create a feature that makes sense? [. . .] that is easy to communicate? [. . .] [that is] a USP, something the others do not have? [or that leads to a] product improvement [regarding] convenience or ease of use?

3. Clear positioning.

The right positioning of the product and its features is responsible for success in the market. The R&D manager stated:

> I am convinced that [bad featuring] has to do with (a) wrong positioning, if you do not know your target group and (b) features that are comparable to the lights on a Christmas tree [in other words: gimmicks].

According to the R&D manager, the definition of the target group and a high quality set of features are essential.

Marketing writes a product briefing with the general description of the product. Product management positions the new product according to company goals and market needs and presents the results to the team. Tools for the product's positioning are mapping techniques, segmentation, competitor analysis, risk analysis matrixes (investments) and price points. Constant monitoring of the market reveals potential innovations and the development of features into standards. The analysis results in an understanding of what are standard attributes and what are features. Then, a first provisional division of products in a product line is made.

4. Feature decision.

The **reactive feature decision (4a)** is simple: it is an assemblage of existing parts, 'a variation on the same topic' as the manager calls it. The product manager perceives the reactive decision as unproblematical:

> In fact it is annoying to talk about decisions [. . .], there is not so much to decide [. . .] you decide to go left or right. Most decisions are not really decisions but more logical conclusions that follow the facts.

The decision space for the manager in reactive feature decisions is very limited, which can be annoying because of their intrinsic limitations. He sees the choice of the features as a logical conclusion of the product ranges the company already has. On the other hand, management is anxiously looking for new features, that are investigated in proactive feature decisions.

The team discusses in an idea session new feature developments, that have the potential to replace the filter in its function as a USP. This most challenging 'quest' is called the **proactive feature decision (4b)**.

5. Iterations.

After step four, an iterative process starts in which product management is responsible for the agenda. In official meetings, the features with highest priority are discussed. The product gets more shape with every iteration.

6. 'Decision rules'.

'Uncertain' features are evaluated with the help of a few techniques, rules or guidelines. The most important decision rules are described below.

- **QFD**. Quality Function Deployment (QFD) is meant as a tool to translate consumer wishes into technical specifications. The Philips article team uses QFD specifically to evaluate product features. The designer explained:

  > First step in new product development is always an idea generation and a quality function deployment session. [QFD] is a rational approach mainly to determine if the implementation of a certain feature makes sense.

According to the product manager, Quality Function Deployment (QFD) is a helpful tool to guide product definition. He explained:

> The good thing is, that it works not mainly in evaluating the attributes by numbers, but the method makes communication easier between the different people. With QFD you can describe exactly what a feature is, because you are forced to give such a feature an unequivocal name. If you don't, then it does not fit within the matrix.

The method helps the managers to select features 'that make sense' by facilitating communication. QFD also imposes a few problems: (1) innovations like the filter are difficult to grasp by the method; (2) people are invited to manipulate the results by rating one feature very high and all others low; (3) the method induces groupthink problems: the group spirit biases common sense judgements; and (4) people get tired of QFD: 'Do we have to think of something new again?'

Those criticisms are the reason for the product manager to use QFD as an assisting tool of which the outcome must still be discussed:

> We use QFD, but that does not mean that we follow the results of the sessions blindly. [. . .] If you don't watch out, you easily overlook the problems with it. This is extremely dangerous. You need to test [QFD results] always against your 'gut feeling'!

- **Evaluation criteria.** The R&D manager reduced feature choice to three criteria: quality improvement, cost reduction and customer advantage:

> It is important to test the ideas early in the development process according to the three most important criteria: (1) is there a quality improvement? (2) does it save costs? or (3) can we create an advantage for our customer? If one of the criteria is fulfilled, then O.K., go ahead with the idea – if none of the criteria is fulfilled then forget it!

New features must be sufficient on at least one of the three criteria.
- **Clear definition of product features.** According to the designer there must be a clear separation between the basic function and the feature to distinguish the real features from the 'empty features' (gimmicks). He suggests a balance between basic function and features:

> A good product has a stable design, a good basic function and [for the consumer] an understandable set of features. All three dimensions are in balance, without hindering each other. In consumer electronics those three are not in balance – in some examples the number of features hinders the design or the other way around; in other products the ease of use of the basic function is hindered by design – this situation screams for regulations.

He assumed that in consumer electronics the basic function of the product is not clearly defined. For instance, in the performance of the receiver of a radio, the range between bad and good performance is relative. When is the sound good? A jug on the other hand boils water, which is a simple, understandable function for everybody. It is not possible to boil water 'more' or 'less' well.

A balance must be created between basic functions, features and design, when the basic function and its capabilities are defined. The designer also suggested manufacturing products that are fully automatic on the one hand, but that can also be manually operated. The reflex camera serves as an example. It solves a problem of the consumer in an intelligent way:

> You can use technology in an intelligent way, for instance, reflex cameras. [Reflex cameras are full of features], but if you look at the product, you do not see many buttons. The essence is taking pictures, the computer does the calculating.

Consumers do not necessarily have to understand the features necessary to take good pictures. For experts, the camera works also without all those automatic functions. The new 'simple' remote controls of television sets fit within this idea. The consumer has all the possibilities without them hindering the daily routine.
- **Price points.** Each new feature must fit within the scheme of price points. The first steps of the model reveal a list of options of those features that can be considered in a new product. Jugs, for instance, can be: with or without water level indicator, with or without an on/off lamp, corded or cordless, with a lid

that locks or with a lid that needs to be pushed and with or without a filter. Those five features alone open possibilities for $2^5= 64$ products. Still, no company offers 64 models of an electrical kettle. The product manager explained how he reduces the possibilities down to six or seven models:

> The six or seven possibilities are more or less based on what we already had. The new range follows an older range. You choose according to what the competitors offer at that moment and according to estimated cost prices. Of course it can happen that [there is a nice feature] that raises the product price to 83 guilders. [However, 83 guilders] is not a price point and 89 guilders is too expensive, [This is] bad luck! The product must be 79 guilders. [. . .] We do not look too precisely, but [. . .] every extra feature must clearly be a new price point.

Examples for price points of electrical kettles are Fl. 69.-, Fl. 79.- or Fl. 89.-. If the new feature causes the product to exceed a price point, it is not selected, or the team has to cut costs in another place. In fact the criteria 'price points' and 'competitors' restrict the decision space to a minimum. However, if a feature is good, then there is room for discussion.

- **Costs versus features.** Costs are very restrictive criteria. They compete constantly with the criteria 'potential added value':

> We realised, [for instance, due to the filter] that added benefit sells a lot more than it costs. [. . .] The pure cost price of a product, the sum of its parts and the assemblage, [. . .] that is a very annoying topic. It is no fun to talk about cost reductions, everybody gets sick of it, [. . .] really frustrating. Imagine, we talk about cost reductions of 2 per cent, which is nothing on the single product, but a lot regarding all of the products. However, as soon as the dollar or the pound change, you lose everything. So sometimes we get the feeling of working for nothing. [. . .] Talking about costs can also be contradictory, for instance, if quality must be higher, since products that come back with damages raise the [reparation] costs. Then the actual costs of the product need to be increased . . .

The company is constantly busy with cutting costs wherever possible. The discussion is systematised in the development process. Cutting costs and raising customer value at the same time is a basic dilemma of the feature-decision process, which is annoying according to the product manager. Experience showed that the 'added benefit' argument counts for more than the restriction of price increase.

- **Consensus within the team.** Philips managers agree, decisions about features are more often a result of negotiations than of formal procedures. Decisions. . .

> are rarely taken by voting, almost always they follow after a discussion and result in a consensus.

The feature set of a product is good, if there is a general consensus in the team. If there is strong opposition, something is not sufficient. Intuitive reasoning (feeling) therefore plays an important role. As the R&D manager says:

> After three years of experience I have now more or less the feeling if the development goes in the right direction. [. . .] One indicating factor is the attitude of the development team. If everybody in the team shares the good feeling about the new product, then you can bet on the fact that the product will be a success. If one in the team has a bad feeling about the product, then I can be sure something is wrong.

According to him, a consensus leads to a product with a good set of features, while unsolved conflicts indicate that the feature set is insufficient.

7. Practices to support the decision.

The team tries to reach a consensus about the values of the new product's features. One unique important feature is chosen to be the attraction of the product. The following guidelines help the managers to make a decision in case of doubtful features:

- **Expert advice whenever needed.** The product manager invites a special adviser (market research, quality control, fundamental research, etc.) to collect information and give his opinion in an official team meeting.
- **Experimental products.** New features are first tried out on products that are not essential to profitability.

  We put the feature first in a product that is not that important for our return; with such products it is less risky to experiment. With the 'bread and butter range' of the company it is not that easy. In those models, a feature is a way of no return.

- **Consumer complaints.** Figures about consumer complaints are one way to measure quality in an objective way. The analysis of the complaints discloses whether a feature improved the product's reliability or not.

8. Relationship to supply.

This is essential for the development of a new kettle. Make or buy decisions regarding features belong to the top priority issues in this phase of development. Financial consequences have to be set off against the risk of becoming too dependent on a single market partner. Two issues need to be mentioned regarding the relationship to supply: make or buy decisions and the power balance between the market partners.

- **Make or buy decision.** According to the R&D manager, the development of components can be seen as a core competence of the company, like technological know-how or the ability to organise the process efficiently. Which components need to be developed in-house and which can best be bought therefore is a strategic issue:

  Core competencies can be components, technologies, but also organisational processes. If we are in a mature market with a heavy pressure on the price, it is most suitable to decide to buy the core competence. If we are in a more promising market, we have to check if we are able to deal with the core competence ourselves. If we are, then it is best to go ahead with our own possibilities. If we are not, we have to ask if it fits into the strategic plan that we learn to achieve the necessary knowledge within a reasonable time. If that seems feasible, we can make co-developments for the first period and then go independently. If this is not desirable for whatever reasons, then we have to look for partnerships and co-makerships.

In mature markets, it is cheaper to buy than to develop components. In 'more promising', growing markets, independent development or co-development is preferred.

- **The power relationship with the supplier:** If the company decides not to develop a certain component, long-term relations need to be formed. Clear agreements about the outcomes of the co-operation help to reduce the risk of losing the rights of common ideas. There are two solutions to the problem: (1) exclusive rights for the innovation over a period of one or two years or (2) rights until the investment is earned back. The latter helps mainly to prevent price erosion. However, if a really communicable product advantage is possible and profitable, independent development is favoured.

9. Development and technical specification.
Problems in the design phase can put the project back to step 5. Features that are chosen as USPs require special treatment during the actual design of the product.

- Design around the USP. The product is developed around the USP feature. The article team knows how important it is, that a new feature has the potential to communicate without sales personnel or instruction books. In the case of the filter, the name 'filterline' on the outside of the product indicates that the jug has a filter. Now the designers experiment with different colours for the feature. Filters are removable to give people the opportunity to take them in their hands. If there is more than one feature to promote on the surface of a product, the designer recommended using removable stickers to describe the features. This is a creative solution to express the attractions of the product in the store without hindering the product's aesthetics at home.

10. Market introduction.
Two feature-related practices are important for the introduction of a new product. The promotion of different features in markets that are in different stages of their life cycle and the selection of distribution channels.

- **Different features for growing and mature markets.** In a mature market (like that which jugs represent in the UK), a very good extra, single feature (like the filter) can change the whole competitive situation. In a growing market, though, features play a different role. The marketing manager explained:

  > In a growing market, all the features are interesting, the product is compared to totally different product categories as the usual pots you put on the stove. Then, features like the 'three way safety' and the 'movability' [cordless and therefore independent from the stove] become as important as the new filter.

The ideal feature set for a growing market like Germany is different from the set of features expected in the British market. In countries where the whole product concept is new or where the water is so clean that, for instance, a filter is irrelevant, the basic features are relatively more important than single-feature innovations. In markets like the UK, therefore, new features must be advertised, while in growing markets, where the concept of electricity and water often creates suspicion (because electricity together with water signifies danger), more basic features, such as, for instance, the 'three way safety' can be emphasised.

- **How to select retailers.** The retailers are extremely important for the introduction of electrical kettles and Philips therefore needs to select carefully the products they make for different retailers. Otherwise price wars are risked that usually turn out to be disastrous for both retailer and manufacturer alike:

We sell, for instance, a Philips model with and without water level indication. This makes a difference of about one Dutch guilder manufacturing costs, and in the UK that is about a one pound difference in retail price. Retailer A takes the model with the indication and sells it for 20 pounds, retailer B sells the one without for 19 pounds. In this way we manage to keep them out of each other's way, otherwise they would both sell the product first for 18 pounds, and then start a price war.

Philips tries to gain strength in relation to retail by adding new features, but also with gratifications, incentives, point of sales promotions and advertisements. The better the market position of the Philips product, the less dependent is the producer on the retailer. The struggle in gaining power has several dimensions:

1. Create an efficient market push (marketing instruments) and a substantial demand pull (the consumer knows the product and asks for it). The management of DAP chooses a few products and calls them superstars. Those top products are supposed to pull the rest of the models to combine forces. Within the range of electrical kettles, the cordless 'filterline' jug is a superior example of a superstar.

   The status of a superior product (such as the filterline electrical kettle) is of course extremely important. Those products compete with all other brands that are placed on the shelves. If you are number one or two in a market, then the representative has a totally different position at the retailer than when he is one of many. We sell a product four to five times before a consumer uses it at home!

2. According to the managers, retailers expect new products each year. However, they are satisfied with small changes. This can be another feature or a different styling, but also another colour and a few more graphics. In the eyes of the retailer, small changes are sufficient for a product to be 'new'.
3. Philips enters into OEM (Original Equipment Manufacturer) business only with companies that have the same quality image as Philips. With those direct clients the manufacturer has close contact and they can order products 'custom assembled'. A clear OEM policy requires also that the competition between the various OEM customers does not endanger its own profits.

The reorganisation within Philips increased the ability of the company to survive in a flexible environment. One aspect in that general process is the effort to minimise the restrictions imposed upon the company by external interests. As a market-oriented, innovative company they strive to be a player in the market, rather than the party that is played with.

21
The Royal China Group A[1]

Background

The Royal China Group (RCG) was created in 1983 as a result of a merger between two famous and well-established Stoke-on-Trent pottery companies each of which had distinct traditions and operating methods. Even today, the tradition of rivalry between the two organisations continues, as the manufacturing operations remain in the original sites. General management, marketing (including central warehousing and distribution), finance and personnel, however, are centralised at one of the original manufacturing locations.

Two of the four Royal China manufacturing units have manufactured fine china and earthenware since the end of the eighteenth century. The company is proud of its dual heritage and tradition. This includes the famous pattern books, the Royal Warrant (still awarded on a personal basis), the two museums, the craft traditions of hollowware manufacture and hand decoration and, above all, the two internationally-respected company names, 'Royal China' and 'Cromwell'.

These corporate identities have distinct customer followings and traditions. This reflects their origins as discrete pottery companies. Customers tend to relate to Royal China or Cromwell rather than RCG.

The two identities support a full range of fine china, earthenware, tableware and cookware. RCG, therefore, competes in most sectors of the mid-priced to premium priced tableware and cookware markets. RCG has no desire to compete with lower-priced products in wider distribution, as they believe such a policy would be incompatible with their image, skills and traditions. Their products include the most exclusive bone china tableware, medium-priced tableware, fine ornamental ware, giftware, casual earthenware, kitchenware and oven to tableware.

Definitions

The industry differentiates between its products or 'bodies' on the following basis:
Fine China: a general term for quality bone china and porcelain.
Bone China: a hard vitreous material having properties of strength, translucency and whiteness. Bone Chine normally includes approximately 50 per cent bone ash,

---

[1] Although based upon a real business situation, the Royal China Group and its personnel are fictional. As people, places, products and data have been modified all information provided in the case is for teaching purposes only and should not be used for factual information.

25 per cent china clay and 25 per cent feldspar. It is almost exclusively manufactured in the UK (porcelain being the common type of fine pottery in continental Europe).
Porcelain: a hard vitreous material somewhat weaker than bone china. It is characterised by a hard glaze and semi-translucency. Hard porcelain normally includes some 50 per cent china clay.
Earthenware: the basic potters clay of many varieties and compositions, but best-known is the traditional cream-coloured earthenware which was the 'dominant design' for the industrialisation of tableware. Earthenware is a naturally porous, opaque material which is then glazed to produce a non-porous product.
Stoneware: similar to earthenware but manufactured with a higher proportion of stone. The resulting product is harder and more expensive to produce than earthenware.

The Heritage of the Original Companies

Prior to 1983 there was no such organisation as the Royal China Group. Royal China and Cromwell had been distinct Staffordshire companies and rivals for over 200 years.

Royal China

Royal China was the original name of one of the two companies. The company was formed during the American War of Independence. Its first commissions were to supply fine china tableware to the gentry of England. Royal China's fine china products were originally inspired to supply fine china to the exclusive 'one thousand families of England'.

In 1822 Royal China secured the Royal Warrant from George IV. It was believed at the time that the fat King's real objective was to further spite his wife by ordering the finest dinnerware for Carlton House where he entertained his mistresses. (He had recently had his Queen put on trial for infidelity and excluded from his coronation, by having her locked out of Westminster Abbey.)

With the coming of the Industrial Revolution and the development of the middle classes, the company successfully transferred its famous name to both medium-priced china tableware and earthenware kitchenware. This allowed Royal China to develop a volume business by diversifying into medium-priced tableware and kitchenware. Today, Royal China's heritage remains manifest in ornamental ware and premium-priced tableware. Profitability problems are now being experienced with the lower-priced products, given foreign and domestic competition.

Cromwell China

Cromwell China was formed in the 1830's to exploit the emerging process technology of continuous production. This process innovation drove down production costs and created a market for affordable earthenware. Cromwell was one of the first Staffordshire manufacturers to commercialise the now famous blue and white earthenware. In an age without photography, Cromwell perfected and popularised the under-glaze blue, earthenware designs, representing the romanticism of the 'grand tour', the mystery of Arcadia and the fascination with classical China. These now traditional designs are found on pine dressers across the country, reflecting the change in status from utility ware to collectors' items and giftware.

Cromwell was relatively late in developing a manufacturing base for fine china. From the late nineteenth century, however, Cromwell began to produce some of the finest tableware in the country based upon unique shapes and the skills of dedicated craftsmen and decorators. While Royal China was steadily developing its kitchenware base, Cromwell carefully built its reputation in the premium china tableware market sector. Today, Cromwell China has few rivals in this premium sector. Cromwell china is now to be found on the most exclusive tables in the world. Even the 'Palace' was willing to grant a Royal Warrant, but only on the condition that the name Cromwell was removed from the 'backstamp'!

The problem the company has yet to resolve is the balance between the two main product groups, fine china and earthenware, which required different manufacturing skills and marketing programmes.

In summary, Royal China had started as an exclusive fine china manufacturer who subsequently developed further down-market, whilst Cromwell started mid-market and developed further up-market.

Recent History

Sadly, the recent history of the group reflected many changes of direction in terms of marketing strategy. Part of the problem was the tradition and heritage which tended to work against customer orientation; traditional management and workers alike tended to regard themselves as custodians of a unique tradition, and as such they were not always responsive to changing market requirements. There tended to be an attitude of 'we will supply you as and when we are ready'. Consequently, customer service and delivery were major problem areas for RCG. Company humour held that as delivery dates were frequently long, order forms should be modified to include a space for customers to give their next of kin!

Longer-serving RCG middle management tended to blame external events such as foreign competition or the policies of the holding company for the declining fortunes of RCG, rather than questioning their own attitudes and recipes for the business. This situation was aggravated by the appointment of three new directors within the past year, all of whom had been transferred from other positions within the holding company. Nevertheless, corporate performance had been adversely affected by the frequent changes of ownership, as different owners attempted to extract cash, sell assets or rush for growth, depending upon the needs of the parent company.

The Financial Situation

The information presented here relates to the UK and export business only (North America excluded).

Table 21.1 Net sales and margins by product type (£000's at MSP², 1994 fiscal year)

	C'Well	Royal China	Totals	Gross profit	% Sales/MSP
China tableware	4,249	6,203	10,452	3,171	30
E'ware/Cookware	3,167	7,309	10,476	5,128	49
E'ware/Tableware	3,433	–	3,433	1,468	43
Giftware	1,006	752	1,758	791	45
Ornamental	–	883	883	529	60
Total	11,855	15,147	27,002	11,087	41

² Manufacturers selling price

Table 21.2 Net sales and margins by product type (£000's at MSP, 1993 fiscal year)

	C'Well	Royal China	Totals	Gross profit	% Sales/MSP
China tableware	3,347	7,435	10,782	3,881	36
E'ware/Cookware	3,814	7,210	11,024	5,512	50
E'ware/Tableware	3,065	–	3,065	1,318	43
Giftware	1,205	665	1,870	842	45
Ornamental	–	761	761	479	63
Total	11,431	16,071	27,502	12,032	44

The following sales trends result (1993/1994):

China tableware	−3%
Earthenware cookware	−5%
Earthenware tableware	+12%
Giftware	−6%
Ornamental ware	+16%

RCG: Balance sheet and profit and loss statement

By 1994, RCG's 'full range strategy' was becoming increasingly difficult to sustain, given the changes in the market environment, competitive activity and the costs and complexity of servicing the many different product lines. By 1994 the group was experiencing financial difficulties. These can be summarised as:

- Negative profitability
- Low capital investment in new technology
- Decreasing sales and market shares (so far as these could be guesstimated)
- Falling margins
- Minimal marketing investments in brand/corporate equities

Table 21.3 RCG balance sheet

Balance Sheet As at:	31/3/93	31/3/94
Assets	£000's	£000's
Current Assets		
Cash	205	46
Raw Materials	2,870	2,552
WIP	3,833	3,552
Finished Goods	9,345	10,692
Accounts Receivable	3,645	3,142
Prepaid Expenses	79	159
Other Current Assets	137	122
Total Current Assets	20,114	20,265
Net Fixed or Plant Assets		
Land and Buildings freehold	1,607	1,549
Land and Buildings leasehold	286	266
Equipment and Machinery	2,880	2,471
Vehicles	95	80
Other Fixed Assets	12	12
Total Net Fixed Assets	4,880	4,378
Total Assets	24,994	24,643
Liabilities and Owners Equity		
Current Liabilities		
Trade Creditors	2,722	3,243
Other Creditors	345	124
Accrued Expenses	619	679
Other Current Liabilities	673	490
Total Current Liabilities	4,359	4,536
Long Term Liabilities		
Intercompany Loans*	14,349	14,349
Bank Borrowings	4,995	5,688
Other L-T Liabilities	70	70
Total L-T Llabilities	19,413	20,107
Total Liabilities	23,772	24,643
Reserves	1222	0
Total Liab and Owner's Equity	24,994	24,643

* Loan from TTI at 5%.

Table 21.4 RCG income statement

Income Statement £000's Royal China (UK and Export)	Year Ending 31/3/93	31/3/94
Gross Revenue	33,853	33,622
Discounts	6,351	6,620
Net Revenue	27,502	27,002
Cost of Goods	15,470	15,915
Gross Profit	12,032	11,087
Direct SBU Expenses		
Selling and Distribution	1,386	1,370
Ad, Promotion and Exhibitions	754	804
Retail Commissions	1,932	1,806
Direct Retail O/H's	1,980	1,940
Export Commissions	392	402
Factory Shops	596	602
Total Direct	7,040	6,924
Indirect Expense		
Central Warehousing	877	903
Design & NPD	309	402
Administration and General	1,468	1,520
Depreciation	545	521
Other Operating Expenses	428	556
Total Indirect	3,627	3,902
Total Operating Expenses	10,667	10,826
Net Operating Income	1,365	261
Interest Expense	900	1,127
Net Income before Corp. Tax	465	(866)
Tax @ 33%	153	0
Net Income	312	(866)

The company is also experiencing increasing logistical problems with manufacturing, warehousing and distribution. This adversely affects the quality of customer service, which in turn reduces the likelihood of customer repeat purchase. The expense of financing the increasing working capital requirements has also to be considered. The seemingly ever-increasing mountain of finished stock (44 per cent of which is discontinued lines or unbalanced stock, such as cups without saucers) is a primary concern to the managing director.

The owner, Toy Town International (TTi), is a major toy conglomerate who acquired RCG three years ago as part of a diversification strategy. TTi have already made it clear that they would 'restructure' or dispose of the company (in part or in total), unless a revised strategic plan could convince them of the potential of their investment. Given the independence of the North American marketing operations, the requested strategic plan is to be focused on the domestic and export operations of the original two Staffordshire companies. TTi have requested that full account be taken of the financial realities of the business.

The People and Politics of RCG

RCG's organisational structure is set out below.

Figure 21.1 RCG's organisational structure

RCG's senior management team include:

- The Managing Director
- The Logistics Director
- The Operations Director
- Two Manufacturing Directors (Royal China and Cromwell)
- The Financial Director
- The Marketing Director
- The Personnel Director

The three directors appointed by TTi within the last year include the managing director and the finance director, who were transferred from their positions within TTi's existing operations. TTi has also created a new logistics position at director level, to address the issues of factory loading, inventory and delivery. The logistics director is rumoured to be the pending replacement for the current operations director. The new directors are all under 42 years old and well versed in TTi's culture of control and expertise at 'squeezing the assets'. The remaining directors and senior managers are mainly longer-term RCG employees, who formally worked for the separate companies.

The directors and three senior mangers form an operating group which meets every Monday at 8 a.m. The three senior managers are:

- The manager responsible for the management accounts
- The sales manager
- The design manager

Figure 21.2 The operating group

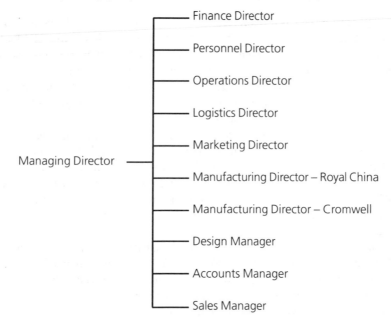

Once a month the operating group is joined by TTi's Group Financial Director who chairs the monthly meetings in the full splendour of the former Royal China boardroom. The atmosphere is rich in heritage (as well as tobacco smoke as the MD likes to encourage his habit), as the board room is adjacent to both the Company Museum and HH's panelled office (HH refers to the preferred way of addressing the new managing director).

The management team is divided both by experience and by loyalty. Whilst there is a broad consensus between those directors who have been appointed directly by TTi within the last year, the remaining directors suspect their colleagues of being party to a possible TTi alternative agenda. The situation is not conducive to a stable management team. Tensions surfaced once the survival and forward strategy questions became the key agenda issues. Two sides emerged, known as the 'Toy-men' and the 'China-men' (in this traditional industry women were yet to be represented at senior management level).The Toy-men tend to complain of the lack of urgency of the China-men with regard to the financial situation, whilst the China-men complain of the 'short-termism' of the Toy-men.

Management meetings tended to reflect this difference, with the Toy-men emphasising this year's results in terms of cash flow and asset management, whilst the China-men emphasise factory and craft skills, new products, investment in new technology, markets and distribution channels. Apart from 'Toy-men and China-men' driven differences, there are differing personal views as to the forward direction of the business which will be explored later in the case.

The view from HH's chair

Harold T. Holt (HH as he expected to be called, given that he disliked being called Harold) was fresh from a successful US assignment with TTi Inc. HH had something of a reputation for being a no-nonsense action man. His physical appearance, being tall and slim, supported this image, as did his mode of speech. This frequently sounded like a new street language to outsiders. HH's linguistic impact was mainly the result of a unique combination of business jargon and the frequent use of initialisations in workplace situations.

HH considered his new position as managing director of RCG as an important step to group general management within TTi, preferably back in the USA. HH believed that the RCG acquisition had not worked out the way TTi had originally planned. This meant that RCG was unlikely to be classified as a TTi core business. HH believed that his role was to ensure the survival of RCG into the twenty-first century, or if this failed to dispose of the group with minimum embarrassment to TTi.

One unprofitable year later he realised that he was unlikely to achieve these objectives in the short term. Moreover, TTi's Group Financial Director, Tod Krumm, had made it clear to him that TTi could not be seen to fail in one of their first major acquisitions. A strategic plan was now required, which he (HH) was responsible for delivering and implementing.

HH recognised that this would require a classic recovery strategy, comprising both a short-term survival plan and a longer-term expansion plan focusing upon the potential of the business. One of his problems was to reconcile the requirements of rationalisation and retrenchment with the requirements of development and growth. Stubbing out his 12th cigarette of the day, he surveyed the range of fine china samples arranged around his office in formal display cabinets, and wondered whether this heritage was an unrealised long-term asset or a short-term millstone. On reflection, he decided to give Rob Hall, his financial director, the responsibility for co-ordinating a survival plan, and Stephen Vincent, his marketing director, the responsibility for co-ordinating a longer-term plan.

Industry and environmental trends

External factors had also contributed to RCG's current situation. Although RCG's access to objective market information was limited, they were aware of the following general market, competitive and customer trends.

1. The major European manufacturers and the 'big' two UK manufacturers (Wedgwood and Royal Doulton) are investing in incremental process innovation in order to reduce the adverse price differential to foreign (mainly Japanese) competition.
2. Major European manufacturers are continuing to develop captive retail outlets, given the reluctance of the trade to invest in a numerous and complicated product range as well as the need to control the disposal of seconds ware.
3. Price competition is being aggravated by the abuse of seconds ware, when 'Phantom' seconds are used to conceal price discounting.
4. The development of specialist companies following niche marketing strategies. For example, Portmeirion, with its wide range of botanical designs targets the kitchenware market, whilst Steelite, using 'bodies' with a higher tolerance of breakage, targets the catering market. The major UK manufacturers also target specific market sectors. Examples include Aynsley in giftware, Masons (Wedgwood) in stoneware, Denby in kitchenware and Spode in exclusive fine china and earthenware. Other niches have been created by the mail order companies concentrating upon collectable items.
5. The increasing penetration of European markets by Asian manufacturers establishing strong positions in lower-priced market sectors. This penetration is based upon a mix of lower production costs and contemporary, traditionally inspired designs, allied to investments in distribution systems. Japanese companies such as Noritake are using a low-price market entry strategy as a base to move up-market supported by improved quality and design.
6. The increasing penetration of the UK market by European manufacturers often supported by efficient production plants and investments in marketing, design and distribution infrastructure. The German manufacturer Villeroy and Boch is one example. Their activity includes innovation in floral wide-border designs, captive retailing, hotel and restaurant ware and efficient delivery and after-sales service.
7. Declining purchases by tourists (mainly North American), traditionally a major force in the UK market. This probably reflects the more competitive nature of the US market (increasing the differential between the relatively high UK prices and the more competitive US domestic market). It also reflects the success of the European North American distribution companies.
8. The concern that traditional UK manufacturers may be squeezed between the lower-priced Asian competition, medium-priced added-value European competition and the niche UK manufacturers.
9. Changes in the status and customer perceptions of tableware products. Some relevant trends, RCG believed, included:
   - The decline of the 'once in a lifetime' purchase pattern, reflecting an infrequent usage attitude to fine china. (This overlaps with the 'bridal market',

comprising wedding gifts of complete dinner services.) Trends in the table-ware market appear to be moving towards the frequent use of more informal patterns, prompting a trend towards pre-packed products in single items or small sets, rather than the traditional full dinner or tea service.

- Allied to the last point, the repositioning of kitchenware as informal table-ware, following a tendency for the kitchen to take over the main living areas.
- The trend towards country living and casual but elegant designs pioneered by such opinion leaders as Laura Ashley.
- The decline of family life and the importance of the 'dinner table' in favour of the TV meal.

The industry appears to be experiencing changing market segmentation within a static/declining market. RCG are finding it difficult to source objective market data and are perplexed as to the nature of the market segments. The industry is replete with misleading definitions and unhelpful and unreliable information as to the size, segmentation and trends of the UK tableware and cookware markets. Indeed, it is doubtful if these are viable terms. In the late 1980's, the major manufacturers, in a attempt to solve these problems, agreed to pool confidential manufacturers' sales (volume and value), with the co-operation of the industry federation. Sadly, the experiment proved difficult and this initiative was abandoned.

Market data

Market data is confusing in this market, given the unco-ordinated nature of data capture, as illustrated by:

- Obscure market definitions and the resulting overlaps
- Confusion between manufacturers' sales values and retail sales values
- Confusion between UK manufacturers' outputs and UK consumption (manu-facturers' sales less exports plus imports)
- No access to European or Asian market data

What can be said in general terms relating to the UK market is that:

- The trend of UK consumption for china and porcelain tableware, kitchenware and giftware of all types (from ornamental ware and classic figurines through to cheap souvenirs and earthenware mugs sold at petrol stations) shows a decline of 25 per cent over the last four years in volume terms .
- A smaller decline of 8 per cent for earthenware tableware and kitchenware is recorded for the same period. The effect of the UK recession seems to have been most severe on mid-priced china tableware.

RCG's limited market and competitive data is now summarised under the titles of Tableware, Cookware, Giftware and Ornamental ware.

Tableware

Although experiencing global competition, tableware is the *raison d'être* of the traditional European manufacturers. Tableware has traditionally been segmented by price using as a marker the retail price of a five-piece place setting, or a 25-piece dinner service. The major price points relating to the traditional 25-piece dinner service are £100 or less, £100–350 and over £350. This simplistic price segmentation is complicated by consumer requirements for both formal and informal tableware. In other words, at the top end of the market a purchaser may be willing to buy both a Wedgwood or Spode dinner service for occasional, formal use and Portmeirion or Evesham for everyday, informal use. At the mid-point of the market the preference may be for a popular Royal Doulton pattern, such as 'Carnation' for formal use and Johnsons Brothers earthenware, or un-branded pottery for everyday use. Any number of variants to this basic model are possible. For example, Evesham cookware and tableware (not an inexpensive product range) may be used for formal, occasional use together with simple pottery for informal use.

The value of the UK tableware market at MSP for *medium and premium priced products* (over £100 per 25-piece tableware and cookware) is estimated to be some £125m. RCG estimated the sub-sectors as:

Tableware and cookware	£108m
Hotel and catering	£11m
Mugs	£6m
Total	**£125m**

The lower-priced tableware sector is estimated at a further £175m with a significant sub-sector accounted for by lower-priced catering ware and mugs. Given the trend amongst the UK manufacturers to push price increases in the last few years, the medium/premium sector of the tableware market is experiencing value growth rather than volume growth.

RCG offer a range of tableware patterns across the premium and mid-priced segments. They are experiencing strong global competition in the mid-priced sector. This, together with the domestic strength of Royal Doulton and store own-label products such as Marks & Spencer, has prompted RCG to consider withdrawing its bone china patterns from the mid-priced sector in order to concentrate attention on earthenware, which retails at similar price points but is more profitable and less competitive. In the premium tableware sector, the problem of being perceived (normally incorrectly) as second best to Wedgwood or Spode is creating an increasing credibility gap with both the trade and the final end-user.

Comparing fiscal 1993 performance with fiscal 1994, sales at MSP for china tableware have declined by 3 per cent, whilst margins have slumped to an all time low of 30 per cent of net sales. One growth area, however, is the resurgence of the traditional blue and white earthenware, competing in the mid-priced tableware sector. RCG was taken by surprise by an exceptional 30 per cent increase in orders in the last fiscal year. As a result RCG were able to deliver and invoice only 40 per cent of these orders. Overall sales for earthenware tableware therefore increased by 12 per cent over fiscal 1993.

The direct UK competition for the company in the tableware market includes those other prestigious manufacturers who contest the premium fine china sector and position their earthenware products in the mid-priced sector. Although the group have a number of ranges in the mid-priced bone china sector, the more traditional members of RCG's management team tend to react unfavourably if they are compared directly with Royal Doulton, whom they regard as being all things to all people (not perhaps a negative comment as typified by their very successful Carnation pattern). Indeed, Royal Doulton can boast of being the world's largest manufacturer of bone china. (Royal Doulton includes Minton, Royal Crown Derby and Royal Albert.)

RCG prefer to compare themselves with either Wedgwood (includes Masons and Johnson Brothers) or Spode, given the similarities in heritage, traditional shapes, hand decoration and the commitment to earthenware.(Earthenware examples are Wedgwood's Countryware and Creative Tableware and Spode's Blue Italian.) In addition RCG's tableware business tends to polarise, like Wedgwood and Spode, between premium fine china and mid-priced earthenware.

In one respect, however, there is no comparison. This refers to competitive logistics. Direct competitors have attempted to address the potentially complex logistical issues by concentrating upon the faster-selling patterns in terms of delivery priorities. This is also true of the European competitors (such as Velleroy and Boch) who are offering a delivery service of days rather than weeks. This contrasts unfavourably with RCG's high proportion of late or incomplete deliveries.

Cookware

RCG are well aware that they had no reliable information as to the size and trends of the Cookware sector (or indeed if such a discrete sector can be identified), given the overlap with tableware. Some 46 per cent of total RCG gross margin, however, was generated by cookware. They suspected that only part of the increasingly distinctive cookware sector is monitored under the Business Monitor's definition of tableware. The remainder, they believed, is recorded as 'other giftware'.

RCG's major cookware competitor is Royal Worcester's Evesham. RCG's 15-strong salesforce has attempted to out-distribute Evesham by extending distributions to non-traditional outlets, including cookware shops, garden centres and gift shops. To support this strategy RCG's cookware lines have been heavily promoted by deep price discounts and the 'manufacture of seconds' (in effect bestware, presented as seconds to justify price cutting).

Trends in cookware include:

- The increasing influence of European design.
- Pre-packaging for giftware.
- Intensifying UK competition.
- Increasing demands for products compatible with ovens and micro-waves.
- The blurring of distinctions between cookware and tableware (e.g. oven-to-table ware).
- Traditional manufacturers entering the premium end of the cookware market.

For example, Spode is adapting premium earthenware designs to specific cookware applications.

- Dedicated cookware companies, such as Portmeirion, are occupying price-points immediately below the RCG range.
- At the cheaper end of the cookware sector, companies such as Denbyware are discounting to generate volume sales.

The two market leaders, Royal Worcester and RCG, are therefore struggling to maintain volumes. As a result, RCG's cookware volumes have decreased by 5 per cent on last year, despite price discounts of up to 33 per cent, which do little to build popularity in the industry.

Giftware

Until recently, Giftware had been a predictable range of mainly bone china 'collectibles', ranging from bud vases, collectors' plates and miniature cottages. As customer attitudes changed, giftware became a more dynamic business.

The total giftware market in 1993 was believed to be worth some £160m at MSP, of which medium to higher-priced giftware (£10.00 per item and above) accounted for some £100m. This diverse category could be segmented as follows:

Table 21.5

Figurines and jugs	£23m
Other sculpture	£16m
Florals giftware	
(e.g. Aynsley)	£5m
Nurseryware	£6m
Other general giftware	£50m
Sub Total	£100m
Low priced giftware	£60m
Total	**£160m**

RCG's presence in the giftware sector was confined to the mid-priced to premium-priced sectors. Traditionally, their mid-priced products were typified by the 'bud vase' range of bone china objects and a number of limited series collector plates. RCG's giftware sales were 6 per cent below the previous year.

In a sense, however, all of RCG's products, except complete dinner services, could be regarded as giftware in the wider sense. The company's own concession stores (the eyes and ears of the company) were the first to highlight the trend towards boxing and gift-wrapping of individual items and sets of tableware (rather than services). RCG had observed that competitors such as Spode and Masons were creating large traditional earthenware pieces as stand-alone giftware items.

Figurines
Royal Doulton dominates the figurine and character jug sector (Toby Jugs) with in excess of 50 per cent of the market. The Royal Doulton range of figurines retails

from £30 to £250 per figure and is distributed across the spectrum of distribution channels, including their retail concessions, specialist china and glass retailers, gift shops, jewellers and mail order.

Mail order refers to Lawleys by Post, which is Royal Doulton's entry into the booming direct mail china business. This sector has expanded as a result of the activities of the mail order specialists and the 'mints' (Bradford Exchange, Compton Woodhouse, Hamilton Mint and Franklin Mint). In addition Royal Doulton has a well-developed collectors club which has developed into an international operation.

The Spanish Lladro range of figurines underlines the international dimension to this sector. These distinctive figurines are characterised by larger than average size, a non-traditional, less delicate design and the use of pastel colour blends. Lladro have been successful with their collectors club which is supported by promotional activities such as mailings and 'Figure of the Year' promotional offers.

Wedgwood's Coalport range of figurines is the traditional contender. Lladro and Coalport each have approximately a 10 per cent share of the figurine sector. The middle and lower-priced sectors of the figurine market are dominated by resin products (cottages and animals), which have the advantage of lower costs and consistency of product. There is evidence that the trend towards cheaper alternatives to ceramics may be repeated with figurines. The resin manufacturers have created a significant business at the expense of the traditional fine china manufacturers. These companies include Lilliput Lane, Border Fine Arts and Country Artists.

RCG now have only a token figurine presence in their concession stores. The design team believe that the heritage of the group lends itself to the recreation of limited edition figurines at the top end of the market. These would be priced above competition (between £500 and £1,000).

Florals

The Florals sub-sector of giftware is dominated by Aynsley with its range of some 200 specialist boxed bone china giftware products. Five patterns form the basis of the range which retail from £5 to £100. Aynsley may also be forced to consider adding resin products to their range.

Nurseryware

Doulton and Wedgwood account for some 90 per cent of the nurseryware sector. Wedgwood markets a complete range from £5 to £45 per item. Their established brands include the Beatrix Potter characters of 'Peter Rabbit' and 'Mrs Tiggywinkle', as well as 'Thomas The Tank Engine'. Royal Doulton have similar well-established products including 'Brambly Hedge', 'Bunnykins' and 'Snowman'. Staying abreast of children's events, including books, videos and films, is critical to success in this sector.

General giftware

General giftware and lower-priced merchandise is stocked by a wide range of outlets, including tableware and cookware outlets, general retailers, jewellers and gift shops, given the opportunity to increase impulse purchase and stock turn. Accordingly, RCG products in gift outlets were frequently merchandised alongside such items as mugs, resin cottages, glass and resin animals, cat and kitten collector plates, imitation jewellery and local pottery.

Ornamental ware

RCG's ornamental ware included prestigious commissions and unique limited editions. These items were hand made, hand decorated and required specialist skills and production processes (for example, an extended sequence of separate 'firings'). Some pieces would sell for thousands of pounds, often acquired by museums. Ornamental ware showed a 16 per cent increase on the previous year. In the last few years, however, ornamental ware had been rationalised with the loss of many skilled craftsmen.

Ornamental ware had an importance to RCG quite out of proportion to the sales generated. There are a number of reasons for this:

1. They are the link to the original craft skills on which rested the prestige and heritage of the company.
2. They are the spearhead for the company's public relations and exhibition strategy.
3. They associate the company with the most prestigious contemporary designers.
4. They form an umbrella under which the more prestigious tableware lines can benefit in terms of premium pricing.
5. There is only one other British manufacturer who can compete with RCG in this field.

Channels of Distribution

Table 21.6 Summary of channel trends

Ceramic tableware and giftware Sales by value	1993 %
Department and chain store	35
Specialist china and glassware	20
Supermarkets	17
Hardware and kitchen stores	15
Mail order and factory shops	13

- Given the stocking costs of full sets of tableware, in-depth distribution of quality fine china (apart from manufacturers' concession stores) was limited to the London West End stores, regional departmental stores and approximately 70 specialist independent stores, who are members of the Guild of Fine China.
- The major chain stores (for example, Chinacraft, Chinacave, Reject China) fully exploit their buying power and the weakness of the UK manufacturers. They require preferential service for limited stock, considerable discounts and the purchase of distressed merchandise at or below cost of goods.
- Department stores are increasingly limiting their product range to lower-priced tableware and giftware. This often takes the form of own-label, pre-packaged, boxed ware.

- Kitchen ware and cookware shops tend to be independent and stock higher stock-turn items, including oven-to-table ware, earthenware and giftware.
- Up-market gift shops are seeking stock-turn from boxed cookware and earthenware items, whilst more down-market outlets also stock earthenware mugs, resin cottages, glass animals and collectors' plates.
- Competition is placing increasing emphasis on factory shops, as discounted retail prices for both seconds and bestware are normally more profitable than sales to third party channels. Competitors are also developing 'off-site factory shops' to move high stocks of finished products. RCG operates two such outlets on original production sites.

Table 21.7 RCG Sales by outlet type (UK and export, excluding North America; base 1994 – £000's)

Outlet type	Net sales	Gross sales (before discounts)
Key accounts (MSP) (mainly chain stores)	3,867	5,569
Field accounts (MSP) (mainly independent and regional chains)	5,550	6,937
Retail concession stores (RSP)	8,604	11,615
Factory shops (RSP)	3,009	3,009
Export (MSP)	3,507	3,682
Hotel, catering and commissions (MSP)	2,465	2,810
Total	27,002	33,622

The concession stores

In the case of RCG this latter category refers to the 75 'shop in shop' Royal China stores in major multiple groups across the country. In order to operate such stores the company was paying a 21 per cent commission on net retail sales to the host store group, as well as conforming to their merchandising and promotional policies. These 75 RCG concession stores compare with some 197 operated by Royal Doulton.

RCG's concession stores generate total sales (RSP) of £8,604,000. Some 37 of these stores are located in branches of Debenhams or House of Fraser. Other host stores included Beatties, Fenwicks, Beals, Lewis, Allders, D.H. Evans and the prestigious Bentalls, Selfridges and Harrods. Average sales per store were £115,000 in 1994. Sales volumes relate to concession size, with the highest value sales achieved in Harrods and Selfridges; and the lowest in Debenhams, Beals and D.H. Evans.

Concession stores are one of the few distribution channels where RCG can sell ware at retail prices. The company, however, is responsible for the store commissions payable, the staffing costs and stock financing costs (normally comprising the full range of company products). Concession stores are also important as a legitimate method of disposing of seconds ware. Some 33 per cent of sales through RCG's concession stores comprised sale stock and seconds promoted at Christmas, January and during the summer Sales periods.

Table 21.8 Comparisons with competition included:

Royal Doulton	197 Concessions
	33 Lawleys
	6 Factory shops
Wedgwood	150 Concessions
	4 Factory shops
Royal Worcester	80 Concessions
	4 Factory shops
Portmeirion	15 Retail shops
Rosenthal/Thomas	12 Concessions
Villeroy & Boch	45 Concessions

Concession stores also provide the industry with:

- A vehicle for promoting their image and corporate identity (often the only significant promotional activity).
- Direct customer feedback as to customer requirements and market trends.
- A mechanism for market testing new patterns and marketing mixes.
- The opportunity for co-operation with other tableware manufacturers (normally crystal glass companies who might share the costs of concession trading).

Some of the host stores, however, are re-appraising their approach to concession trading. Feedback from the field has established that this applies mainly to Debenhams. RCG recognise that this is a problem becoming increasingly specific to themselves as they are the lowest (in revenue terms) of the main fine china concessions.

Other RCG distribution issues

- The number of distribution channels and product alternatives complicates pricing decisions. Trading terms are confusing as:
- There is no clear differentiation between bestware and seconds.
- There is no integrated promotional philosophy between the concession stores and third party accounts.
- There are no consistent terms for major accounts.
- In difficult times, concealed price decreases designed to generate volume orders are adversely impacting on the profitability of the business. Examples of such 'promotional' activity are the extension of 'sales periods', the promotion of best-ware as seconds and stock disposal below direct cost.
- RCG's exports (excluding North America), suffer from low margins and delayed deliveries. This de-motivates foreign distributors and understates overseas potential in a situation where English fine bone china and traditional blue and white earthenware is highly regarded in such markets as Germany, Japan and Australia.

22

The Royal China Group B

The Alternatives Proposed by RCG Managers

The Financial Director's view

HH liked Rob Hall. This was not a view shared throughout the management team, many of whom regarded him as excessively secretive and liable to move the goal posts of financial control at any time. Rob, for better or worse, was the representative of TTi's culture of control and, given his training and experience, was not happy with expansionist views.

Sharing the same brand of cigarettes, HH and Rob spend a few moments discussing the problems of the retail division. This included Rob's projections for a reduced retailing operation. Rob then spread out on HH's conference table the long list of product margin print-outs which the company, despite much disbelief and strong criticism, had finally managed to complete three months before. These showed gross and net margins by product group, gross after deducting direct costs and net after deducting direct and indirect costs. Rob then outlined a somewhat complex rationalisation programme based on the view that a retreat to a limited number of niche markets was a better fit with the resources of the business.

HH was aware that this approach would probably lead to a single manufacturing unit for both china and earthenware. It was time, Rob suggested, to stop attempting to be all things to all people in the classic tradition of the full-range UK manufacturers; to stop pretending that the two former companies now comprising RCG could both survive in their current form into the twenty-first century.

HH also favoured a slimmer, more profitable business. His concern was that Rob's financially-based rationalisation programme should be complemented by a market logic. He knew from his US experience the dangers of being too margin-driven, rather than market-driven. Rob was proposing a series of rationalisation phases based upon product group gross and net margins. Each product group had been allocated to a 'status group', depending upon such factors as volume, complexity and life cycle. Target gross and net margins were then established for each group. If the target margins were not achievable the product group was a candidate for elimination.

The implications of this approach

Apart from the difficulties that the process might result in an unbalanced range (e.g. cups without saucers), there was the danger that successive products would fail to meet the margin criteria, as rationalisation wave followed rationalisation wave. Consequently, by the end of the process an unacceptable proportion of the corporate overhead might be insupportable, as they were reallocated across a diminishing revenue base. HH also anticipated resistance from the traditionalists inside the company. He anticipated that Rob's proposals as they stood would involve the merging of the two historic identities and breaking the unwritten rule that neither of the two original companies would manufacture the other's 'back-stamp'. The undiluted rationalisation proposals, he suspected, would create unnecessary problems of low employee morale. HH therefore required the rationalisation proposals to be balanced against a longer-term appraisal of the business.

Nevertheless, both HH and Rob felt that this was probably a viable start point for a short-term survival plan. What was now required was a clear statement of business potential to underpin a longer-term strategy. The longer-term strategy HH felt should be co-ordinated by Stephen Vincent, the marketing director, and his team. In the meantime, HH asked Rob (knowing that he would be talking to group HQ later in the day), to talk to Stephen about the need to push for immediate price increases to meet the proposed target margins for all product groups. This HH believed to be a fast track route to the survival phase of the strategic plan.

Marketing

Stephen is nearing retirement and is seen as a mentor for his team of 'Young Turks' who ran the Retail, UK sales, Export and Design units. His background is in international marketing and consultancy. As a consultant he was retained by the previous corporate owners to establish a North American distribution company for the two original companies. These now operate as independent North American distribution companies.

The marketing group is organised into distinct commercial units. These are:

- Retail (Concessions and Factory Shops)
- Export sales
- UK field sales
- UK key accounts
- Customer service
- Design and new product development.
- Support marketing activities (advertising, promotions, exhibitions and marketing research)

The UK field sales and design managers were also members of RCG's operational management group.

Stephen equates marketing strategy with product and distribution strategy

Given the structure of his division, Stephen tends to think in terms of commercial business units. He is aware of the rationalisation programme proposed by Rob (given that he plays golf most weekends with Rob's deputy). He considers Rob's approach to be premature, as there is as yet no framework for such a rationalisation exercise.

Stephen believes that a framework could be provided by deciding priorities in terms of product groups and commercial business units. He suggested to his marketing manager, Jackie Clarke, that she co-ordinate the business unit plans of his managers, taking into account the following matrix.

Table 22.1 The proposed planning matrix

Commercial Business Unit	Market sector				
	China T/W	Earth T/W	Cookware	Giftware	Ornamental Ware
Retail					
Factory shops					
Export					
UK Key and field accounts					
Hotel/catering					
Direct response					
Other					

Stephen urged his managers to be creative with their unit plans and consider all the alternatives. The individual responses of his managers in qualitative terms will follow shortly.

Stephen is aware that each manager will promote their own area of responsibility, rather than take part in an objective exercise. As a start point he asked Jackie to circulate the latest profit contribution statement for the commercial units (profit contribution by commercial unit, after allocation of direct costs). The managers frequently challenged these figures. They believed that the revenue base was influenced by preferential allocations of limited stock between the business units. The retail manager considered his allocations particularly unfair, given the stock clearance targets handed down by HH, together with the practice of charging the retail division for the cost of stocks in branches and factory shops.

The contributions by commercial business unit for fiscal 1994 are set out below:

Table 22.2 Contribution by business unit

Royal China Group £000's; 1994	Key Account Field/Hotel	Export	Factory Shops	Retail Concessions	Total
Gross sales	15,316	3,682	3,009	11,615	33,622
Net Sales M/RSP	11,882	3,507	3,009	8,604	27,002
Cost of Goods	7,755	2,420	1,711	3,785	15,671
Stock Shrinkage	0	0	34	210	244
Gross Margin	4,127	1,087	1,264	4,609	11,087
GM% net sales	35	31	42	54	41
Commissions	0	402	0	1,806	2,208
Ad. and promotion	624	180	0	0	804

Royal China Group £000's; 1994	Key Account Field/Hotel	Export	Factory Shops	Retail Concessions	Total
O/H's and wages					
Sell. and Distrib.	1,120	250	602	1,940	3,912
Total Direct	1,744	832	602	3,746	6,924
Unit Contrib.	2,383	255	662	863	4,163
%/net sales	20	7	22	10	15

Stephen also asked Jackie to consider mechanisms for co-ordinating and evaluating the unit plans. He suggested that she consider the market life-cycle portfolio matrix, as well as a methodology to establish the relative attractiveness of the various market segments.

The views of the individual managers of the commercial units

The Retail Manager's plan

Ian Smith, the manager of the retail concessions and factory shops, was recruited from IKEA two years ago for his retailing experience. He is adapt at motivating the 210 people reporting to him. It is well-known that HH is thinking of him as the next marketing director. Ian controls the retail business with the help of three regional concession managers and a factory shop manager.

Unlike his staff and the Production and Personnel Directors, he sees the so-called crisis in his area as an opportunity to reposition his retailing operation along more profitable lines. Ian estimates that his business will shrink by 30 per cent in revenue terms, if the retail division has to lose up to 20 concession stores over the next 18 months. Although this sounds dramatic, Ian considers that it is the smaller and less prestigious concessions that are at risk.

Crucial to his philosophy is the view that in retailing terms RCG sells only three core product lines. These are:

- Bestware
- Seconds
- Clearance ware

Ian's view is that marketing strategy is about planning the marketing mix on this basis. Marketing seconds, for example, requires a discrete approach. The distinctions between cookware, tableware or giftware are of lesser importance.

The retail division's proposals are to restructure the retailing operation around these priorities. They recognise that the majority of the concession stores in Debenhams, and perhaps House of Fraser, are unlikely to survive. This discontinuity in strategy requires creative thinking, for out of crisis comes opportunity.

The proposed forward strategy for the division is:

- Retreat to high-volume prestigious concessions.
- Support the remaining concessions with additional investment in fixtures and fittings and promotional activity.

- Support those host stores who follow a policy of minimum discounting and quality image projection with joint media and promotional support.
- Progressively reduce the mix of seconds to bestware to 20:80 rather than the 30:70 at present.
- Make up any short-fall by requesting new product development of both earthenware tableware and earthenware cookware. Ian was aware that any request for additional earthenware products would run into two major problems:
  1. The lack of earthenware capacity.
  2. The need for investment in a 'vitreous body', to meet consumer requirements for compatibility with microwaves, dishwashers and high temperature ovens and freezers. Following his presentation to HH on his appointment, he knew that this request had resulted in an active new product programme, despite the relatively non-prestigious nature of microwave cooking which did not impress the design department.
- Lobby the marketing director and HH to ensure that the company's third party accounts do not promote and undercut the concession stores. This is developing into an area of contention between the UK major accounts and the retail division.
- Request funding to establish eight RCG-owned retail stores in key city locations (one of these to be a West End 'Flagship' store; no seconds). In other locations, stores would follow the guidelines for the mix of seconds to bestware.
- Develop the existing on-site factory shops into tourist campuses comprising:
  - Bestware shop
  - Seconds (factory) shop
  - Museum and valuation service
  - Factory tours
  - Restaurant and tea room
- Open up to five off-site RCG factory shops for clearance ware.

This final initiative is designed to reduce finished stocks and control the disposal of large quantities of unbalanced/defective stock. Such stock is currently offered to third party traders who may flood the market with 'seconds', seriously damaging the image and reputation of RCG. At present large quantities of slow-moving stock are disposed of through chain stores, who expect first refusal on such opportunities. Stock disposal and the wider issue of discounts remain areas of contention between the retail division and the salesforce.

The Field Sales Manager's plan

The 15-strong field salesforce reports to Greg Field. Greg has worked for RCG for the last 14 years, in export sales and recently as national accounts manager. It was Greg who had the difficult task of merging the original two salesforces and assisting with the opening of a centralised warehouse. Like Ian, he is directly responsible for the profit of his unit. He contrasts his 'real responsibilities' with those of the design manager, who he maintains, is not constrained by any budgets or targets.

Greg views the pending down-sizing of the retail division with a certain degree of satisfaction. He believes that vertical integration into retailing soaks up resources and generates lower margins compared with third party sales (when all the overheads are allocated).Greg sees the company's problems in terms of products, as his salesforce requires a full product range to sustain its credibility. Greg takes the view that RCG is already operating as a niche marketer when compared with competitors such as Royal Doulton and Wedgwood.

His priority is to defend and expand the all-important cookware range, given that 39 per cent of RCG's revenue and 46 per cent of RCG's gross margin is generated by cookware, which in turn supports the overheads such as finance, personnel and design. The block to progress, Greg believes, is the personality of the design manager, who blocks any initiative that might result in volume products. He has little time for either Stephen or HH, both of whom seem unwilling to address the new product development opportunity. Greg requires pressure on the design department to develop successors to the current cookware range which is looking tired and dated in comparison with competition. This request has been pending for the last five years. The current new product development programme for cookware is limited to the provision of microwave versions of the existing range. Given the delivery and stocking problems caused by adding variants to the existing product line (which Stephen and HH never ceased to stress), Greg cannot understand the rationale to double the existing cookware range, rather than providing an innovative alternative.

Greg blames the design manager for this situation. Despite a long-term relationship, he regards communication with Alan (the design manager) as almost impossible. This is not helped by the design manager's habit of referring to him in meetings as 'Mr Asda' whenever a request is made for products with volume potential. Greg now regards the design manager as almost permanently 'out to lunch', as his American counterpart had suggested to him over dinner the week before.

Greg has frequently highlighted the trend towards giftware. The salesforce wish to exploit this trend by repositioning selected tableware items as giftware, as well as developing specific giftware ranges to cover the mid/premium-priced market sectors. In particular the salesforce have highlighted the potential for large pieces of earthenware giftware in specialist outlets. Greg feels frustrated as he is aware that the design team are confining their efforts to up-market tableware patterns and ornamental ware.

It would be wrong to regard the salesforce as only interested in volume. They are close to customers on a daily basis and believe that they are best positioned to assist RCG management with the difficult decisions involved with deciding between alternatives If choices are required, Greg and the salesforce recommend:

- Withdrawal from the volume tableware market (where margins after discounts are depressed and deliveries problematic.
- Switch resources to earthenware, cookware and giftware.
- Co-operate more enthusiastically with major retailers in terms of joint promotions and advertising, given that RCG's media and promotional activities are minimal.
- Rebuild the ornamental business with particular reference to figurines which have real volume potential. RCG, with its heritage and tradition, they believe is well positioned to compete with Royal Doulton. The trade, Greg knows, would welcome an additional UK supplier.

- Rebuild the collectibles business and develop this by creating a RCG direct mail Collectors' Club. Having investigated the rapidly developing direct mail businesses of Royal Doulton, Lladro and the mail order specialists, Greg has put forward a plan for a RCG direct response business which he believes has the following advantages:
  - The ability to charge the full retail price without discounts and the problem of seconds.
  - The advantages of creating a collectors club. This refers to the possibilities of multiple purchases from individual customers.
  - Product would be made to order, with cash paid up-front and minimal inventory problems.
  - The ability to mount specific marketing communications programmes so that there was an economic rationale for media advertising.
  - RCG can associate itself with popular external artists.
  - Greg estimated that the revenue from such an operation could exceed £5m within three years with a 60 per cent margin (50 per cent higher than the current total RCG gross margin).

Unfortunately, at the management meeting to consider his proposals, HH had told him in no uncertain terms to go out and sell-off the finished goods stock mountain and then concentrate on the existing business, which was behind target as a result of his lack of focus on current business ('LOFOCB', HH pronounced it Lo'fob).

The design manager was more caustic and threatened to resign if RCG ever seriously considered becoming a mail order company, focusing on what he called 'the resin cottage and cat and kitten plate market'. HH had then appealed for calm and passed Greg the pile of finished stock print-outs, complete with HH's very comprehensive notes in the margin.

Greg didn't leave the meeting before giving full vent to the feelings of his salesforce. This referred to being provided with unsaleable stock on the one hand, whilst important customer orders were being cancelled as a result of stock shortages on the other. Greg delighted in telling HH that the way to solve the short-term problem was to stop cancelling his team's hard won orders because of logistical incompetence. He also suggested that the longer-term opportunities would be best addressed by a customer-led new product development programme, rather than by the current 'internal secret process'. His final comment was to invite HH to accompany his salespeople for a glimpse of reality. He then left the meeting without the finished stock print-outs.

Subsequently, Greg was a marked man. On his departure from the meeting an angry HH, more concerned with the short-term problems of survival, told Stephen that he had better attend sharply to the serious morale problems in his division and send certain of his staff on a course on working capital management, if he could not communicate to them the importance of 'JOTRAW' (joining occasionally the real awake world). It was often said of HH that he only managed his best comments in anger! Nevertheless, Greg had made the point that any strategic plan would not be taken seriously by the sales team (including retail and export), unless a rapid solution was found to the de-motivating effects of cancelling orders as a result of stock shortages.

The Design Manager's perspective

Alan Ashbourne, the design manager, takes the view that he will not be dictated to by transient sales managers. (Greg had been with RCG for almost the same time as Alan, but Greg had worked for the 'other company', so in Alan's view, Greg's time there didn't count.) The salesforce, Alan believes, has yet to understand that the survival of the company depends on sustaining its distinctive competitive advantage . . . which is traditional design. Previously, there had been many failed efforts to 'modernise' and generate volume businesses inspired by the salespeople and their discount philosophy. People like Greg, Alan believed, would never be happy until the product range was available on garage forecourts or sold through mail order catalogues.

Product development inspired by the salesforce, he considers as the ultimate nightmare, which can only result in a stream of dead-end products of no particular advantage to anybody but trade buyers, whose only interest is short-term advantage. Marketing in this industry is not about giving the customer what he thinks he wants (most of the time they have no clear idea as to what they do want); any fool of a sales manager can follow today's numerous customer whims, ignore the core competence and heritage of the business and bankrupt the company. In this instance the company itself is the best arbiter and creator of product design. Once this initiative is lost the path to disaster follows.

In response to increasing pressure to research new patterns against target customers, Alan would refer his peers to the rapid feedback obtained from RCG's captive retail outlets. If pushed further he would repeat his common response, 'You name me one successful pattern that was based upon consumer research and I'll show you 20 that were not'.

Alan's opinions also applied to the retail and export divisions. In short, he regarded himself and his small team as the 'conscience of the company', in an environment of constantly changing out-of-touch senior managers. His experience was that within 18 months or so there would be another owner and another management team to educate. The danger period was the first year of a new regime, as it took approximately a year for them to begin to understand the business.

Alan also acted as the spokesperson for the trustees of the two RCG museums. In this role he was widely respected. Indeed, on one occasion he had taken issue with an inexperienced HH and Rob at one of the first management meetings under the new HH/TTi regime. He was obliged to point out to them that the revised RCG balance sheet had incorrectly included the value of the collections in the two museums, despite the fact that they were not corporate assets. HH now treated him with caution, having nearly made a serious public relations error in his immediate search for a strong balance sheet.

Alan had wide support from many in the two original companies. He represented tradition and succession (25 years in the industry). This was underlined by his own name on the Royal Warrant. Alan had taken on, by default, the public relations function, and broadcast regularly on Radio Stoke without any reference to HH or Stephen (as he had always done so). His long experience of the industry enabled him to speak his mind and propose an alternative agenda without reference to Stephen or the other managers in the marketing group. Part of this agenda had a strong appeal to HH and TTi.

Some of Alan's views include the following:

- The 1983 merger had been a disaster, robbing both companies of their identity and rationale. The rationale for the merger was to create a smaller version of Royal Doulton to build critical mass. Alan believes that RCG's cost structure, with the exception of cookware, cannot support this approach.
- The delivery problems he believes to be largely the result of the TTi drive towards centralisation. They had only come about when the new central warehouse had been created in the name of efficiency, which was somehow mistaken for improved customer service. All that has happened, he maintains, is that the pride in the two businesses has been lost and the combined sales and production people have lost their way. His solution was to go back to basics and stop manufacturing finished stock for central warehouse inventory. Stock should be held at the early stages of production and then decorated on receipt of firm orders. This was an old concept in the industry, mainly used for limited runs of complex products (know as stock at 'Glost').
- This manufacturing philosophy underpinned Alan's approach to the NPD programme. Nothing was willingly developed that was seen as incompatible with this process. This in effect excluded mass market products, where a core inventory range is essential. It was well-known that HH and his new Operations Director were giving serious consideration to this approach for part of the product range, given the need to reduce finished stocks and rationalise the range. Rob was also known to favour this approach for a wider range of products, given the reductions in inventory charges.
- HH was, therefore, reluctant to change the NPD approach in the short term and he was particularly sensitive to the charge of not really understanding the business; or as Alan put it, 'what's the point of squeezing the assets, if you don't need the assets in the first place?' (He was not given to initialisation.)
- The way forward for Alan was a de-merger. At least one of the original companies (preferably his original company) could then revert to being a specialist, highly prestigious manufacturer of tableware supplying the North American market and decorating to order. His figures could demonstrate that this was a more profitable option. This, however, was relatively easy given the current financial problems of the company.
- New product development in the premium sector of the industry is about fashion leadership, based upon a clear identity. Successful European manufacturers have a clear stable of products or 'a look' based upon body, shape, colour and pattern. Indeed, there was a time when any product's heritage could be established at first glance.
- New products that don't fit into a traditional category are orphan products, without identity; and it is this heritage and identity that generate demand. The nature of demand in the USA illustrates the truth of this point. If we give up this approach, we give away not only our birthright, but our opportunity to generate profits based upon distinctive world famous products.
- Most problems, Alan maintained, have been caused by TTi and the previous owners, who have difficulty understanding the dynamics of this traditional

business. They had to understand that this is a niche marketing business. The chosen niche for this company is prestigious fine china supplied to markets that are willing to pay a premium for the very best in English bone china.

- No compromise should be made to those advocates of modern, short-term, mass-market designs that cause such problems for short-sighted management.

In the meantime, the new product development process was of increasing concern to Stephen for a number of reasons:

- The conflict between Greg and Alan required a resolution.
- The lack of any formal system to control each stage of the NPD process from concept to final launch.
- This in turn lead to some new products being 'introduced' to the sales force at almost the same time as the customer.
- Stephen's view that customers should be involved in the NPD process at an early stage. This contrasted with the secrecy surrounding the current process.
- The need in his opinion for external ideas. All patterns were currently generated in-house under Alan's direction.
- The large number of projects with no clear priorities.
- The indifferent record of success.

The Export Manager's plan

Chris Brooks had worked for Royal Doulton as a marketing assistant before Greg discovered him at an industry exhibition four years ago and persuaded him to join RCG as promotions manager. Chris, still in his 20's, jumped at the chance of running his own unit, when the previous export manager was transferred to UK key account management. In this position he knew that he could also make good use of his knowledge of German.

Although seen as a rising star, he is keeping his head down following HH's first visit to the German distributor in Cologne. HH had apparently spent an uncomfortable lunch with this prestigious distributor (and his key staff), being criticised for not taking the export business seriously. As the lunch progressed he was made to feel that he alone was the embodiment of all that was wrong with the British commercial way of life. By the time dessert came, HH felt the eyes of the distributorship staff studying him as if he were a classic eighteenth-century dinner set in the company museum.

HH remained unsure what part, if any, Chris had played in his demise. On his return, however, he told Chris that he was whinging too much about the delivery problems, instead of taking immediate positive action. He suggested that Chris was spreading the available stock over too many markets and not concentrating it on the major export market . . . Germany. He went on to request 'IMPAD' (immediate positive action for Germany) to be monitored by quarterly IMPAD reports.

Chris felt that the views of the German distributor just about summed it up. Export seemed to be the lowest priority for the business. To Chris, who operated in a limited number of mainly European markets, there was no reason why his six key country accounts should not get the same degree of management support as the six major UK key accounts, given that the revenues generated were almost identical. Rather, it seemed to be a struggle to focus management attention on this part of the business, particularly so during this difficult period for the company. Nor was this helped by Rob's approach, who maintained that export was marginal business, especially as there were a number of additional costs not charged to the export group. This was a chicken and egg situation, Chris believed, as until he could increase volumes his margins would remain relatively depressed.

Chris maintained that there were significant opportunities to develop the export markets where RCG had in one form or another been represented for the past 20 years. These markets, in order of importance were Germany, Japan, Benelux, Australia, France and Spain.

The neglect of the last few years had, however, reduced RCG's operations in these countries to a token presence with the exception of Germany, Japan and Australia. This token presence was generating £3.7m per annum.

Table 22.3 Revenues by market

	£m
Germany	1.3
Japan	0.6
Benelux	0.5
Australia	0.5
France	0.4
Spain	0.2
Other	0.2
Total	3.7

Chris recognised that he had to be realistic, given the claims on corporate resources. In order to re-establish the credibility of the export business he proposes to concentrate on priority markets and products. The key points which he will recommend to Stephen include:

- Agree with HH to concentrate on Germany, but add France as the second priority market.
- Target Japan as the third priority market, and attempt to hold the status quo in other markets.
- Use the German and French distributors to cover the Benelux countries.
- As most of the non-priority markets are still using two distributors (from the days of the two original companies), consolidate all RCG business with a single exclusive distributor.
- Appoint a European manager to control and motivate the distributors in Germany, France and Benelux and co-ordinate the Distributor/RCG presence at the major European trade fairs.
- Given the problems with stock availability, concentrate on a common core range of European dinnerware and a distinct core range for Japan.
- As such core ranges will have to be discrete to Europe and South East Asia, this will require NPD briefs for the design department.

- The core ranges will comprise the distinctive English products (which Alan refers to as the soul of the company). These are the classic traditional fine bone china and earthenware tableware. There are no distinctive requirements for cookware.
- Propose that HH personally returns to Germany with a resolution of their problems.

The Marketing Manager's approach

Jackie Clarke has worked her way up through the retail division. Prior to being promoted to the position of marketing manager, she had been the retail area manager for the Midlands for four years. Given her experience of retail promotions, she tended to concentrate on marketing communications. She was disappointed that public relations seemed to remain the responsibility of the design manager. She has no responsibility for profit, as this is the role of the commercial unit managers, such as Ian and Greg. She works closely, however, with Stephen in consolidating the commercial unit's plans and budgets.

As part of this co-ordination role, she assists the unit managers with their strategic plans. For example, she is attempting to complete an evaluation of market sector attractiveness versus internal strengths and weaknesses. To help her with this project she devised a pro-forma designed to build cumulative scores for each market sector; the higher the score the more attractive the sector.

The identified market sectors are:

- China tableware
- Earthenware tableware
- Giftware
- Ornamental ware
- Cookware

The procedure to obtain an overall market score is:

- Each of the identified market sectors is divided into premium-priced, medium-priced and low-priced sub-sectors.
- The 15 resulting sub-sectors are then rated against a battery of internal and external factors on a five-point scale, where 5 refers to an excellent corporate fit, and 1 to a very poor corporate fit.
- Each factor is weighted (1–3) in relation to its perceived importance, where 3 is most important.
- Ratings, when multiplied by factor weights, produce an overall score for each of the market sub-sectors.

Jackie's pro-forma matrix for one of the identified market segments is set out below. These forms she decided would be completed by the unit managers in conjunction with herself.

Marketing department RCG

Table 22.4 Evaluation of relative market attractiveness

| | | Example: China Tableware | | |
		Premium	Medium	Low
Factor	Weight			
Access to dist. channels	2			
Intensity of competition	3			
High quality requirements	2			
Stocking costs	3			
Delivery logistics	1			
Production synergy	2			
New product support	2			
Marketing costs	1			
Synergy with tradition and heritage	3			
Ability to avoid discounting	2			
Existing customer base	1			
Current sector share	1			
Continuity to existing business	1			
Above-average margins	3			
Volume potential	2			

Table 22.5 Evaluation of market attractiveness

Factor	Weight	China Table			Earth Table			Giftware			Ornamental			Cookware		
		prem	med	low	prem	med	low	prem	med	low	prem	med	low	prem	med	low
Access to dist channels	2	10	8	6	10	10	10	6	6	6	8	8	6	10	8	8
Intensity of competition	3	12	15	9	12	9	6	9	6	6	15	12	9	6	6	3
High quality req.	2	10	10	6	10	10	6	8	8	6	15	12	9	6	6	6
Stocking costs	3	9	9	9	9	6	6	6	6	6	12	12	12	8	6	6
Delivery logistics	1	4	4	4	4	4	4	3	3	3	3	3	3	3	3	3
Production synergy	2	8	6	4	8	6	4	6	6	4	6	6	4	8	4	4
New product support	2	6	4	4	6	4	4	4	2	2	10	8	6	6	4	4
Marketing costs	1	5	3	2	5	3	3	4	2	2	3	3	3	3	2	2
Synergy trad/ heritage	3	15	12	9	15	12	6	12	9	3	15	12	9	9	9	6

	Factor Weight	China Table			Earth Table			Giftware			Ornamental			Cookware		
		prem	med	low	prem	med	low	prem	med	low	prem	med	low	prem	med	low
Avoid discounts	2	10	6	2	10	6	2	10	6	4	10	10	6	4	4	4
Existing customers	1	5	5	1	5	4	1	4	3	1	5	4	1	3	2	2
Sector share	1	3	3	2	3	3	2	2	2	1	5	4	3	4	2	2
Cont. exist. Business	1	5	5	1	5	4	1	3	2	1	5	4	3	3	2	1
Above aver. margins	3	15	9	2	12	9	2	9	6	4	15	12	9	12	9	6
Volume potential	2	4	8	10	4	8	10	4	4	8	2	2	2	10	8	10
Totals		121	107	71	118	98	67	90	71	57	129	112	85	95	75	67

The view of the advertising agency

Although RCG normally spent more on packaging and literature than they do on advertising, RCG's Birmingham advertising agency have their own proposals for marketing strategy.

They believe that the industry suffers from introspection. The real issue they believe is the nature and motivation of consumer demand. Although HH has ruled out any further consumer research, given the time constraints involved in the strategic marketing process, the agency believe that the limited qualitative research undertaken to date is sufficient to draw broad conclusions as to the nature of consumer-based market segmentation.

LEARNING NOTE on qualitative research

A) The uses of qualitative research

- For in-depth information on attitudes, opinions, motivations.
- For background information when little information is available.
- To identify and prioritise behaviour patterns.
- To define problem areas more fully.
- For complex issues which cannot be addressed by quantitative research.
- To pilot more comprehensive quantitative research, in order to ask the relevant questions.
- Preliminary screening of ideas and concepts.

Examples:

- New product concept exploration.
- Reasons for brand loyalty.

- Understanding of key customer purchase variables.
- Understanding of possible modes of market segmentation.
- Probing of motivations, e.g. 'Why did you vote for the Green party?'

B) Limitations

- Not statistically valid.
- Expensive, may be lengthy one-on-one interviews.

C) Common methodologies

- Group discussions/focus groups.
- Depth interviews.

Based upon their own qualitative research, the agency presented to Stephen and his team their views as to the consumer segmentation of the UK tableware market. The summary chart is set out below.

The agency view of market segmentation.

1. The 'Once in a Lifetimers'
   - Example, a dinner service received as a wedding present
2. The Compulsive Collectors
   - Of specific patterns or shapes
3. The Entertainers
   - Tableware as a marker of status
4. The Ideal Homers
   - Admire, rather than use
5. The Aspirational Country Cottagers
   - Romantic, traditional, Laura Ashley appeal
6. The Bargain Basement Crocks
   - Quest for the cheapest 'crockery'
7. Modernists
   - Simple, cheerful designs; ideal for the dishwasher and microwave
8. Plate and Mug Dossers
   - Don't believe in tables
9. The Replacers
   - Unfortunately they withdrew the pattern five years ago!
10. Nesters
    - Daily use and life style expression

Subsequent charts went on to quantify and profile each customer group. From this basis they requested Stephen's approval to proceed to creative recommendations for consumer advertising, packaging, literature and promotional activity, targeting groups 3, 4 and 5.

RCG now need to undertake a systematic marketing planning process similar to the process set out in Chapter 2. Stephen needs to assemble the information base from his internal and external sources, consider the objectives and alternatives, and present HH with the recommended strategy.

Your Tasks (for both parts A and B)

This case provides the opportunity for students to become involved in most aspects of the strategic marketing process. It will be helpful to:

1. Produce a summary marketing audit for RCG covering both external and internal factors.
2. Identify the Strategic Business Units (SBUs), and/or the Product Market Units (PMUs).
3. Formulate a mission statement and objectives for both the company and its identified SBU's.
4. Apply the principles of Market Segmentation, Targeting and Positioning.
5. Decide upon the strategic marketing alternatives open to the company and rationalise your choice of strategic direction by illustrating how your marketing strategy relates to both the target market sectors and the internal competencies.
6. Recommend a marketing mix (mixes) to support your alternatives.
7. Discuss the importance of such intangible factors as culture, conflict, crisis and heritage on strategy development.
8. Identify those components of your marketing strategy that relate to the recovery phase and to the expansion phase.
9. Recommend to HH a methodology for managing innovation and product development in this traditional industry.
10. Summarise the priorities for RCG's marketing information requirements.

Epilogue

The Challenge for Marketers

We have seen that marketing and marketers are facing a variety of challenges and criticisms. Some relate to the relevance and boundaries of the marketing concept itself. Others relate to the adequacy of strategic planning tools and to the competence of their users.

Star (1989), for example, claims that the problem with marketing stems from 'functional limitations on the implementability of the marketing concept'. As an example he comments that marketers know that 'consumers who share a common set of attitudinal, perceptual and sociological characteristics are more likely to share a particular set of needs than, say, consumers in the same age or income group'. Yet when it comes to implementing campaigns, consumer segments to be targeted are invariably specified in terms of age, income or social grade. Clancy and Krieg (1990) also criticise marketers for their failure to select appropriate marketing strategies when introducing new products. They say there is a 'tendency to evaluate too few options for every decision in the marketing mix and then to do this evaluation by focusing on whatever option produces the biggest number'. They claim that today's information technology should allow marketers to evaluate – in terms of effect on profitability, not merely numbers of customers or sales – the impact of selecting thousands of different market segments to target, different product concepts and different promotional messages.

Chaston (1990) suggests that management in industry frequently has negative perceptions of the marketing function and its contribution to corporate success. He attributes this to marketers placing too much emphasis on the importance of their own role and to poor marketing practice. According to him, marketers are guilty of, among other sins:

- Resisting attempts to place controls on their performance
- Lacking financial managerial skills
- Indulging in creativity without analysis
- Using market research to justify preconceptions
- Starving other departments of resources
- Having insufficient understanding of business

The challenge for marketers, therefore, is to begin by getting better at the core strategy skills. At one and the same time, marketers must become more numerate and yet more creative; rigorous and yet more visionary; specialist and yet more generalist.

Bibliography

Aaker, D. (1984). *Strategic Marketing Management*. New York: Wiley.

Abell, D. & Hammond, J. (1979). *Strategic Market Planning*. Englewood Cliffs: Prentice-Hall.

Ackoff, R. L. (1986). *Management in Small Doses*. New York: Wiley.

Ansoff, H. I. (1957). Strategies for Diversification. *Harvard Business Review*, 25, Sept.-Oct., 5.

Ansoff, H. I. (1968). *Corporate Strategy*. New York: McGraw-Hill.

Ansoff, *et al.* (1970). Does Planning Pay. *Long Range Planning*, 3, 2, 2-7.

Argenti, J. (1976). *Corporate Collapse*. New York: McGraw-Hill.

Ash, D. & Bowman, C. (1989). *Readings in Strategic Management*. London: Macmillan.

Baden-Fuller, C. & Stopford, J. (1992). *Rejuvenating the Mature Business: The Competitive Challenge*. HBS Press.

Baker, M. J. *et al.* (1991). *The Marketing Book, 2nd Edition*. Oxford: Butterworth-Heinemann.

Baker, M. J. (1993). Bank Marketing – Myth or Reality? *International Journal of Bank Marketing*, 11, 6, MCB University Press Ltd.

Berry, L. (1990). Ten Commandments of Services Marketing. *Bank Marketing*, August.

Brown, S. (1995). Life begins at 40? Further thoughts on marketing's 'mid-life crisis'. *Marketing Intelligence & Planning*, 13, 1, 4-17.

Chaffee, E. (1985). Three Models of Strategy. *Academy of Management Review*, 10, 89-98.

Chaston, I. (1990). *Managing for Marketing Excellence*. Maidenhead: McGraw-Hill.

Christopher M., Payne, A. & Ballantyne, D. (1991). *Relationship Marketing. Bringing quality, customer service and marketing together.* Oxford: Butterworth-Heinemann Ltd.

Clancy, K. & Krieg, P. (1990). From Myopic Maximisation to Panoramic Optimisation: New Directions in Financial Services Marketing and Marketing Research in the 1990's. *Marketing and Research Today*, August.

Cravens, D. W. (1994). *Strategic Marketing, 4th Edition*. Homewood Illinois: Irwin.

Davidson, J. H. (1972). *Offensive Marketing*. London: Cassell.

Davidson, H. (1993). Bubbling Benetton beats recession. *The Sunday Times*, April.

Drucker, P. (1954). *The Practice of Management*. London: Heinemann.

Drucker, P. (1973). *Management: Tasks, Responsibilities, Practices*. New York: Harper & Row.

Drucker, P. (1985). *Innovation and Entrepreneurship*. London: Heinemann.

Duncan, R. (1972). Characteristics of organisational environments and perceived uncertainty. *Administrative Science Quarterly*, 17, 313-327.

Faulkner, D. & Bowman, C. (1992). Generic Strategies and Congruent Organisational Structures: Some Suggestions. *European Management Journal* 10, 4.

Fifield, P. & Gilligan, C. (1995). Strategic Marketing Management, *Chartered Institute of Marketing Diploma Work book*. Oxford: Butterworth-Heinemann.

Freeman, R. (1984). *Strategic Management*. Boston: Pitman.

French, J. R. P. & Raven, B. (1959). The bases of social power, in Cartwright, D. (Ed) *Studies in Social Power*. Ann Arbor: Michigan Press.

Goddard, J. (1985). *London Business School Journal*. Winter 85.

Goold, M. & Campbell, A. (1987). *Strategies and Styles*. Oxford: Blackwell.

Greenley, G. E. (1989). *Strategic Management*. Hemel Hempstead: Prentice-Hall.

Greiner, L. (1972). Evolution and Revolution as Organizations Grow. *Harvard Business Review*, July-August.

Gummesson, E. (1987). The new marketing-developing long-term interactive relationships. *Long Range Planning*, 20, 4, 10-20.

Gummesson, E. (1994). *Is relationship marketing operational?* Proceedings of the 23rd EMAC Conference, Maastricht.

Henry, J. & Walker, D. (1991). *Managing Innovation*. London: Sage Publications for The Open University.

Johnson, G. (1989). Rethinking Incrementalism. *Strategic Management Journal*, 9, 75-91.

Johnson, G. & Scholes, K. (1989). *Exploring Corporate Strategy*. Hemel Hempstead: Prentice-Hall.

Kanter, R. M. (1983). *The Change Masters*. New York: Basic Books.

Kerin, *et al.* (1990). *Strategic Market Planning*. Boston: Allyn and Baker.

Ketelhöhn, W. (1993). *International Business Strategy*. Oxford: Butterworth-Heinemann.

Ketelhöhn, W. (1993). An Interview with Aldo Palmeri of Benetton: The Early Growth Years. *European Management Journal*, 11, 3.

Kotler, P. (1972). A Generic Concept of Marketing. *Journal of Marketing*, 36, April, 46-54.

Kotler, P. (1991). *Marketing Management: Analysis, Planning, Control and Implementation, 7th Edition*. Englewood Cliffs, NJ: Simon & Schuster.

Kotler, P. & Levy, S. (1969). Broadening the Concept of Marketing. *Journal of Marketing*, 33, July, 3-12.

Lancaster, G. & Massingham, L. (1993). *Essentials of Marketing*. London: McGraw-Hill.

Levitt, T. (1974). *Marketing for Business Growth*. New York: McGraw-Hill.

Levitt, T. (1983). The Globalisation of Markets. *Harvard Business Review*, 83, May-June, 92-102.`

McDonald, M. H. B. (1989). *Marketing Plans, 2nd Edition*. Oxford: Butterworth-Heinemann.

McDonald, M. H. B. (1992). Strategic Marketing Planning. *Market Intelligence and Planning*, 10, 4, 4-22, MCB University Press.

McNamee, P. B. (1992). *Strategic Management*. Oxford: Butterworth-Heinemann.

Miller, D. (1990). *The Icarus Paradox: How Excellent Organizations Can Bring About Their Own Downfall*. New York: Harper Business.

Mintzberg, H. (1978). Patterns in Strategy Formulation. *Management Science*, 24.

Mintzberg, H. (1987). The Strategy Concept I: The Five P's of Strategy. *California Management Review*, Fall 87, 11-24.

Mintzberg, H. (1987). The Strategy Concept II: Another Look at Why Organizations Need Strategies. *California Management Review*, Fall 87, 25–32.

Mintzberg, H. & Quinn, J. (1991). *The Strategy Process*. Englewood Cliffs, NJ: Simon & Schuster.

Mintzberg H. & Walters, J. A. (1982). Tracking Strategy in an Entrepreneurial Firm. *Academy of Management Journal*, 82, 465-499.

Ohmae, K. (1982). *The Mind of the Strategist*. New York: McGraw-Hill.

O'Shaugnessy, J. (1988). *Competitive Marketing: A Strategic Approach*. Unwin Hyman.

Pascale, R. (1990). *Managing on the Edge: How Successful Companies Use Conflict to Stay Ahead*. London: Viking Penguin.

Pearce, J. & Robinson, R. (1985). *Strategic Management, 2nd Edition*. Irwin.

Pearson, G. (1994). The Marketing/Strategy Interface, in Wilson, I. *Marketing Interfaces*, London: Pitman.

Peters, T. J. (1987). *Thriving on Chaos*. London: Macmillan.

Peters, T. J. & Waterman, R. H. (1982). *In Search of Excellence*. New York: Harper & Row.

Piercy, N. (1992). *Market-led Strategic Change*. Oxford: Butterworth-Heinemann.

Piercy, N. & Giles, W. (1989). The Logic of Being Illogical in Strategic Marketing Planning. *Journal of Marketing Management*, 89, 5, 1, 19-31.

Porter, M. E. (1985). *Competitive Advantage*. New York: The Free Press.

Prahalad, C. K. & Hamel, G. (1990). The Core Competence of the Corporation. *Harvard Business Review*, May-June, 79-91.

Quinn, J. B. (1980). *Strategies for Change: Logical Incrementalism*. Homewood, Ill: Irwin.

Rumelt, P. (1974). *Strategy, Structure and Economic Performance*. Division of Research, HBS.

Schonberger, R. J. (1987). *World Class Manufacturing. The lessons of simplicity applied*. New York: The Free Press.

Slatter, S. (1984). *Corporate Recovery*. London: Penguin.

Stacey, R. D. (1993). *Strategic Management and Organisational Dynamics*. London: Pitman.

Strauss, B. (1994). *Total quality management: Customer orientation without marketing?* Proceedings of the 23rd EMAC Conference, Maastricht.

Star, S. H. (1989). Marketing and Its Discontent. *Harvard Business Review*, December.

Thölke, J.M. (1994). *Product Features and Product Feature Strategies: An Exploratory Study Paper for UMIST workshop: Meeting the Challenges of Product Development*. Manchester.

Thomas, M. (1993). Marketing - in chaos or transition?, in Brownlie, D. *et al.* (Eds), Rethinking Marketing, *Warwick Business School Research Bureau*, 114-23.

Thompson, J. L. (1990). *Strategic Management*. London: Chapman and Hall.

Tuchman, B. W. (1962). *The Guns of August*. New York: Macmillan.

Utterback, J. M. (1994). *Mastering the Dynamics of Innovation*. HBS Press.

Vandermerwe, S. (1993). *From Tin Soldiers to Russian Dolls*. Oxford: Butterworth-Heinemann.

Walters, D. W. (1988). *Strategic Retailing Management*. Hemel Hempstead: Prentice Hall.

Wilson, I. (1994). *Marketing Interfaces*. London: Pitman.

Wilson, R. *et al.* (1992). *Strategic Marketing Management*. Oxford: Butterworth-Heinemann.

Wood, L. (1990). *The end of the Product Life Cycle? Education Says Goodbye to an Old Friend*. Proceedings of the Marketing Education Group Annual Conference, Oxford Polytechnic.

Worthington, S. (1994). *Metal Cars and Plastic Cards – What's the Connection?* Proceedings of the Marketing Education Group Annual Conference, University of Ulster.